Quiet Water

MAINE

AMC's Canoe and Kayak Guide to 157 of the
Best Ponds, Lakes, and Easy Rivers

3RD EDITION

ALEX WILSON & JOHN HAYES

Appalachian Mountain Club Books
Boston, Massachusetts

AMC is a nonprofit organization, and sales of AMC Books fund our mission of protecting the Northeast outdoors. If you appreciate our efforts and would like to become a member or make a donation to AMC, visit outdoors.org, call 800-372-1758, or contact us at Appalachian Mountain Club, 5 Joy Street, Boston, MA 02108.

outdoors.org/publications/books

Distributed by National Book Network.

Front cover photo of Long Pond © Julia Sidman
Back cover photo of Long Pond and title page photo © Jerry Monkman
Interior photographs © Alex Wilson and John Hayes, except where noted
Maps by Alex Wilson and John Hayes © Alex Wilson and John Hayes
Illustrations © Marrin Robinson
Book design by Eric Edstam

Library of Congress Cataloging-in-Publication Data
Names: Wilson, Alex, 1955– author. | Hayes, John, 1944– author.
  Title: Quiet Water Maine : AMC's Canoe and Kayak Guide to 157 of the Best
    Ponds, Lakes, and Easy Rivers / Alex Wilson & John Hayes.
  Description: 3rd Edition. | Boston, Massachusetts : Appalachian Mountain Club
    Books, 2017. | Previous edition: c2005.
  Identifiers: LCCN 2017003493| ISBN 9781628420661 (pbk.) | ISBN 9781628420685
    (mobi) | ISBN 9781628420678 (ePub)
  Subjects: LCSH: Canoes and canoeing--Maine--Guidebooks. |
    Lakes--Maine--Guidebooks. | Ponds--Maine--Guidebooks. |
    Kayaking--Maine--Guidebooks. | Maine--Guidebooks.
  Classification: LCC GV776.M2 W55 2017 | DDC 797.12209741--dc23 LC record available at
https://lccn.loc.gov/2017003493

The paper used in this publication meets the minimum requirements of the American National Standard for Information Sciences-Permanence of Paper for Printed Library Materials, ANSI Z39.48-1984. ∞

Outdoor recreation activities by their very nature are potentially hazardous. This book is not a substitute for good personal judgment and training in outdoor skills. Due to changes in conditions, use of the information in this book is at the sole risk of the user. The author and the Appalachian Mountain Club assume no liability for accidents happening to, or injuries sustained by, readers who engage in the activities described in this book.

Interior pages contain 30% post-consumer recycled fiber.

Cover contains 10% post-consumer recycled fiber.

Printed in the United States of America,
using vegetable-based inks.

6 5 4 3 2 1   17 18 19 20 21

MIX
Paper from
responsible sources
FSC® C005010
www.fsc.org

I want to go soon and live away by the pond, where I shall hear only the wind whispering among the reeds. It will be success if I shall have left myself behind. But my friends ask what I shall do when I get there. Will it not be employment enough to watch the progress of the seasons?

—Henry David Thoreau

MAP LEGEND

▲ Tent site

▲ Lean-to

⩊ Picnic area

[Ⓐ] Campground

[⊟] Boat access

[P] Parking area

⣴ Marsh

☼ Peak

▬ Dam

Divided highway	═══════
State highway	━━━━━
Paved road	▬·▬·▬·▬·
Less-traveled road	═══════
Rough dirt road	▫ ▫ ▫ ▫ ▫ ▫
Foot path	------------
Railroad tracks	┼┼┼┼┼┼

LOCATOR MAP: MAINE

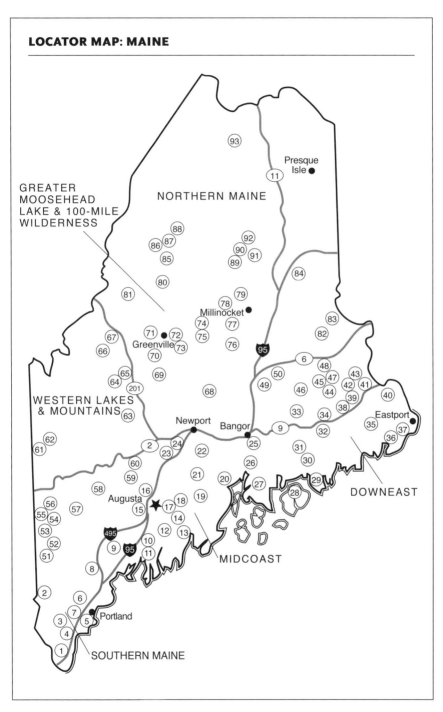

Numbers on map correspond to trips; for a complete list, see "Contents," beginning on page vi.

Contents

SECTION 3: DOWNEAST

SECTION 4: WESTERN LAKES & MOUNTAINS

SECTION 5: GREATER MOOSEHEAD LAKE & 100-MILE WILDERNESS

SECTION 6: NORTHERN MAINE

NATURE ESSAYS

At-a-Glance Trip Planner

#	Trip Name	Page	Access Location	Area/ One-Way Length	Estimated Time (round-trip)
	SOUTHERN MAINE				
1	York River and Smelt Brook	2	York	6 miles one way	6 hours
2	Salmon Falls River	5	Acton	2 miles one way	3 hours
3	Estes Lake	7	Sanford	387 acres; 4 miles one way	6 hours
4	Mousam River	10	Kennebunk	3 miles one way	4 hours
5	Scarborough Marsh	12	Scarborough	3,100 acres	5 hours
6	Presumpscot River	15	Westbrook	5 miles one way	5 hours
7	Hollis Center Arm of the Saco River	19	Buxton	428 acres; 3.5 miles one way	5 hours
8	Lower Range Pond	21	Poland	290 acres	3 hours

NOTES
[1] MPH or HP limit
[2] few motorboats
[3] no personal watercraft

Hiking Trails	Swimming	Motor Boats	Fire Permit Required	Trip Type
N	N	Y[2]	N	marshy tidal stream
N	N	Y[2]	N	slow-flowing, shallow, marshy stream
N	N	Y	N	dammed-up section of river; marshy streams
N	N	N	N	dammed-up section of river
N	N	Y[2]	N	meandering, slow-flowing, salt-marsh streams
N	N	N	N	dammed-up section of river; marshy channels
N	N	Y	N	dammed-up section of river
Y	Y	Y[1]	N	deep, clear kettle pond; some marshy areas

#	Trip Name	Page	Access Location	Area/ One-Way Length	Estimated Time (round-trip)
	MIDCOAST				
9	Runaround Pond	26	Durham	91 acres	3 hours
10	Merrymeeting Bay and Cathance River	28	Bath; Bowdoinham	9,600 acres	all day
11	Nequasset Lake	34	Woolwich	392 acres; 1 mile one way	4 hours
12	Dresden Bog	37	Dresden	341 acres	3 hours
13	Duckpuddle Pond and Pemaquid River	41	Waldoboro	293 acres; 2 miles one way	5 hours
14	Dyer Long Pond	45	Jefferson	423 acres	4 hours
15	Jimmie Pond and Hutchinson Pond	47	Manchester	107 acres; 100 acres	4 hours
16	Messalonskee Lake, Belgrade Stream, and Long Pond	50	Belgrade; Mount Vernon	3,510 acres, 6 miles one way; 2,714 acres	all day
17	Lower Togus Pond	55	Augusta	515 acres	5 hours
18	Turner Pond	57	Somerville	193 acres	4 hours
19	Stevens Pond	60	Liberty	336 acres	4 hours
20	Upper Mason Pond and Goose River	62	Belfast	75 acres; 6 miles one way	6 hours
21	Sandy Pond	66	Freedom	430 acres	4 hours
22	Carlton Pond and Carlton Bog	69	Troy	430 acres	4 hours

NOTES

[1] MPH or HP limit

[2] few motorboats

[3] no personal watercraft

Hiking Trails	Swimming	Motor Boats	Fire Permit Required	Trip Type
N	N	N	N	shallow, marshy pond
N	N	Y	N	tidal freshwater bay; marshy rivers
N	N	Y	N	wooded reservoir and inlet stream
N	N	N	N	shallow, weedy pond; difficult access
N	N	Y²	N	shallow, marshy pond; long, marshy stream
N	N	Y²	N	long, shallow pond; wooded shore
Y	N	Y²	N	Jimmie: deeper pond, wooded shore; Hutchinson: shallow, marshy pond
N	N	Y	N	marshy lake; slow-flowing stream
N	N	Y²	N	long, shallow, marshy pond
N	Y	N	N	shallow, marshy pond
N	Y	Y¹	N	pond with many islands; some marshy areas
N	N	Y²	N	shallow, marshy pond; marshy stream
N	N	Y²	N	shallow, marshy pond; floating and fixed islands
N	N	Y²	N	shallow, marshy pond; large amounts of aquatic vegetation

#	Trip Name	Page	Access Location	Area/ One-Way Length	Estimated Time (round-trip)
23	Canaan Bog, Carrabassett Stream, and Black Stream	71	Canaan	380 acres; 7 miles one way	6 hours
24	Douglas Pond and Sebasticook River	75	Pittsfield	566 acres; 2 miles one way	5 hours

DOWNEAST

#	Trip Name	Page	Access Location	Area/ One-Way Length	Estimated Time (round-trip)
25	Fields Pond	79	Orrington	182 acres	3 hours
26	Silver Lake	82	Bucksport	630 acres	5 hours
27	Wight Pond	88	Penobscot	135 acres	2 hours
28	Mount Desert Island: Long Pond, Seal Cove Pond, Eagle Lake, and Jordan Pond	90	Bar Harbor; Mount Desert Island; Southwest Harbor; Tremont	897 acres; 283 acres; 436 acres; 187 acres	5 hours; 3 hours; 3 hours; 1 hour
29	Jones Pond	99	Gouldsboro	467 acres	3 hours
30	Donnell Pond	102	Franklin	1,120 acres	all day
31	Scammon Pond, R. Lyle Frost WMA	105	Eastbrook	396 acres	3 hours
32	Bog Brook Flowage, Bog Brook WMA	111	Beddington	625 acres	6 hours
33	Great Pond and Dead Stream	113	Great Pond	679 acres; 1 mile one way	4 hours
34	Mopang Lake and Second Mopang Lake	114	Devereaux TWP; T30 MD BPP	1,487 acres; 145 acres	5 hours
35	Rocky Lake, Rocky Lake Stream, East Machias River, and Second Lake	117	Berry TWP	1,555 acres; 6 miles one way;	all day

NOTES
[1] MPH or HP limit
[2] few motorboats
[3] no personal watercraft

Hiking Trails	Swimming	Motor Boats	Fire Permit Required	Trip Type
N	N	Y[2]	N	shallow, marshy pond; streams
N	N	Y	N	marshy pond; slow-flowing river
N	N	Y[2]	N	marshy pond and stream
N	N	Y[2]	N	pond dotted with islands
N	N	Y[2]	N	long, narrow pond
Y	Y	Y	N	long, narrow, deep lakes
N	N	Y	N	pond with several islands
Y	N	Y[3]	N	large, irregularly shaped pond with several islands
N	N	Y[2]	N	shallow, weed-choked pond
N	N	Y[2]	N	shallow pond and marshland
N	N	Y[1]	N	scenic pond; meandering, marshy stream
N	N	Y[2]	Y	large lake with islands, coves, marshy stream
N	N	Y[2]	Y	large lake with many islands and coves; marshy streams

#	Trip Name	Page	Access Location	Area/ One-Way Length	Estimated Time (round-trip)
36	Rocky Lake II	121	Whiting	1,126 acres	6 hours
37	Orange River, Orange River WMA	123	Whiting	5 miles one way	5 hours
38	First, Second, and Third Chain Lakes	125	Wesley	336 acres; 589 acres; 157 acres	5 hours
39	Clifford Lake and Silver Pug Lake	127	Greenlaw Chopping TWP; T26 ED BPPP	954 acres; 198 acres	6 hours
40	Bearce Lake	131	Meddybemps	275 acres	2 hours
41	Pocomoonshine Lake, Mud Lake, and Crawford Lake	134	Crawford; Princeton	2,464 acres; 100 acres; 1,677 acres	all day
42	Big Lake, Clifford Stream, Little River, and Little Musquash Stream	138	Greenlaw Chopping TWP	10,305 total acres; 9 miles one way	all day
43	Big Musquash Stream	140	Grand Lake Stream PLT	6 miles one way	5 hours
44	Third Machias Lake	147	T43 MD BPP	2,778 acres	all day
45	Fourth Machias Lake	150	Sakom TWP	1,539 acres	6 hours
46	Nicatous Lake	152	T3 ND	5,165 acres	all day
47	Pocumcus Lake, Junior Lake, and Sysladobsis Lake	155	T6 ND BPP	2,201 acres; 3,866 acres; 5,376 acres	multiday
48	Scraggly Lake (Southern) and Pleasant Lake	159	T6 R1 NBPPP	2,758 acres; 1,574 acres	all day
49	Cold Stream	162	Passadumkeag	5 miles one way	4 hours
50	Folsom Pond, Crooked Pond, and Upper Pond	165	Lincoln	282 acres; 220 acres; 506 acres	5 hours

NOTES

[1] MPH or HP limit
[2] few motorboats
[3] no personal watercraft

Hiking Trails	Swimming	Motor Boats	Fire Permit Required	Trip Type
N	N	Y[2]	Y	large, shallow lake with several islands and coves
N	N	N	N	small lake and marshy stream
N	N	Y[2]	Y	long, connected lakes
N	N	Y[3]	Y	lake with large peninsula, many coves, and islands
Y	N	N	N	small, shallow lake
N	N	Y[2]	Y	shallow lakes with many islands; boggy streams
N	N	Y[2]	Y	large, shallow lake with many islands and marshy coves; rivers through marshlands
N	N	N	N	slow-flowing, meandering, marshy stream
N	N	Y[2]	Y	long, shallow lake with marshy inlet
N	N	Y[2]	Y	shallow lake with marshy inlet stream
N	N	Y[3]	N	large lake with 98 islands
N	N	Y[2]	Y	large lakes with many marshy coves
N	N	Y[2]	Y	large, shallow lakes with marshy coves
N	N	Y[2]	N	meandering stream through treeless marsh
N	N	Y[2]	Y	shallow ponds

#	Trip Name	Page	Access Location	Area/ One-Way Length	Estimated Time (round-trip)
WESTERN LAKES & MOUNTAINS					
51	Brownfield Bog, Major Gregory Sanborn WMA	168	Brownfield	467 acres; 1.5 miles one way	3 hours
52	Pleasant Pond and Saco River	171	Fryeburg	239 acres; 2 miles one way	4 hours
53	Kezar Pond	173	Fryeburg	1,447 acres; 1 mile one way	4 hours
54	Five Kezar Ponds (Middle Pond, Back Pond, Mud and Unnamed Pond)	176	Waterford	72 acres; 62 acres; 45 acres	2 hours
55	Horseshoe Pond	179	Lovell	132 acres	2 hours
56	Virginia Lake	181	Stoneham	128 acres	2 hours
57	North Pond	183	Norway	147 acres	3 hours
58	Bunganock Pond and Bunganock Brook	186	Hartford	51 acres; 1 mile one way	2 hours
59	Parker Pond	189	Vienna	1,610 acres	5 hours
60	Bog Stream, Mercer Bog WMA	191	Mercer	3 miles one way	3 hours
61	Umbagog Lake, Lake Umbagog NWR	193	Errol, NH	7,850 acres	multiday
62	Upper Richardson Lake and Lower Richardson Lake	198	Richardsontown TWP; TWP C	4,200 acres; 2,900 acres	multiday
63	Flagstaff Lake	201	Flagstaff TWP	20,300 acres	multiday
64	Gilman Pond	205	Lexington TWP	242 acres; 2.5 miles one way	4 hours

NOTES
[1] MPH or HP limit
[2] few motorboats
[3] no personal watercraft

Hiking Trails	Swimming	Motor Boats	Fire Permit Required	Trip Type
N	N	N	N	shallow ponds filled with aquatic vegetation
N	N	Y[2]	Y	shallow, marshy pond reached by Saco River
N	N	Y[2]	N	large lake with extensive marshes
N	N	Y[1]	N	wooded ponds; minerotrophic fen
Y	N	Y[1]	N	narrow pond in wooded valley
N	N	Y[3]	N	small, wooded pond
N	N	Y[2]	N	shallow marsh, slowly filling in
N	N	N	N	shallow, weedy pond and stream
N	N	Y	N	large, clear lake
N	N	N	N	wide, shallow, heavily vegetated stream
N	N	Y	N	large, shallow, marshy lake with numerous coves and rivers
N	N	Y	Y	deep, clear lakes
Y	N	Y[2]	Y	large, shallow lake with numerous coves and islands
N	N	Y[2]	N	shallow pond with inlet and outlet streams

#	Trip Name	Page	Access Location	Area/ One-Way Length	Estimated Time (round-trip)
65	Pierce Pond and Upper Pierce Pond	208	Pierce Pond TWP	1,650 total acres	5 hours
66	Spencer Lake and Fish Pond	211	Hobbstown TWP	1,819 total acres	5 hours
67	Attean Pond, Holeb Pond, and Moose River Bow Loop	214	Attean TWP	2,745 acres; 1,055 acres; 34-mile loop	multiday

GREATER MOOSEHEAD LAKE & 100-MILE WILDERNESS

#	Trip Name	Page	Access Location	Area/ One-Way Length	Estimated Time (round-trip)
68	Branns Mill Pond	219	Dover-Foxcroft	271 acres	4 hours
69	Bald Mountain Pond	221	Bald Mountain TWP	1,152 acres	all day
70	West Shirley Pond	224	Shirley	275 acres	4 hours
71	Indian Pond	227	Big Moose TWP; Indian Stream TWP; Sapling TWP	3,746 acres	all day
72	Prong Pond	230	Beaver Cove	427 acres	4 hours
73	Long Pond	233	Bowdoin College Grant West TWP	643 acres	4 hours
74	Second, Third, and Fourth Roach Ponds	235	Shawtown TWP; T1 R12 WELS	970 acres; 570 acres; 266 acres	multiday
75	First, Second, and Third West Branch Ponds	239	Shawtown TWP	119 acres; 214 acres	4 hours
76	Seboeis Lake	242	T4 R9 NWP	4,201 acres	all day
77	Cooper Brook Deadwater, Lower Jo-Mary Lake, Middle Jo-Mary Lake, and Turkey Tail Lake	248	T4 Indian Purchase TWP	1,912 acres; 1,152 acres	multiday
78	First, Second, and Third Debsconeag Lakes and Debsconeag Deadwater	252	T2 R9 WELS	320 acres; 189 acres; 1,011 acres	multiday

NOTES
[1] MPH or HP limit
[2] few motorboats
[3] no personal watercraft

Hiking Trails	Swimming	Motor Boats	Fire Permit Required	Trip Type
Y	N	Y[2]	N	deep, clear ponds
N	N	Y[1]	Y	deep, clear lake
Y	N	Y[2]	Y	large, shallow lakes, one dotted with islands; marshy stream
N	N	Y[2]	N	shallow, marshy pond and stream
Y	N	Y[1]	Y	deep, clear pond
N	N	N	N	shallow, marshy pond
N	N	Y[2]	Y	long, large, deep lake
N	N	Y[2]	Y	shallow pond with marshy areas
Y	N	N	Y	long, narrow pond
Y	N	Y[1]	Y	wilderness ponds
Y	N	Y[2]	Y	shallow ponds with wooded, marshy shores
N	N	Y[2]	N	large, deep lake
N	N	Y[1]	Y	shallow, marshy lakes and streams
N	N	N	Y	deep lakes with some marshy areas

#	Trip Name	Page	Access Location	Area/ One-Way Length	Estimated Time (round-trip)
79	Upper Togue Pond, Lower Togue Pond, and Abol Pond	258	T2 R9 WELS	294 acres; 384 acres; 70 acres	5 hours
80	Lobster Lake	261	Northeast Carry TWP	3,475 acres	all day
81	Canada Falls Lake	265	Pittston Academy Grant	2,627 acres	all day

NORTHERN MAINE

#	Trip Name	Page	Access Location	Area/ One-Way Length	Estimated Time (round-trip)
82	Baskahegan Lake	270	Brookton TWP	6,944 acres	all day
83	Crooked Brook Flowage	273	Danforth	1,645 acres	5 hours
84	Mattawamkeag Lake	275	Island Falls	3,330 acres; 4 miles one way	all day
85	Chesuncook Lake, West Branch Penobscot River, and Pine Stream Flowage	278	Pittston Academy Grant; T3 R12 WELS; T3 R13 WELS	26,200 total acres; 20 miles one way; 15miles one way	multiday
86	Loon Lake, Big Hurd Pond, and Little Hurd Pond	284	T6 R15 WELS	1,140 acres; 250 acres; 180 acres	all day
87	Caucomgomoc Lake, Rowe Pond, Round Pond, Daggett Pond, and Poland Pond	287	T7 R14 WELS; T7 R15 WELS	5,081 acres; 250 acres; 375 acres; 461 acres; 490 acres	multiday
88	Allagash Lake and Johnson Pond	291	T7 R14 WELS	4,260 acres; 197 acres	multiday
89	Lower South Branch Pond and Upper South Branch Pond	295	T5 R9 WELS	93 acres; 84 acres	4 hours
90	Grand Lake Matagamon	298	T6 R8 WELS	4,165 acres	multiday

NOTES
[1] MPH or HP limit
[2] few motorboats
[3] no personal watercraft

Hiking Trails	Swimming	Motor Boats	Fire Permit Required	Trip Type
Y	N	Y[1]	N	small ponds with some marshy areas
N	Y	Y[3]	N	deep lake with marshy coves and sand beaches
N	N	Y[2]	Y	large, shallow lake
N	N	Y	Y	large, shallow lake with marshy coves and several islands
N	N	Y[2]	Y	shallow, marshy lake
N	N	Y	Y	winding river and large, shallow lake with islands
N	N	Y	Y	huge, scenic lake; northern forest streams with marshlands
N	N	Y[3]	Y	lake and shallow ponds with marshy coves
N	N	Y[3]	Y	shallow lake, ponds, and connecting streams
N	N	N	N	clear, sand-bottomed lake
Y	N	N	N	small, deep, oligotrophic ponds
Y	N	Y[2]	N	large, deep lake with some marshy area

#	Trip Name	Page	Access Location	Area/ One-Way Length	Estimated Time (round-trip)
91	Sawtelle Deadwater and Mud Pond	303	T6 R7 WELS	218 acres; 6 miles one way	6 hours
92	Scraggly Lake (Northern)	307	T7 R8 WELS	842 acres	all day
93	Deboullie Pond, Pushineer Pond, Gardner Pond, and Togue Pond	310	T15 R9 WELS	266 acres; 55 acres; 288 acres; 388 acres	multiday

NOTES
[1] MPH or HP limit
[2] few motorboats
[3] no personal watercraft

Hiking Trails	Swimming	Motor Boats	Fire Permit Required	Trip Type
N	N	N	Y	long, narrow, marshy stream
Y	N	Y[3]	N	deep, clear lake
Y	N	Y[2]	Y	small, deep ponds

Preface

The first edition of *Quiet Water Canoe Guide, Maine,* published in 1995, was the third in a series that now includes guides to New Hampshire and Vermont; Massachusetts, Connecticut, and Rhode Island; New York; and New Jersey and Eastern Pennsylvania. Alex Wilson started the series in 1992 with the New Hampshire and Vermont guide then followed with the southern New England guide in 1993. John Hayes co-authored the Maine guide with Alex in 1995, followed by the New York guide in 1996, and became co-author, again with Alex, of subsequent editions of the other guides.

We took the opportunity in the second and third Maine editions to add new material, including more than a dozen new trips to great locations such as Flagstaff Lake, West Shirley Bog, Mercer Bog, Goose River, and to AMC's newly acquired locations in the 100-Mile Wilderness.

For the third edition, we dropped the entries for Shapleigh, Smarts, and Hansen Ponds, and Branch Pond due to access issues, and we dropped the entries for Josh Pond and Josh Stream due to new development.

The third edition now has 93 trips covering 175 bodies of water, a 22 percent increase in the number of trips from the first edition.

Because descriptions inevitably go out of date, we also rechecked all bodies of water to ensure that new development had not crowded the shores; we revised directions to reflect new road names; and we added GPS coordinates to access points. When possible, we avoided places with substantial development, but we worried more about the effect of personal (motorized) watercraft and high-speed boating on safety, the quietwater experience, and the environment.

Introduction

Quiet waters—lakes, ponds, estuaries, and slow-flowing streams—receive much less attention than whitewater rivers. If you seek the adrenaline rush of paddling cascading rivers, plenty of excellent resources exist, but this is not one of them. The peaceful solitude of out-of-the-way lakes and ponds lures us to quietwater paddling. This guide will lead you to wood ducks swimming through early morning mists; to moose belly-deep in lily pads; to playful antics of river otters as you round a bend in a winding inlet channel; to the thrill of an osprey diving and retrieving a silvery fish in its talons; and to old-growth white pine towering above crystal-clear ponds, helping us imagine what our forests looked like centuries ago.

With quietwater paddling, you can focus on *being* there instead of *getting* there. You don't need a lot of fancy, high-tech gear, although a light canoe or kayak makes portaging over beaver dams a lot easier. Binoculars and field guides to fauna and flora make up our most important gear—after boats, paddles, and personal flotation devices (PFDs).

This guide will lead you to a body of water and describe why you might want to paddle it. Generally, we tried to include places that have abundant wildlife or extensive marshlands or beautiful scenery; most entries have all three. We hope that our research will allow you to spend your valuable time paddling instead of driving around for hours, trying to find elusive accesses. We designed the Quiet Water series for paddlers of all experience levels, to help you better enjoy our wonderful water resources.

THE SELECTION PROCESS

This guide includes only a small percentage of the lakes, ponds, estuaries, and slow-flowing rivers in Maine. In our selection process, we looked for great scenery; limited development; few motorboats and personal watercraft; a varied shoreline with lots of coves and inlets; and interesting plants, animals, and geological formations.

We include a variety of water types: big lakes and rivers for longer excursions, and protected ponds and marshes for when you have limited time or when weather conditions preclude paddling larger bodies of water. We wrote this book not only for vacationers planning a weeklong trip hundreds of miles from home but also for local residents wanting to do some paddling on their afternoons off.

The book contains a wide geographic spread of small and large bodies of water. We asked people about the best places to paddle; we consulted DeLorme's *Maine Atlas & Gazetteer*; we bought other books about paddling; and we systematically searched the United States Geological Survey (USGS) 7.5-minute topographic maps of the state.

Although we tried to include the very best places to paddle, we doubtless missed some really good locations. If you have suggestions for other lakes, ponds, and streams to consider for future editions, please write to Alex Wilson at alex@atwilson.com or John Hayes at jhayes@pacificu.edu.

SAFETY, EQUIPMENT, AND TECHNIQUE

We all long for the idyllic paddle on mist-filled, mirror-smooth surfaces of quiet ponds at daybreak. But if you spend any time paddling lakes and tidal rivers, you also will encounter far less tranquil conditions. Estuaries can have swift tides that, coupled with wind, can be very dangerous. On many of the larger bodies of water in this book, strong winds can arise quickly, whipping up 2- to 4-foot waves in no time—waves big enough to swamp an open boat. If you capsize in cold water even a moderate distance from shore, hypothermia—a cooling of the body's core that can lead to physical and mental collapse—can set in quickly. If you have just driven a long way to reach a particular lake and find it dangerously windy, choose a more protected body of water or go hiking instead.

Safety First

All Northeast states require each boater to carry a U.S. Coast Guard–approved (type I, II, or III) personal flotation device (PFD). A good PFD keeps a person's face above water, even if that person has lost consciousness. A foam- or kapok-filled PFD also will help keep you warm in cold water. Children ages ten and under must wear PFDs, which must be the right size to prevent slipping off; adult PFDs are not acceptable for children. Although the law does not usually require adults to wear PFDs, we strongly recommend you do so, especially when paddling with children. If you don't normally wear your PFD while paddling, at least don it in windy conditions, when crossing large lakes, or when you may encounter substantial motorboat wakes. It could save your life.

You should also bring along a waterproof first-aid kit. The best kit is one you assemble yourself; make sure it has bandages and moleskin for blisters, an antihistamine for allergic reactions, sunscreen, an extra hat, a pain reliever, and any special medications you might require

As for clothing, plan for the unexpected. Even with a sunny-day forecast, a shower can appear by afternoon. On trips of more than a few hours, we bring along rain gear and dry clothes in a waterproof stuff sack as a matter of course. Along with rain coming up unexpectedly, temperatures can drop quickly, especially in spring or fall, making conditions ripe for hypothermia. Lightweight nylon or polypropylene clothing dries more quickly than cotton, and wool still retards heat loss when wet. Remember that heads lose heat faster than torsos. Bring a hat.

Also bring a whistle, which you may need to use if you need help, since the sound of a whistle travels farther than the sound of a human voice, especially if it's windy. Bring enough food to maintain your energy level, and carry one liter of water for short trips and two or more liters for long trips. Avoid shallow, marshy waters during waterfowl hunting season. For hunting season dates, check Maine's fish and wildlife website: maine.gov/ifw/hunting_trapping.

Other safety tips include:

- Get off the water during lightning storms. Lightning almost always strikes the highest object in the vicinity, which would be you in a boat on a lake.
- Know what to do if you capsize—and have experience doing it.
- Avoid dehydration by drinking plenty of liquids.
- Avoid areas with a lot of high-speed boating.
- Check the weather forecast before going out.
- If appropriate, check times of low and high tides.

Equipment

For quietwater paddling, avoid high-performance racing or tippy whitewater canoes or kayaks. Borrow a boat before buying; selection will be easier with a little experience. Whether you prefer a canoe or a kayak, look for a model with good initial and secondary stability. A boat with good initial stability and poor secondary stability will tip slowly, but once it starts, it may keep going. The best canoes for lakes and ponds have a keel or a shallow "V" hull and a fairly flat keel line to help track in a straight line, even in a breeze. Kayaks perform extremely well in rough water, particularly if equipped with a foot-operated rudder and a sprayskirt to keep from taking on water.

If you yearn for out-of-the-way paddles requiring portages, get a Kevlar (strong, lightweight carbon fiber) boat if you can afford it. We paddle a rugged, high-capacity 18-foot, 4-inch Mad River Lamoille canoe that weighs just 60 pounds; a 15-foot, 9-inch Mad River Independence solo canoe that weighs less than 40 pounds; a 14-foot Wenonah Wigeon kayak that weighs 38 pounds; and a 14-foot Wilderness Systems Chaika kayak that weighs 32 pounds. These older boats have been replaced by newer but similar models. If you plan to paddle alone, consider a sea kayak or a solo canoe in which you sit (or kneel) close to the boat's center. You will find paddling a well-designed solo canoe far easier than paddling a used two-seater by yourself. The touring or sea kayak—with its long and narrow design, low profile to the wind, and two-bladed paddling style—is faster and more efficient to paddle than a canoe.

A padded portage yoke in place of the center thwart (a strut placed crosswise, left/right)on a canoe is essential if you plan on carrying much. With un-padded yokes, wear a life vest with padded shoulders. Attach a rope, called a painter, to the bow so you can secure the boat when you stop for lunch, line it up or down a stream, and—if the need ever arises—grab onto it in an emergency. We both have embarrassing stories about not using a painter to secure the boat. Wind can cause Kevlar boats to disappear very quickly, and it's not fun to watch your boat bobbing away in a stiff wind!

Choose light, comfortable paddles. For canoeing, we use a relatively short (48- or 50-inch), bent-shaft paddle. Laminated from various woods, the paddle has a special synthetic tip to protect the blade. Bent-shaft paddles allow more efficient paddling because downward force converts more directly into forward thrust. Straight-shaft paddles also work well. Always carry at least one spare paddle per group, particularly on longer trips, in case you break a paddle or a porcupine gets hold of one.

Paddling Technique

On a quiet pond, does it matter if you use the proper J-stroke, the sweep stroke, or the draw? No. Learning some of these strokes, however, can make paddling more relaxing and enjoyable. We watch lots of novices zigzagging along, frantically switching sides while shouting orders fore and aft. People have told us about marriage counseling sessions devoted to paddling technique!

If you are new to the sport and want to learn canoeing or kayaking techniques, buy a book or participate in a paddling workshop, such as those offered by the Appalachian Mountain Club (see activities.outdoors.org), equipment retailers, and boat manufacturers. We include recommended books on canoeing and kayaking in Appendix B.

Start out on small ponds. Practice paddling into, with, and across the wind. On a warm day close to shore, with your PFD on and others to help you out of difficulties, practice capsizing. Intentionally tipping your boat will give you an idea of how easily it can upend. Try to get back into the boat when you are away from shore. Bailing water out of a kayak while treading water is impossible without a hand pump; you can have one mounted permanently on your boat, or you can carry a portable one. You should be able to right a canoe with two people, getting most of the water out. (Keep a bailer fastened to a thwart.) Getting back in the boat is another story. Good luck!

PADDLING WITH KIDS

When canoeing with kids, try to make it fun and keep calm. Even though you may be plenty warm from paddling, children can get cold while sitting in the bottom of a boat. Remember that everyone should have PFDs on at all times, and PFDs will help keep children warm. Kids also need protection from sun and biting insects. Watch for signs of discomfort. Set up a cozy place where young children can sleep. After the initial excitement of paddling fades, a gently rolling canoe often puts children to sleep, especially near the end of a long day. Also, for longer excursions, make sure to bring dry clothes for everyone in a waterproof sack.

How to Use This Book

For each trip in the book, we provide a list of basic information, a map, directions, and a short description of what you'll see.

TRIP INFORMATION

At the start of each trip description, we include location, DeLorme and USGS map information, area covered by the trip, an estimate of time required for a leisurely paddle, habitat type (i.e., type of environment you will encounter), types of game fish, predominant animals, and types of vegetation you should expect to see, contact information, and special notes about development or hazards to avoid. For information on public and private campgrounds, see the extensive lists in the DeLorme atlas.

Choose larger bodies of water and longer rivers when you have more time and a good weather forecast. Under windy conditions, paddle smaller bodies of water or rivers. Most entries include substantial shallow-water marshlands.

Note that although we list fish species for each destination, specific or general advisories against eating or reducing consumption of caught fish from all bodies of water exist, particularly for pregnant and nursing women and children. Advisories do not apply to stocked hatchery fish. We include specific and general advisories in Appendix A.

MAPS

We recommend you use DeLorme's *Maine Atlas & Gazetteer*, available at bookstores, outdoor retailers, and delorme.com. We key each entry included in this book to the DeLorme atlas, which divides Maine into 70 detailed 10-by-15-inch maps at a scale of 1: 135,000. The maps include most—but not all—access locations, campsites, road names, campgrounds, and parks, as well as other pertinent information. For more detail and information on topography, marsh areas, and so on, refer to the 7.5-minute, 1: 24,000-scale USGS topographic maps listed in each section.

GETTING THERE

We give directions from the nearest city or major highway to the access. We provide distances between points, with the cumulative distance given in parentheses. We assume you will use a detailed highway map, such as DeLorme's atlas. We also include GPS coordinates, taken onsite with a dashboard-mounted GPS unit; we report latitude and longitude values in degrees and minutes. If it's more convenient to use degrees as one number, take just the minutes and divide by 60 to get a decimal. For example, to convert 42° 45.602′, divide 45.602 minutes by 60 minutes per degree to get 0.760031°. Then add this decimal to 42° to get 42.760031°.

WHAT YOU'LL SEE

The trip descriptions, each a few paragraphs long, give details about the area's natural features. Those details include birds, animals, and plants you should expect to see, and in some cases we describe prominent geological features. Bringing field guides to birds, plants, and animals—along with waterproof binoculars—would be a great help in identifying and enjoying what you see.

Happy paddling!

Stewardship and Conservation

Diverse wetlands—among the richest, most readily accessible ecosystems—provide wonderful opportunities for paddlers to learn about nature. You can visit crystal-clear mountain ponds, slow-flowing rivers, and unique bog habitats. You can observe hundreds of species of birds; dozens of mammal, insect, turtle, and snake species; and hundreds of plant species. Some quite rare species, such as a delicate bog orchid or a family of otters, provide a real treat when you observe them. But even ordinary plants and animals lead to exciting discoveries and can provide hours of enjoyable observation.

In this book's essays, we describe a few interesting plants and animals you might encounter. We intersperse these descriptions, and accompanying pen and ink illustrations by Marrin Robinson, throughout. We hope the information in these short essays will enhance your own observations.

DO WE REALLY WANT TO TELL PEOPLE ABOUT THE BEST PLACES?

People have asked us how we could, in good conscience, tell others about the more remote, pristine, unspoiled places. After all, increased visitation would make these places less idyllic. We spent many an hour grappling with this difficult issue as we paddled along. We believe people who experience wild, remote areas firsthand will come to value them and build support for their protection.

For many lakes and ponds, protection would mean the purchase of fragile surrounding areas by state or local governments, or by private organizations, such as the Appalachian Mountain Club or The Nature Conservancy. On other bodies of water, restricting high-speed boating would offer the best form of protection.

Wetlands perform extremely important functions, such as recharging groundwater, helping control floods, supporting fishing and waterfowl hunting, and providing habitat for many rare and endangered species, as well as for hundreds of other species. Even low-impact uses, such as canoeing or kayaking, can substantially affect fragile marsh habitat. Paddling can disturb nesting loons and eagles, rare turtles, and fragile bog orchids. And even a canoe or kayak can carry invasive plants and other harmful organisms from one body of water to another. Be sure to clean off your boat before you visit other water bodies.

You can go even farther than the adage: "Take only photographs, leave only footprints." Carry along a trash bag and pick up the leavings of less thoughtful individuals. If each of us did the same, we would all enjoy more attractive places to paddle. While motorboaters tend to have a bad reputation when it comes to leaving trash, paddlers should have the opposite reputation, which could come in handy when seeking restrictions on high-impact resource use.

For information on low-impact camping and other uses of fragile habitats, see Rich Brame and David Cole's book, *Soft Paths: How to Enjoy the Wilderness Without Harming It*, 4th ed. (Stackpole Books, 2011). Also, visit the website of Leave No Trace (lnt.org), an organization dedicated to teaching people how to minimize their outdoor impact.

Besides reducing our impact on the environment, we can actively work to protect fragile bald eagle, osprey, otter, and other wildlife populations. If we want to preserve these species and their habitats for future generations, we will demand that elected and appointed officials make wildlife preservation and ecosystem protection a higher priority. We can also join conservation organizations—such as AMC, Sierra Club, The Nature Conservancy, Maine Audubon Society, Natural Resources Council of Maine, and many others—so that when those organizations speak about preserving the environment, their voices carry the weight of tens of thousands of like-minded members.

Many of the waters featured in this book have more protection now than when the first edition was published in 1995. Some bodies of water now impose a 6 or 10 HP limit on motors, or prohibit internal-combustion motors, or prohibit personal watercraft, or impose speed limits. The land around a number of our most treasured water resources has received protection from development forever. Appalachian Mountain Club, The Nature Conservancy, and land trusts continue to protect more of the shoreline along many key ponds and lakes. Because Maine is so large by East Coast standards, however, and because glaciation has covered it with so many bodies of water, much remains to be protected from continued development and from high-speed boating. When we update this guide in a few years, we hope to report even more progress in protecting these lakes and ponds.

We heartily applaud Maine for banning lead sinkers and jigs weighing less than 1 ounce in 2013. Along with the banning of lead shotgun pellets for waterfowl hunting in 1991, lead-induced loon mortality should begin to decrease. According to Maine Audubon, the ingestion of lead pellets or sinkers is responsible for about one-third of loon mortality.

AMC'S CONSERVATION EFFORTS

Because New England lakes and ponds are beautiful, their real estate value is high, which can lead to excess development and harm to the environment. In response, the Appalachian Mountain Club has worked hard to protect the undeveloped shorelines of the Northeast. AMC, with other environmental organizations and land trusts, has successfully secured millions of dollars in funding from federal and state budgets and bonds to protect critical lands with high aesthetic, recreational, and ecological waterfront values. AMC has been a leader in protecting riparian lands during the licensing of hydropower projects, knowing that in return for using the public waters, the hydroelectric dam owners have an obligation to create shoreline management plans and mitigate their operational effect on the watershed. AMC's Maine Woods Initiative (see "AMC in the Maine Woods," page 322) has protected over 70,000 acres of forest land, including 17 lakes and ponds, and much of the headwaters of the West Branch of the Pleasant River.

PUBLIC ACCESS

Private land, typically that of large paper companies, surrounds most of the wild lakes in eastern and northern Maine. Nearly all of these companies allow recreational use, for which we should be very thankful. In eastern and central Maine, access and camping are generally permitted at no cost. In some areas, you must obtain landowner permission to camp; never camp on land posted No Trespassing. You must also obtain a fire permit in most areas.

Since this book's first edition in 1995, forestland ownership in Maine has undergone tremendous change. After decades of stasis, punctuated by the sale of an occasional large parcel from one timber company to another, the announcement by Sappi Limited (originally incorporated as South African Pulp and Paper Industries Limited in 1936) in 1998 that it would sell 905,000 acres of timberland triggered an unprecedented sell-off of northern forestlands. About 5.5 million acres, or nearly 30 percent, of northern Maine changed hands between 1998 and 2003; the 8,600 square miles sold is 2.5 times the size of Yellowstone National Park and equals the area of New Hampshire and of the Adirondack Forest Preserve. While some lands sold to The Nature Conservancy included conservation easements, the vastness of the sales from one timber company to another, to investment companies, or to land developers galvanized the conservation community.

In response, in 2003 AMC launched its Maine Woods Initiative, a land protection effort that balances outdoor recreation, education, conservation, and sustainable forestry in the 100-Mile Wilderness region. For more information, see "Maine Woods" on page 255.

On 3.5 million acres in northern Maine, roughly north of Moosehead Lake and west and north of Baxter State Park, a coalition of landowners called the North Maine Woods controls and charges fees for recreational access. Most of its 14 checkpoints with heavy use are open from 5 A.M. to 9 P.M. For current operation hours and fees for camping and access, visit northmainewoods.org or call 207-435-6213.

Logging trucks have the right of way on these private roads. We've seen tandem trucks barreling along, carrying mammoth loads. Keep out of their way for safety reasons and out of courtesy to those who make their land available for our recreational use. A related consortium of landowners, including AMC, have formed the KI-Jo Mary Multiple Use Forest for a 175,000-acre area between Millinocket, Greenville, and Brownville. For checkpoint and campsite information, see the "KI-Jo Mary" tab at northmainewoods.org.

LEAVE NO TRACE

Appalachian Mountain Club is a national education partner of the Leave No Trace Center for Outdoor Ethics. The center is an international nonprofit organization dedicated to responsible enjoyment and  active stewardship of the outdoors by all people, worldwide. The organization teaches children and adults vital skills to minimize their impact when they're outdoors. Leave No Trace (LNT) is the most widely accepted outdoor ethics program used today on public lands across the nation by all types of outdoor recreationists. LNT unites five federal land management agencies—United States Forest Service, National Park Service, Bureau of Land Management, Army Corps of Engineers, and United States Fish and Wildlife Service—with manufacturers, outdoor retailers, user groups, educators, organizations such as AMC, and individuals.

These seven principles guide the LNT ethic:

Plan ahead and prepare. Know the terrain and any regulations applicable to the area you're planning to visit, and be prepared for extreme weather or other emergencies. This will enhance your enjoyment and ensure you've chosen an appropriate destination. Small groups have less impact on resources and the experience of other backcountry visitors.

Travel and camp on durable surfaces. Travel and camp on established trails and campsites, keeping in mind rock, gravel, dry grasses, or snow make durable surfaces with least impact on the environment. Good campsites are found, not made. Camp at least 200 feet from lakes and streams, and focus activities on areas where vegetation is absent. In pristine areas, disperse use to prevent creating new campsites and trails.

Dispose of waste properly. Pack it in, pack it out. Inspect your camp for trash or food scraps. Deposit solid human waste in cat holes dug 6 to 8 inches deep, at least 200 feet from water, camp, and trails. Pack out toilet paper and hygiene products. To wash yourself or your dishes, carry water 200 feet away from streams or lakes, and use small amounts of biodegradable soap. Scatter strained dishwater.

Leave what you find. Cultural or historic artifacts—as well as natural objects such as plants or rocks—should be left as found.

Minimize campfire impacts. Cook on a stove. Use established fire rings, fire pans, or mound fires. If you build a campfire, keep it small and use dead sticks found on the ground.

Respect wildlife. Observe wildlife from a distance. Feeding wildlife alters their natural behavior. Protect wildlife from your food by storing rations and trash securely.

Be considerate of other visitors. Be courteous, respect the quality of other visitors' backcountry experience, and let nature's sounds prevail.

AMC is a national provider of the Leave No Trace Master Educator course. AMC offers this five-day course, designed especially for outdoor professionals and land managers, as well as the shorter two-day Leave No Trace Trainer course, at locations throughout the Northeast. For more information, visit outdoors.org/education/lnt. For LNT information and materials, contact Leave No Trace Center for Outdoor Ethics at 800-332-4100 or visit lnt.org.

FIRE PERMITS

Because Maine depends on forest products, the state takes great care to reduce fire risk. One does not need a fire permit in state parks and in private campgrounds; most other sites require permits. Designated campsites include two types: authorized campsites where you may carefully build a fire without a permit; and fire-permit campsites where you must obtain a permit. Use of a camp stove does not require a permit.

To obtain a permit, contact the Maine Forest Service Regional Headquarters for campfire permits: Ashland Regional Office 207-435-7963; Old Town Regional Office 207-827-1800; Augusta Regional Office 207-624-3700. *The Maine Atlas & Gazetteer* identifies authorized and permit campsites by closed and open tent symbols, respectively. Because the Maine Forest Service sometimes changes these designations, we recommend purchasing a new Maine Atlas periodically. We do not distinguish between the two types of campsites on the maps in this book.

LODGING OPTIONS

Along with camping on or near most bodies of water covered in this book, other lodging options often exist nearby. Information on inns is available from the Maine Innkeepers Association at maineinns.com.

In remote northern and eastern parts of the state, scattered sporting camps that harken back to a bygone era offer comfort and protection from biting insects. Most sporting camps have five to twenty cabins and a central lodge for meals; some are set up for housekeeping. For information on sporting camps, refer to Alice Arlen's *Maine Sporting Camps: The Year-Round Guide to Vacationing at Traditional Hunting and Fishing Lodges*, 3rd ed. (Countryman, 2003). A list is also available from the Maine Sporting Camp Association at mainesportingcamps.com.

Appalachian Mountain Club runs Gorman Chairback Lodge & Cabins, Little Lyford Lodge & Cabins, and opening in 2017, Medawisla Lodge & Cabins. All AMC properties are located in what is known as Maine's 100-Mile Wilderness. Gorman Chairback and Little Lyford are within 15 miles of Greenville and 25 miles of Brownville, while Medawisla is northeast of Greenville and 7 miles from Kokadjo. All AMC lodge features a dining lodge, bunkhouse, and individual cabins with various sleeping capacities. Some cabins at Gorman Chairback and Medawisla are ADA accessible. Each lodge features a boathouse stocked with kayaks, canoes, personal flotation devices, and paddles, all free for guest use. As part of its Maine Woods Initiative, the AMC maintains trails throughout the area, connecting its property to mountains of the 100-Mile Wilderness. Nearby Gulf Hagas, a National Natural Landmark features miles of gorges and waterfalls. For more information and reservations, see outdoors.org/lodging, or call 603-466-2727.

1 | SOUTHERN MAINE

The most accessible region of Maine for out-of-staters, Southern Maine includes Portland and adjacent Casco Bay. Thirty miles of beautiful coastline extend from Kittery to South Orchard Beach, and lakes abound inland. Myriad activities await explorers in this well-traveled area. You can visit historical sites in the Yorks and climb Mount Agamenticus for a landscape-level view; Old Orchard Beach stretches for 7 miles and has whale-watching opportunities; Kennebunk has a working waterfront harbor; and Biddeford-Saco boasts the pristine Saco River (Trip 7), which offers unlimited, multiday paddling opportunities. Other featured trips include little-traveled Mousam River (Trips 3 and 4), which meanders through a surprisingly undeveloped landscape; Scarborough Marsh (Trip 5), with 31,000 acres of marshland, including 15 percent of Maine's salt marsh; and Salmon Falls River (Trip 2), a meandering marshy stream forming the boundary between Maine and New Hampshire. For this book's third edition, we've also added a tidal section of the York River (Trip 1) and a meandering section of the Presumpscot River (Trip 6).

1 | York River and Smelt Brook

This tidal portion of the York River meanders several miles through a broad meadow. Timing your visit to the tides would make paddling a lot easier. Look for osprey, snowy egret, sandpipers, and marsh wren in spring.

Location: York
Maps: *Maine Atlas & Gazetteer*, Map 1: A4, B4; USGS York Harbor
Length: 6 miles one way
Time: 6 hours; shorter trips possible
Habitat Type: Tidal salt marsh with meandering river and creek
Fish: Saltwater species (see fish advisories, Appendix A)
Take Note: Launching at low tide or when tide is flowing out can be a challenge; for York Harbor tides, visit me.usharbors.com/maine-tide-charts

GETTING THERE

From I-95, Exit 7 southbound, turn left (east), go 0.5 mile, and turn right on Route 1. Go 0.7 mile (cumulative: 1.2 miles) and turn right on Route 91. Go 2.1 miles (3.3 miles) and turn left on Scotland Bridge Road. Go 0.2 mile (3.5 miles) to the access on the left before the bridge. (43° 9.612′ N, 70° 42.522′ W)

WHAT YOU'LL SEE

Wild, tidal, meandering York River and Smelt Brook traverse a sea of grasses in this broad salt marsh. You will experience significant current as you paddle upriver (to the right as you approach the river on Scotland Bridge Road), particularly where the channel narrows as it passes under the bridge. If possible, time your paddling to ride the incoming tide as you paddle upriver; then, after the tide turns, paddle with the current back to your vehicle.

A few houses encroach as you head upstream, but these disappear soon enough. You may see an occasional motorboat with people fishing one of these channels, but mostly you will have the place to yourself.

The salinity drops as you paddle farther from the ocean, and that makes for interesting studies in vegetation. Initially, high salinity selects for salt marsh cordgrass (*Spartina*), but as the salinity drops you will see lots of other species of grass, sedge, and rush. In York River's upper reaches, large patches

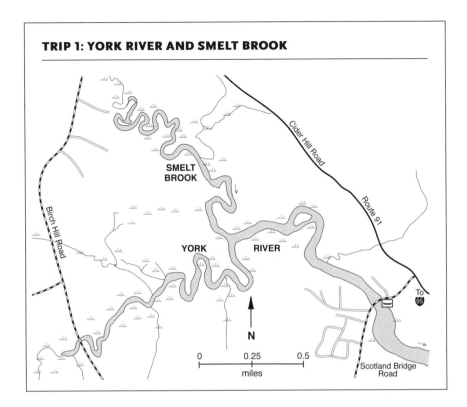

TRIP 1: YORK RIVER AND SMELT BROOK

SMELT BROOK

Cider Hill Road

Route 91

Birch Hill Road

YORK   RIVER

N

0   0.25   0.5

miles

To 95

Scotland Bridge Road

of narrow-leaved cattail (*Typha angustifolia*) line the shore. In late summer and fall, patches of goldenrod with its yellow flowers brighten the shoreline. We saw a few patches of *Phragmites* and hope this invasive species won't displace other vegetation over time.

In spring and early summer, listen for metallic trilling of singing marsh wrens, *Cistothorus palustris*, which prefer nesting in narrow-leaved cattails. Males weave several elliptical nests to attract females and use false nests for roosting. Densities of territorial males can reach one per acre. The denser the vegetation, the more successful the rearing of young. Males destroy the eggs and nests of other marsh wrens and, indeed, of other bird species. With patience and binoculars, you should be able to spot singing males.

Birdlife fills the salt marsh. On a mid-August visit, we watched a sizable group of snowy egrets feeding in some perched wetlands between serpentine oxbows, while dozens of lesser yellowlegs flew from mudbank to mudbank in search of food. An occasional great blue heron launched out from overlooking trees; kingfishers arced out over the water with their rattling call; and hundreds of small sandpipers scampered over exposed mud flats as the tide ran out.

Marsh wrens often weave their nests, like this one, from narrow-leaved cattails.

Farther from water, on higher ground, red oak dominates the tree story, along with white pine, red maple, gray birch, and hickory. Watch for the red-tailed hawks we assume nest in trees along here.

Expect a workout here if you paddle all the way up to the bridges on York River and Smelt Brook. In a long afternoon here, we paddled about 11 miles, unfortunately working against the tide much of the time. On Smelt Brook (right fork a little more than a mile from the access), you can paddle quite a way upstream on a gradually narrowing channel. Downed trees blocked our passage just before reaching the junction of Route 91 and Birch Hill Road at Brixham Lower Corners. We eased under one log but gave up when we reached others just around the bend.

York River's main channel provided open paddling all the way to Birch Hill Road, where we turned around and beat a hasty retreat on the rapidly outgoing tide. With a fairly deep river channel, we doubt you would have trouble here, even at dead-low tide, but high tide provides a much better view out over the broad marsh.

In 2016, an effort was underway to include the York River and its tributaries in the Wild and Scenic Rivers Program, a federal designation that would help protect this important resource.

2 | Salmon Falls River

Narrow, marshy Salmon Falls River, which forms the southern portion of the border between Maine and New Hampshire, meanders behind a small dam, and off into a forest. Look for patches of floating heart among the many species of aquatic vegetation, along with muskrat, ducks, and red-winged blackbirds.

Location: Acton
Maps: *Maine Atlas & Gazetteer*, Map 2: B1; USGS Great East Lake
Length: 2 miles one way
Time: 3 hours
Habitat Type: Meandering, slow-flowing, marshy stream
Fish: Smallmouth bass (see fish advisories, Appendix A)
Take Note: Barely submerged boulders near the dam; thick aquatic vegetation, particularly in mid- to late summer

GETTING THERE

From Milton Mills, New Hampshire, with the U.S. Post Office on the right, go 0.3 mile north on Jug Hill Road, turn right on Hopper Road, and go 0.5 mile (cumulative: 0.8 mile) to the access, just over the bridge on the left. Go 0.5 mile (1.3 miles) to a second access that avoids the backyards and submerged boulders. (43° 29.994′ N, 70° 57.546′ W)

From Sanford, Maine, go northwest on Routes 11 and 109, and turn left on Route 109 at the split. Go 3.6 miles and turn left on Sam Page Road. Go 0.2 mile (3.8 miles) and turn left on Hopper Road. Go 3.1 miles (6.9 miles) to the access on the right. The boulder- and backyard-free access is 0.5 mile back (6.4 miles).

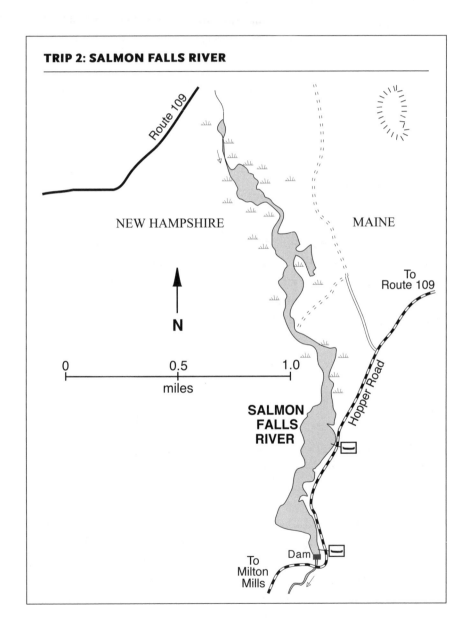

TRIP 2: SALMON FALLS RIVER

Route 109

NEW HAMPSHIRE

MAINE

To Route 109

N

0   0.5   1.0
miles

Hopper Road

SALMON FALLS RIVER

Dam

To Milton Mills

WHAT YOU'LL SEE

Salmon Falls River forms the boundary between lower Maine and New Hampshire. Though a small stream for most of its considerable length, in Milton Mills a dam widens it to paddleable proportions.

Although this section of the river runs only about 2 miles, it seems much longer. The channel meanders aimlessly through endless acres of aquatic vegetation, with some beautiful patches of floating heart, with its diminutive waterlily-like leaves. The sizeable amount of underwater structure supports healthy fish populations, with some huge smallmouth bass lurking under the lily pads.

Paddle here if you enjoy exploring pond life among the lily pads, pickerelweed, arrowhead, sedges, and rushes. In places, vegetation masks the main channel. While what looks like a widened channel dead-ends, the real channel snakes through a dense stand of pickerelweed.

The last time we paddled here, we had to carry over a new beaver dam about 1 mile from the access point. In addition to seeing a new beaver lodge, we saw a muskrat, many ducks, kingfishers, hundreds of red-winged blackbirds, and many dragonflies and damselflies. In the upper reaches, lots of tamaracks grow out of sphagnum hummocks.

The dam access has more parking, but if you put in at the upper site, you will avoid paddling through backyards. Once past these, the evidence of human civilization recedes until you reach the upper stretch of this small reservoir. Putting in up above allows you to avoid the barely submerged rocks that choke the lower section. Go slowly there.

---

3 | Estes Lake

On this section of the Mousam River, backed up behind a dam, look for loons, eastern kingbirds, great blue herons, mallards, and double-crested cormorants. Inlet streams provide a few miles of great paddling through marshlands.

Location: Sanford
Maps: *Maine Atlas & Gazetteer*, Map 2: C4; USGS Alfred
Area/Length: 387 acres; 4 miles of lake, plus a few miles of inlet streams

Time: 6 hours; shorter trips possible

Habitat Type: Dammed-up section of river; marshy streams

Fish: Smallmouth bass, largemouth bass, chain pickerel (see fish advisories, Appendix A)

Take Note: Motors allowed to 10 HP; section south of campground has some development

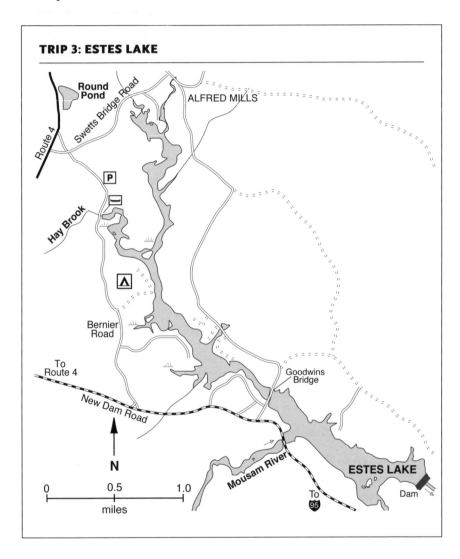

TRIP 3: ESTES LAKE

GETTING THERE

From I-95, Exit 25 southbound, turn left on Route 35, go 0.2 mile, and turn right on Alfred Road. Go 2.9 miles (cumulative: 3.1 miles) and veer left on Old Falls Road. Go 1.9 miles (5 miles) and turn left on Old North Berwick Road. Go 0.7 mile (5.7 miles) and turn right on New Dam Road. Go 2.7 miles (8.4 miles) and veer right on Bernier Road. Go 1.5 miles (9.9 miles), passing Apache Campground, to the Hay Brook bridge. If no room to park, go 0.3 mile (10.2 miles) to the parking area on the right. (43° 27.018′ N, 70° 42.750′ W)

WHAT YOU'LL SEE

Estes Lake, a long, widened section of river, backs up behind a small hydroelectric dam on the Mousam River. Actually, the Middle Branch of the Mousam River forms the northern three-quarters of Estes Lake, as the main river enters the lake near the south end.

Paddling from the access on Hay Brook, you pass through cattails, horsetails, and many other marsh plants. Wood duck nesting boxes dot the shoreline, although we saw only a tree swallow peer out from one of the holes. Eastern kingbirds darted out from exposed perches to snatch insects from the air, and hermit thrushes sang from the understory, along with rufous-sided towhees and common yellowthroats. Aquatic vegetation chokes the shallow water everywhere on Hay Brook.

As you enter the main lake, off to the right you will see Apache Campground and a few houses on the opposite shore. Paddle around to the left, heading north. Besides the many marshy coves to explore, you can paddle up each of the two main tributaries for a couple of miles before they become impassable. The varied vegetation here, ranging from scrubby marsh plants to tall deciduous trees and pine plantations, enhances the scenic character of upper Estes Lake.

You should not see many powerboats here. No access exists for large boats; the Estes Lake Association limits motors to 10 HP, and the large number of barely submerged rocks and stumps make speedboating dangerous. We paddled here on a warm Saturday in late June and saw no other boat, human- or motor-powered.

4 | Mousam River

On this section of the Mousam, expect to see tree-lined shores, great blue herons, kingfishers, double-crested cormorants, and possibly beavers in the evening. Trees, shrubs, and flowers bloom in profusion in spring. Look for large patches of irises.

Location: Kennebunk
Maps: *Maine Atlas & Gazetteer*, Map 2: D5; USGS Kennebunk
Length: 3 miles one way
Time: 4 hours; shorter trips possible
Habitat Type: Dammed-up section of river
Fish: Brook, brown, and rainbow trout (see fish advisories, Appendix A)
Take Note: Shoreline private but with limited development

GETTING THERE
From I-95, Exit 25 southbound, turn left on Route 35, go 0.2 mile, and turn right on Alfred Road. Go 0.8 mile (cumulative: 1 mile) and turn left on Mill Street. Go 0.5 mile (1.5 miles) to the access on right before the bridge. (43° 24.228′ N, 70° 35.238′ W)

WHAT YOU'LL SEE
The Mousam River provides an outstanding paddling resource for much of its length, from Mousam Lake down to Kennebunk Beach. The section included here runs upstream from a dam just west of I-95. The river meanders so frequently, you rarely see much of it at once. Side passages abound, and the main channel has no perceptible current, at least at times of low water.

Throughout this section, standing dead trees seem to sprout from the water, and the typical assortment of aquatic plants and shoreline shrubs adorn the many marshy areas. Rhodora, a beautiful pink wild azalea, blooms in early June, followed by sheep laurel and a viburnum, probably arrowwood. Extensive patches of iris bloom in marshy areas, wherever there's open canopy. If you get as far as the high-tension wires crossing overhead, look for black locusts hanging out over the water. These trees belong to the pea family and sport large clusters of white flowers in June.

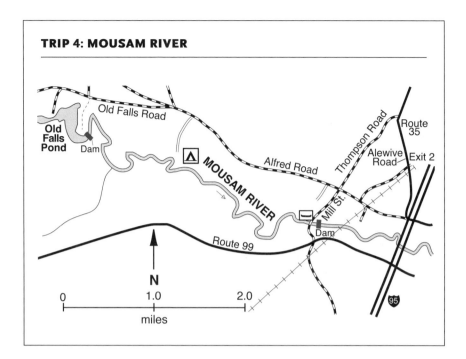

TRIP 4: MOUSAM RIVER

Great blue herons stalk fish and amphibians along the shoreline; double-crested cormorants dive for fish; and herring gulls patrol the air, hunting for dead things floating in the water, always ready to snatch food away from other birds that venture near. Beaver cuttings and lodges occur all along the shore, and this should be a good place to look for river otters.

The privately owned shoreline has very few No Trespassing signs. In the more secluded reaches, you probably could picnic on the flat grassy spots, but please treat the land with respect so it does not get posted off-limits to others who follow. An occasional house or camp punctuates the shoreline, but in places you can paddle 1 mile without seeing any evidence of civilization. This wild river's presence within a few miles of Kennebunk, I-95, and thousands of summer vacationers is remarkable. Boating here on a warm Saturday in June, we saw nary another human.

Large clumps of irises grow along Mousam River's shores.

5 | Scarborough Marsh

This salt marsh features many acres and miles of streams through salt marsh grasses. Paddling at low tide and under windy conditions can be a challenge. The nature center's staff can be helpful about when to paddle here. Look for muskrat, salt marsh and Nelson's sharp-tailed sparrows, glossy ibis, snowy egrets, and great blue herons.

Location: Scarborough
Maps: *Maine Atlas & Gazetteer*, Map 3: B3, B4; USGS Old Orchard Beach, Prouts Neck
Area: 3,100 acres with many miles of streams
Time: 5 hours; shorter trips possible
Habitat Type: Meandering, slow-flowing, marshy streams
Fish: Saltwater species (see fish advisories, Appendix A)
Information: Maine Audubon Society Nature Center, 207-883-5100, maineaudubon.org/find-us/scarborough-marsh; Friends of Scarborough Marsh, scarboroughmarsh.weebly.com

Take Note: Some streams go dry at low tide; wind and tides can make paddling difficult; novice paddlers should avoid this marsh; for tides, visit me.usharbors.com/maine-tide-charts

GETTING THERE

From the junction of Routes 1 and I-295 in Portland, go 8.1 miles south on Route 1 and turn left on Route 9/Pine Point Road. Go 0.8 mile (cumulative: 8.9 miles) to the Audubon Center on the left. (43° 33.948′ N, 70′ 22.482′ W)

WHAT YOU'LL SEE

Preserved by the Wetlands Protection Act of 1972, Scarborough Marsh is a 3,100-acre estuary of fresh, brackish, and salt water filled with birds, mammals, insects, and crustaceans, representing 15 percent of Maine's saltmarsh area.

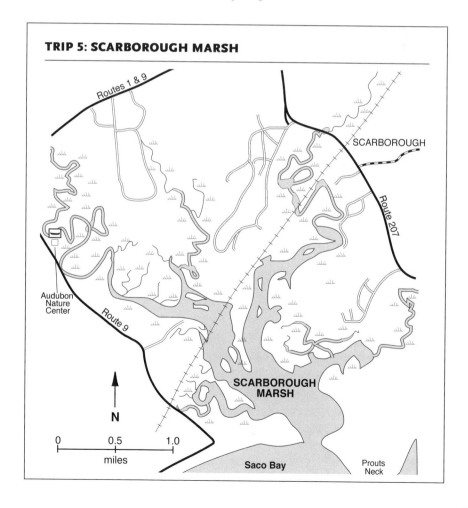

TRIP 5: SCARBOROUGH MARSH

Acres of cordgrass, cattails, rushes, and sedges greet you as you venture onto the serpentine waters of Scarborough Marsh.

Native Americans called marshes *owascoag*, which means "land of many grasses," and indeed, endless acres of cordgrass, cattails, rushes, and sedges, along with many other aquatic plants, stretch into the distance.

We have much to learn about the ecology of estuaries and their value as producers of huge quantities of biomass, with more production per acre than farm fields, pine plantations, or even tropical rain forests. The Friends of Scarborough Marsh, a coalition of citizens and organizations, works to protect and to restore the marsh. The Maine Department of Inland Fisheries & Wildlife oversees Scarborough Marsh and, through a cooperative agreement, allows Maine Audubon to operate a nature center here. The center offers education programs (including canoe and walking tours), nature trails, canoe rentals, and a boat launch site.

The nature center maintains a list of recent sightings in this birdwatcher's paradise. One bird of interest that occurs in relatively large numbers, the glossy ibis, looks black at a distance but iridescent purple at close range. About two feet long with a three-foot wingspan, it uses its long, down-curved bill to poke around marshy areas, hunting up crustaceans or whatever else it can find. It formerly ranged only as far north as the mid-Atlantic states but has recently expanded into Canada.

We have included Scarborough Marsh with some reservations due to its 10-foot tides and wind, which blows almost constantly across the treeless marsh. Paddling against both tide and wind can be quite tiring, and this combination will confront you on windy days, as the serpentine rivers double back on themselves every few hundred feet. We recommend this area to strong paddlers who wear PFDs at all times.

Maine Audubon recommends you paddle out against the tide while fresh then allow the tide to help carry you back in—very wise advice, indeed. With a little planning, you could ride both out and back in on the tide as it turns. Contact the nature center just before your trip to find out the local tide times. The staff also told us horror stories of people who paddle up narrow creeks and get stranded as the tide runs out, leaving the paddlers in hip-deep mud. We recommend you stick to the miles of main river channels, which do not go dry at low tide.

6 | Presumpscot River

The Presumpscot backs up behind a small dam, taming the river to a barely perceptible current. Besides spotting wood ducks and large numbers of painted turtles, this wild place affords a great opportunity to study aquatic vegetation.

Location: Gorham, Westbrook, Windham
Maps: *Maine Atlas & Gazetteer*, Map 5: E3; USGS Gorham, Portland West
Length: 5 miles one way
Time: 5 hours; shorter trips possible
Habitat Type: Dammed-up section of river; marshy channels
Fish: Brook trout, brown trout, landlocked salmon, smallmouth bass (see fish advisories, Appendix A)
Take Note: A small amount of development near the put-in

GETTING THERE
From I-95, Exit 47 northbound, go 1.7 miles west on Route 25 and turn right, followed by a quick left on Business 25. Go 0.8 mile (cumulative: 2.5 miles) and turn right on Bridge Street in Westbrook. Go 0.3 mile (2.8 miles) and turn left

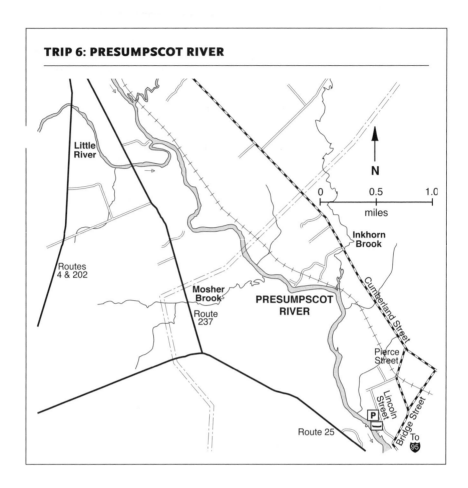

TRIP 6: PRESUMPSCOT RIVER

Little River

Routes 4 & 202

Mosher Brook

Route 237

PRESUMPSCOT RIVER

Inkhorn Brook

Cumberland Street

Pierce Street

Lincoln Street

Bridge Street

P

Route 25

To 95

N

0   0.5   1.0
miles

on Lincoln Street. Go 0.1 mile (2.9 miles) to the carry-in access on the left; park at the skating rink. (43° 40.904´ N, 70° 22.243´ W)

WHAT YOU'LL SEE

The section of the Presumpscot between Saccarappa Falls and Mallison Falls provides a very pleasant upstream paddle against a barely perceptible current. You initially will pass a few houses as you paddle northwest, but these generate little impact on the river's wild feel.

In some areas, trees and shrubs extend right down to the water, but along much of the river, a fringe dominated by bur-reed, arrowhead, pickerelweed, and bulrush buffers the shore. We saw some spectacular bright pink waterlily here, which we believe is a hybrid of the native American white waterlily (*Nymphaea odorata*) and a nonnative horticultural waterlily species, *Nymphaea alba*.

An uncharacteristically unwary painted turtle watches us glide by.

The broadleaf arrowhead (*Sagittaria latifolia*)—also known as duck-potato, Indian potato, and wapato, in reference to its edible tubers—along the river is among the most robust we've come across in our paddling, as is the bur-reed (*Sparganium eurycarpum*). Ferns include royal, interrupted, ostrich, sensitive, and bracken. Shrubs and trees here include alder, glossy buckthorn (an invasive plant), red maple, silver maple, black cherry, red oak, white birch, gray birch, and white pine.

About 1.5 miles upriver from the access, Inkhorn Brook enters from the right, through a distinctive stone tunnel. You can easily paddle through the tunnel, which supports railroad tracks, and enter a secluded, wild cattail marsh. We immediately surprised about a half-dozen painted turtles sunning on some partially submerged logs, not accustomed to intruders. You can't paddle far on Inkhorn Brook, perhaps 100 yards, before downed trees block your way, but it's definitely worth the detour.

Along with the couple-dozen painted turtles during our mid-August trip, we spotted wood ducks, Canada geese, and cormorant. In spring we would expect to see many more species.

Another mile or so upstream from Inkhorn Brook and a few hundred yards before some large power lines cross the river, Mosher Brook enters sharply from the left. Paddling a short distance on this creek, we saw lots of 6- to 8-inch bass. Overhanging shrubs—including, unfortunately, plenty of buckthorn—make this creek less inviting, and you can go only a little way.

Less than a mile from the large power lines, you will reach the confluence of Little River, which enters from the left. You can also paddle up this river, but we only explored to the Mosher Road bridge, perhaps 0.5 mile from the confluence. Continuing on the main river from the Little River inlet, you will reach Mallison Falls and the Mallison Falls Hydroelectric Project in less than 1 mile.

The Presumpscot River, which extends for 27 miles and drops 270 feet from the outlet of Sebago Lake to Casco Bay, played an important role in Maine's history. The Native American name means "many falls" or "many rough places," but once Europeans settled here, the river changed dramatically.

Maine's first dam, the Smelt Hill Dam, was built at Presumpscot Falls in 1732, and settlers subsequently built another nine dams on the river, ultimately impounding 22 of the river's 27-mile length. The Presumpscot River also hosted Maine's first pulp mill, in the 1730s, in Westbrook (near the access) and its first hydroelectric facility, in 1889, at the Smelt Hill Dam.

Damming the river resulted in early conflict between the Colonists and the Rockomeecook, as doing so blocked migrating fish, upon which the tribe depended. In fact, the first armed conflict with American Indians over fish passage occurred here. Chief Polin twice walked to Boston to plead with the governor to remove the dams, ultimately futilely. Polin was killed on the banks of the river in 1756 following the subsequent Chief Polin Uprising. It was also on this river that the first known sale of alcohol to American Indians occurred. Squitregusset, a member of the Aucociscos, sold all of his land on the Presumpscot near Falmouth to settlers for 1 gallon of alcohol per year.

In 2002, past wrongs spanning centuries were partially corrected with the removal of Smelt Hill Dam, allowing an upstream 7-mile migration of smelt and other sea-running fish for the first time in 270 years. Presumpscot River Watershed Coalition advocates removal of another three dams.

7 | Hollis Center Arm of the Saco River

Picturesque, deciduous-covered hillsides border this long and narrow, dammed-up section of the Saco. Look for great blue herons patrolling the shoreline.

Location: Buxton, Dayton, Hollis
Maps: *Maine Atlas & Gazetteer*, Map 2: A5, B5 and Map 3: A1, B1; USGS Bar Mills
Area/Length: 428 acres; 3.5 miles one way; you can also paddle up the Saco River beyond the Route 202 bridge
Time: 5 hours; shorter trips possible
Habitat Type: Dammed-up section of river
Fish: Smallmouth bass (see fish advisories, Appendix A)

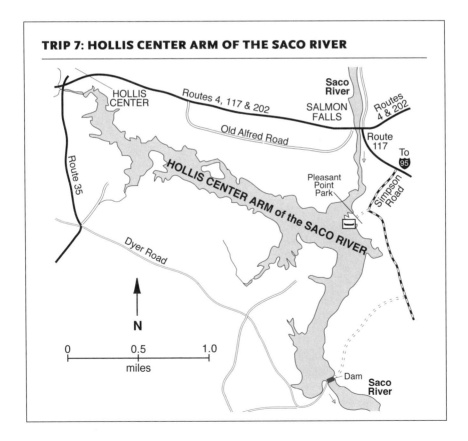

TRIP 7: HOLLIS CENTER ARM OF THE SACO RIVER

Take Note: Wind from the northwest can make paddling difficult; novice paddlers should avoid this area under windy conditions

GETTING THERE

From I-95, Exit 36, go east on I-195 to Exit 1, turn left on Industrial Park Road, go 0.5 mile and turn right on Route 112. Go 5.5 miles (cumulative: 6 miles) and turn left on Route 117, followed by a quick jog right. Go 2 miles (8 miles) and turn left on Simpson Road. Go 0.3 mile (8.3 miles) and turn right through stone pillars into Pleasant Point Park, Buxton. Carry your boat down to the water from the parking area. (43° 35.238′ N, 70° 33.150′ W)

WHAT YOU'LL SEE

The Saco River drains the White Mountains of Maine and New Hampshire, meandering southeast until it dumps into the Gulf of Maine at Saco. Whitewater dominates the river's upper reaches, but once it crosses from New Hampshire into Maine, the Saco becomes a quietwater paddler's dream. From Swans Falls in Fryeburg it meanders slowly for miles down to Hiram and seems nearly

A couple canoes on the Saco River near Hollis, Maine. Photo: Jerry and Marcy Monkman/ Ecophotography

bank-to-bank with canoeists all summer long, inducing anyone who wants a modicum of solitude to seek less-traveled ways. The Hollis Center Arm described here, just south of Salmon Falls and southeast of Hollis Center, backed up behind a dam, sees far fewer paddlers.

The town of Buxton owns Pleasant Point Park, whose gates remain open from sunrise to sunset. Large deciduous trees line the shore and the hillsides around this wide lake, with a smattering of lofty conifers, mainly white pine, interspersed. Huge granite boulders poke up here and there along the shoreline. Numerous coves, some of them quite deep and with jagged shorelines, beg to be explored. With all of the maples, oaks, and other deciduous trees lining the banks and covering the hillsides, this should be a beautiful place to paddle in the fall when the leaves turn. We would avoid this popular recreation spot on midsummer weekends. When we paddled here, we passed several canoes out on the water but saw only one small motorboat.

8 | Lower Range Pond

Although this is a great place to paddle, avoid it on nice summer weekends. Look for loons, ospreys, great blue herons, and ducks. A bald eagle pair has nested here successfully every year since 2004.

Location: Poland
Maps: *Maine Atlas & Gazetteer*, Map 5: A3; USGS Mechanic Falls, Minot
Area: 290 acres
Time: 3 hours
Habitat Type: Deep, clear, wooded kettle pond with some marshy areas
Fish: Brook trout, brown trout (see fish advisories, Appendix A)
Take Note: 10 HP limit; some development; popular swimming area; entrance fee; open 9 A.M. to sunset

GETTING THERE
From I-95, Exit 63 northbound, turn right/east on Route 202, go 0.2 mile and turn left on Route 26. Go 9.4 miles (cumulative: 9.6 miles) and turn right on Route 122/Poland Springs Road. Go 1.4 miles (11 miles) and turn left on Empire Road. Go 0.7 mile (11.7 miles) and turn left into the park. (43° 2.550′ N, 70° 21.198′ W)

TRIP 8: LOWER RANGE POND

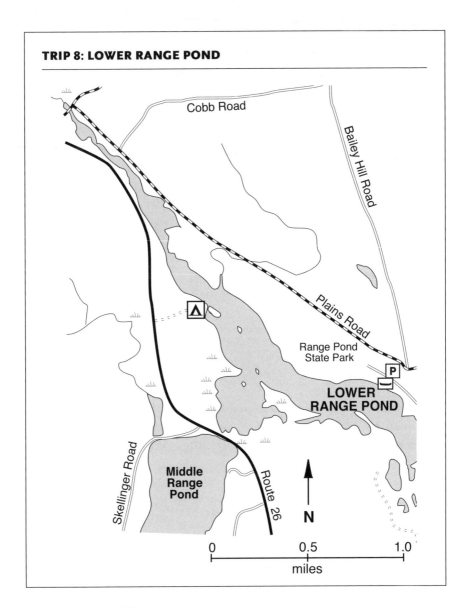

WHAT YOU'LL SEE

On the right day, with the weather just threatening enough to keep most people away, Lower Range Pond offers a great paddling experience. A 10 HP limit keeps this spot relatively quiet. The pond boasts crystal clear water with sandy shores that are superb for swimming, and the marshy coves teem with wildlife.

We visited on a late afternoon midweek in August and had the place to ourselves. But you won't find much solitude here on a nice summer weekend.

Some development intrudes on the pond's north end, including a campground and the YMCA's Camp Connor. The houses along here, with their associated boats and activity, can detract significantly from a quietwater experience. We prefer paddling the south end and the marshy extension off to the southwest, toward Route 26 and Middle Range Pond. (If you carry over the road into Middle Range Pond, be very careful of traffic.) By midsummer, this marshy cove may be too shallow and weed-choked for paddling, except for a deep, winding channel.

During our visit, we saw a variety of wildlife: a loon pair with well-developed chicks, ospreys, great blue herons, black ducks, kingfishers, kingbirds, spotted sandpipers, numerous fish, freshwater mussels, and a fascinating invertebrate: bryozoans. In its own phylum (birds, mammals, and reptiles are other phyla), the bryozoan we saw here is in the genus *Pectinatella*. Individual units, or zooids, of the underwater colonies use tiny hairs, or cilia, to sweep the water for microscopic algae, diatoms, and protozoa. *Pectinatella* colonies grow as large as watermelons, although here they range considerably smaller. The slimy, gelatinous colonies look somewhat like translucent pineapples growing on underwater branches or rocks. Though we see bryozoans only rarely in Maine, we appreciate their presence, as they require extremely pure water and thus serve as indicators of pollution-free lakes and ponds.

In 2004, a bald eagle pair kicked ospreys off an existing nest in a red pine on an island off the campground and has fledged one or two young every year since, with triplets in 2012. This pair is one example of the remarkable recovery of eagles, ospreys, peregrine falcons, and other raptors since Rachel Carson rang the pesticide alarm with her 1962 book, *Silent Spring*.

Close proximity to Maine's most famous spring water bottling plant, Poland Spring, also tells of the water's purity. Paddling around the pond's southern edge, you can hear the hum of pumping machinery coming from the plant. (Poland Spring pumps from a huge underground aquifer, not from the pond.)

Trees include white pine, a few red pine, hemlock, gray birch, red maple, and pitch pine, some unusually large. Extensive areas of pickerelweed, watershield, pondweed, bulrushes, and grasses grow along the shallower shores. In places you will see patches of cattail, American white waterlily, yellow pondlily, and a waterlily-like member of the gentian family: floating heart (with small, heart-shaped leaves and small white flowers).

Kettle ponds, such as Lower Range Pond and its larger neighbors to the south (Middle and Upper Range ponds), formed when the last glacier receded about 10,000 years ago, leaving behind huge chunks of ice buried in glacial till. As the ice gradually melted, the deep depressions filled with water. You can often recognize kettle ponds by their sandy shores and bottoms.

2 | MIDCOAST

The Midcoast region's diverse landscape—the bustling towns of Augusta, Bangor, Bath, and Brunswick; rolling farmland; coastal harbors; and rocky shoreline—gives way to pockets of inland wilderness with surprising paddling opportunities. We feature 16 trips here, including secluded Dresden Bog (Trip 12), just a short distance from the state capital, in the Erle R. Kelley Wildlife Management Area; Lower Togus Pond (Trip 17), which is within Augusta's city limits but remains undeveloped, boasting an abundance of bog vegetation; and Carlton Pond and Carlton Bog (Trip 22), close to Bangor, in the middle of a state waterfowl production area, where you have a great chance to see wildlife, including black terns.

For this book's third edition, we have added four new wonderful paddling opportunities, including Merrymeeting Bay on the Androscoggin and Kennebec Rivers, a major waterfowl gathering spot (Trip 10); marshy Messalonskee Lake, with its rare birds and meandering Belgrade Stream in the Belgrade Lakes region (Trip 16); Upper Mason Pond and Goose River (Trip 20), just north of Penobscot Bay; and Canaan Bog, Carrabassett Stream, and Black Stream (Trip 23) along Route 2, just east of Skowhegan.

9 | Runaround Pond

Runaround Pond is really two creeks filled with aquatic vegetation. Expect to see great blue herons, kingfishers, ducks, painted turtles, muskrat, beavers in the evening, ospreys, and possibly great horned owls.

Location: Durham
Maps: *Maine Atlas & Gazetteer*, Map 5: B5; USGS North Pownal
Area: 91 acres
Time: 3 hours
Habitat Type: Shallow, marshy, dammed-up pond
Fish: Largemouth bass, chain pickerel (see fish advisories, Appendix A)
Take Note: Slow paddling due to aquatic vegetation

GETTING THERE

From Auburn, go south on Route 136. Route 9 enters from the left. Where Routes 9 and 136 split in Durham, go 2.2 miles south on Route 9 and turn right on Runaround Pond Road. Go 1 mile (cumulative: 3.2 miles) to the access on the right. (43° 57.090′ N, 70° 10.152′ W)

WHAT YOU'LL SEE

Runaround Pond—really two shallow, weedy streams—teems with wildlife and aquatic vegetation. It takes a few hours to paddle back to the farthest navigable reaches of each stream, but it's well worth the effort. You should see wood ducks, mallards, great blue herons, muskrats, turtles, fish, and other wildlife. When we paddled here on a beautiful Sunday morning in July, we met only one other canoe. Aquatic vegetation severely limits access for motorboats.

Several large, flat boulders at the access, overhung by red pines, provide perfect spots for a picnic. From the access, you can paddle into a serene little cove by going through one of the two large culverts under the road. The creek emerges in a walled canyon with large white pines above.

As you return to the access and head upstream, huge rafts of beautiful, bright blue–flowered pickerelweed greet you, abuzz with the constant drone of thousands of bumblebee pollinators. Watershield, American white waterlily, yellow pondlily, and a yellow-flowered bladderwort are your constant companions. Tannic acids released during plant degradation color the water a yellow-brown.

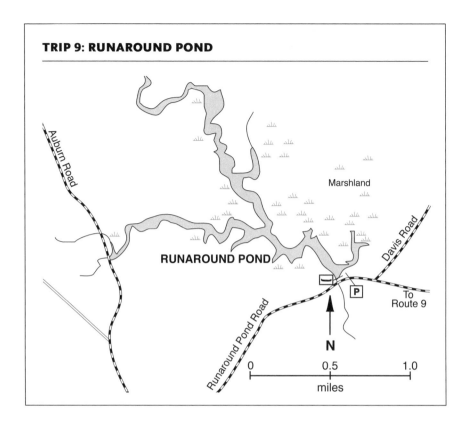

TRIP 9: RUNAROUND POND

Marshland

RUNAROUND POND

Auburn Road

Davis Road

Runaround Pond Road

To Route 9

N

0   0.5   1.0
miles

When the stream channel forks, go left, weaving your way back up the meandering channel. Shrubs and aquatic vegetation choke the wide valley, leaving open only a narrow channel. Back on higher ground, maple dominates the shoreline, along with scattered pine, pointed balsam fir, and red oak. You can paddle all the way to Auburn Road, more than 2 miles, where the stream becomes impassable.

A great horned owl alighted from one of the many side coves as we drew near. Kingfishers scolded us all the way up the stream. Several great blue herons took off as we approached, and wood ducks and mallards exploded from the surface as we rounded the numerous stream bends. We did not expect to see a cormorant on this shallow, weedy stream, but there it was as we rounded a bend. You should see muskrat and turtles, and in the evening look for the numerous beavers whose presence is evident everywhere.

The right-hand fork, not quite as long, has thicker aquatic vegetation, a less open channel, and lots of duckweed obscuring visibility into the water. Nonetheless, it offers much of the same beauty as the left fork and is well worth paddling.

A great horned owl casts a cautious eye in our direction as we paddle by.

10 | Merrymeeting Bay and Cathance River

Six Maine rivers converge here to form Merrymeeting Bay, one of the East Coast's main waterfowl stopovers. Also expect to see bald eagles, ospreys, lots of wild rice, and many marshland species. Fifty fish species live in or pass through the bay; before you drop a line, know which, what size, and how many of each you can keep.

Location: Bath, Bowdoinham, Brunswick, Topsham
Maps: *Maine Atlas & Gazetteer*, Map 6: B4; USGS Bath, Bowdoinham, Brunswick, Richmond
Area: 9,600 acres
Time: All day; shorter trips possible
Habitat Type: Tidal freshwater bay formed by the Androscoggin and Kennebec rivers; marshy side channels and streams
Fish: 50 fish species recorded (see fish advisories, Appendix A)

Take Note: Hazardous conditions due to wind; strong tidal currents; stay well away from the restricted outflow called "The Chops" (northeast of the maps included here)

GETTING THERE

Bay Bridge Road. From I-295, Exit 28 northbound to Route 1 North, go 1.4 miles and merge onto Route 1. Go 3.2 miles (cumulative: 4.6 miles) and exit for Route 24/Bath Road in Brunswick. Go 0.5 mile (5.1 miles) and turn left on Bath Road. Go 0.5 mile (5.6 miles) and turn left on Old Bath Road. Go 2.5 miles (8.1 miles), turn left, and immediately left again on Bay Bridge Road. Go 0.6 mile (8.7 miles) to the access. (43° 56.088′ N, 69° 53.334′ W)

    Cathance River. From I-295, take Exit 37 northbound, turn right (east), and go 1.3 miles to Route 24 in Bowdoinham. Go straight across to the access. (44° 0.474′ N, 69° 53.694′ W)

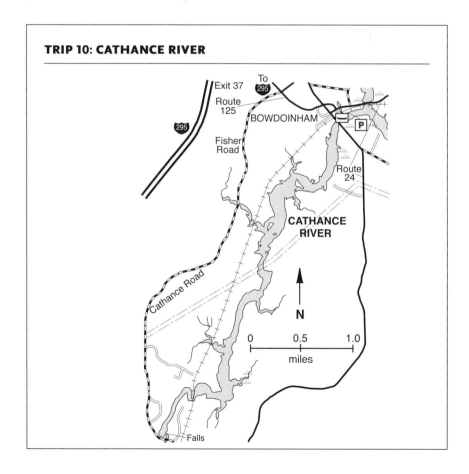

TRIP 10: CATHANCE RIVER

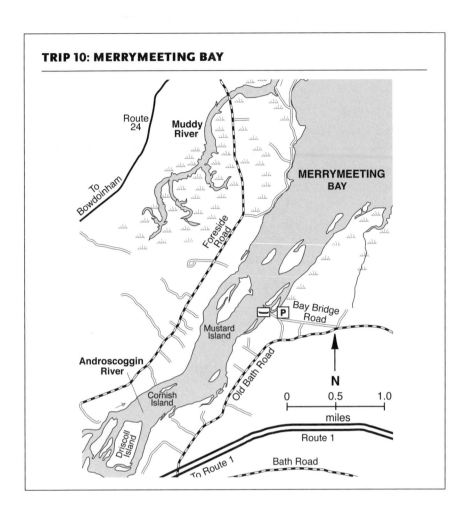

TRIP 10: MERRYMEETING BAY

WHAT YOU'LL SEE

Created by the confluence of six rivers, including two of Maine's largest, Androscoggin and Kennebec, remarkable Merrymeeting Bay sees a huge amount of fresh water pass through it. In fact, rivers emptying into Merrymeeting drain nearly 40 percent of Maine's land area, enough water volume to keep the water fresh—despite its being tidal.

Although Merrymeeting is called a bay, it really isn't, because it doesn't front directly on the ocean. Geologists refer to it as an inland river delta. The very low salinity (less than 0.5 parts per thousand versus 35 for seawater) means it shouldn't really be called an estuary or salt marsh either, although sometimes it's referred to as an estuary. Ecologists refer to it as a tidal riverine ecosystem.

The large tidal flux (about five feet) and predominantly fresh water results in a tremendous variety of fauna and flora. Merrymeeting is the largest stag-

Look for abundant wild rice growing here as you paddle up the scenic Cathance River.

ing area for migratory waterfowl north of Chesapeake Bay. In all our years of paddling, we can't recall ever seeing more wild rice (*Zizania aquatica*) than we found growing here—both on the main bay and along Cathance River, which we spent a long afternoon exploring.

Paddling on Merrymeeting Bay and the lower sections of rivers feeding it is all about understanding—and planning around—the tides. If you time it well, you can paddle with the current both ways on an out-and-back trip.

Cathance River

If paddling upstream (south) on Cathance River from the Bowdoinham access, try to begin your trip a few hours before high tide. You will be able to ride the incoming tide. Then, if the tide turns before your return, you can ride the outgoing tide back to Bowdoinham.

Wild rice—tremendous amounts of it—dominates the Cathance River shoreline. You will also see lots of other grasses, arrowhead, pickerelweed, and in midsummer, bright red cardinal flower blooms (*Lobelia cardinalis*). White pine, hemlock, red maple, several birch species, and some white cedar grow farther from shore.

Merrymeeting Bay presents a wealth of paddling options: islands, coves, and marshy streams.

We watched an immature bald eagle on this stretch, along with an osprey and northern harrier. Merrymeeting Bay is known for its sizable population of bald eagles.

Some development occurs near the Bowdoinham access, but almost none occurs along the 5-mile stretch of river upstream from the falls at Cathance. A number of streams ripe for short explorations enter along this stretch of quietly meandering river. After about 1.5 miles, you will pass under a huge array of high-voltage transmission lines—five or six. As you paddle farther south, the extensive areas of marsh peter out somewhat, with woodland extending right down to the water.

Continuing upstream, the river narrows, and you eventually pass a railroad trestle high overhead, with the falls about another 0.5 mile farther. Water cascades down and around the exposed ledge in several places. During spring, these falls can be dramatic. On the left side of the falls as you approach, you will see metal steps up to a picnic area—Head of the Tide Park in Topsham—which you can also reach by vehicle on Cathance Road. The granite millstones seen here indicate that a water-powered mill once existed on this site.

Paddling the other way on Cathance River from the Bowdoinham access, you can enter the main bay, and by sticking to the right (western) shore as you approach open water, you will reach the mouth of Muddy River. This offers additional pleasant exploration as long as you aren't working too hard against the tide.

Merrymeeting Bay

Putting in at the hand-launch site on Bay Bridge Road, you will enter via a widened section of the Androscoggin River. Large Mustard Island sits immediately across from the access. Farther north, a smaller island with stone shoreline at the southern end looks very inviting for picnics. Farther north on the bay's eastern shore, a small amount of development infringes. On a calm day, miles of shoreline beg to be explored.

During the late 1800s, in winter people harvested millions of tons of ice, referred to by some as "white gold," on the lower Kennebec River and shipped it as far away as the West Indies. By the end of the 1800s, the annual Kennebec ice harvest amounted to as much as 3 million tons. The invention of refrigeration around the turn of the century, of course, put an end to the freshwater-harvested ice industry.

From around 1900 through the Second World War, a substantial boatbuilding industry thrived here, particularly at Bath Iron Works, a little farther downstream on the Kennebec River. At peak production during the war, Bath Iron Works produced a destroyer every 17 days!

Merrymeeting Bay provides a key resource for anadromous fish, or fish that mostly live at sea but return to fresh water to spawn. Endangered shortnose sturgeon and Atlantic salmon, along with Atlantic sturgeon, shad, alewife, and eels all ply these waters. Some fish are protected, so before fishing here, make sure you know what fish can be kept.

When you paddle here, stay well away from the outlet of water known as "The Chops." This narrow slot through bedrock is considered very hazardous to boaters. We recommend sticking more to the bay's western side.

We have not explored the northern end of Merrymeeting Bay, where the Kennebec and Eastern rivers flow in. An access in Richmond on the Kennebec River across from Swan Island and a smaller access on the Eastern River off Route 197 in Dresden provide closer approaches to more northern waters. One could spend days exploring Merrymeeting Bay and its associated rivers, but use caution given the strong tidal currents and broad expanses over which waves can build up.

11 | Nequasset Lake

Little development crowds the wooded shoreline, making this a quiet place to paddle only a stone's throw from busy Route 1. Look for loons, ospreys, bald eagles, great blue herons, ducks, and woodland bird species.

Location: Woolwich
Maps: *Maine Atlas & Gazetteer*, Map 6: B5; USGS Bath
Area/Length: 392 acres; stream length 1 mile
Time: 4 hours
Habitat Type: Wooded reservoir and inlet stream
Fish: Brown trout, smallmouth bass, largemouth bass, white perch, chain pickerel (see fish advisories, Appendix A)
Take Note: Strong winds from north or south can cause dangerous conditions; novice paddlers should paddle the protected stream during windy conditions rather than the open lake; wear PFD; 10 HP limit

GETTING THERE

From Bath, cross the Kennebec River Route 1 bridge to Woolwich. From the end of the bridge, go 0.3 mile and turn left on Route 127. Go 3.7 miles (cumulative: 4 miles) and turn right on Old Stage Road. Go 0.5 mile (4.5 miles) to the access on the left just after the bridge. (43° 58.104′ N, 69° 46.368′ W)

An alternate access exists at the lake outlet (not shown) near the George Wright Road bridge.

WHAT YOU'LL SEE

From the Nequasset Lake access, one can paddle in both directions. We first paddled north up the inlet, Nequasset Brook. The wide channel starts out lined with pickerelweed but soon takes an abrupt left turn into a heavily forested area, where the stream narrows a bit. Hemlocks and maples form a beautiful canopy over the water for most of this heavily wooded, 30- to 40-foot-wide stream.

The stream has plenty of water, with no noticeable current. Marshy areas abound with swamp rose, pickerelweed, waterlilies, ferns, and bladderwort. A variety of trees extends along the wooded shore. Some spots look good for camping back under the hemlocks and pines. The stream meanders around,

TRIP 11: NEQUASSET LAKE

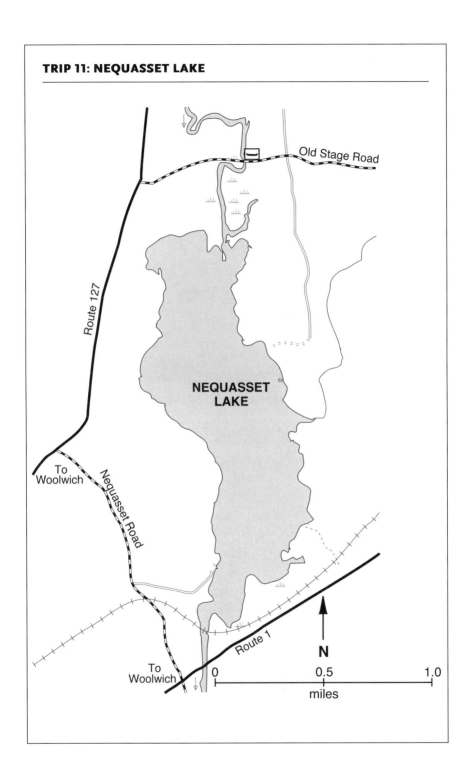

Bald eagles have enjoyed increased nesting success in Maine since this book's prior edition.

heading alternately north, west, south, and west, and then starts over again.

After paddling back about a mile, we came to some fields on the left and a 2-foot waterfall. It looked like one could portage up over the falls and continue paddling. We turned around here. We loved paddling up this quiet, beautiful little stream. A great blue heron and many ducks burst from the water as we rounded the sharp turns, and songbirds called constantly from the woods. Perhaps most numerous were the flutelike notes of hermit thrushes, announcing their territories.

The access stream, every bit as beautiful as the upstream portion, widens from the access down into Nequasset Lake. Lily pads choke several side channels, and at high water levels you can check out the extensive wetland on the left on the way down. The lake's north end contains a fair amount of watershield, a member of the waterlily family whose stalk attaches at the center of a floating oval leaf. A slimy, gelatinous film coats the undersides of leaves and stems.

Mixed hardwoods and evergreens, with many large white pines, line the heavily forested shore of Nequasset Lake, with little development in evidence. Large rocks protrude from shore and lake, inviting swimming. Birds appear everywhere, from great blue herons, hermit thrushs, mallards, and wood ducks on the stream to loons, great crested flycatchers, Eastern kingbirds, kingfishers, yellowthroats, and many more along the lake shore.

Fishermen use this lake regularly, though we only saw a few on a July weekend, most of them fishing quietly. On weekends, you will find more solitude paddling up Nequasset Brook. Although this lake lies close to vacation heaven, you should have to contend with only a modest amount of boating activity during the week.

12 | Dresden Bog

This hard-to-access pond sees few visitors. You will be rewarded with solitude, wood ducks, great blue herons, rich aquatic vegetation, and possibly beavers; look for the latter early in the morning or in the evening. The last time we visited, we saw wild turkeys.

Location: Alna, Dresden
Maps: *Maine Atlas & Gazetteer*, Map 13: E1; USGS Wiscasset
Area: 341 acres; 730 acres in Wildlife Management Area
Time: 3 hours
Habitat Type: Shallow, weedy pond
Fish: Largemouth bass, white perch, chain pickerel (see fish advisories, Appendix A)
Take Note: Very difficult to find access; no motors

GETTING THERE
From I-295, Exit 43, go 8.8 miles east on Route 197, jogging a short right on Route 27, and turn left on Blinn Hill Road in Dresden. Go 1.3 miles (cumulative: 10.1 miles) and stay straight on Bog Road. Go 1 mile (11.1 miles) to the access on the right. Look for a very hard-to-see small brook. Portage over a few beaver dams to get to the pond. (44° 6.318′ N, 69° 40.980′ W)

WHAT YOU'LL SEE
Because access to Dresden Bog requires portaging over a few beaver dams, this beautiful, peaceful area surrounded by the Erle R. Kelley Wildlife Management

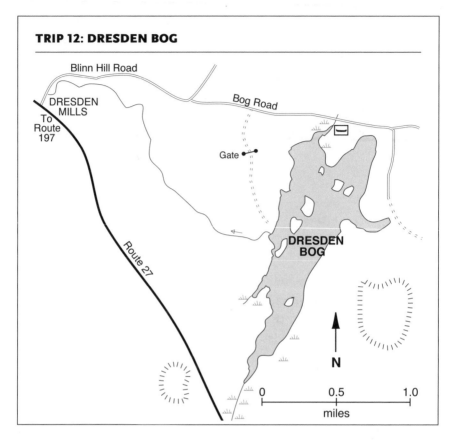

TRIP 12: DRESDEN BOG

Blinn Hill Road

DRESDEN MILLS

To Route 197

Bog Road

Gate

DRESDEN BOG

Route 27

N

0   0.5   1.0

miles

Area, just a short distance from the state capital, receives few visitors.

Paddle down the beautiful little inlet creek, past the beaver dams that bar most people as surely as a gate. Emerging from the marshy entrance, you will be struck by the varied beauty of this place, with many islands dotting the surface, emergent vegetation covering the pond, and mature trees lining the shore.

Many wood duck nesting boxes perch along the shore and out in the water. One hundred years ago, massive cutting of forests in the East and Midwest, as well as unregulated hunting, decimated wood duck populations. Concerned bird watchers, sportsmen, and wildlife management officials began erecting nesting boxes around swamps and rivers, resulting in a dramatic comeback for this beautiful duck.

The wood duck exhibits unusual arboreal behavior. When paddling wooded swamps and rivers, you sometimes see wood ducks perched in trees. Most ducks and geese nest on the ground; in this area, only wood ducks and common and hooded mergansers nest in cavities. Because common and hooded mergansers prefer wooded swamps and somewhat deeper water for diving for fish, we suspect these boxes see mostly wood ducks. For more on the wood duck, see "Wood Duck: Bird with the Spectacular Plumage," below.

We saw several flocks of black ducks and wood ducks feeding in the south end of this very shallow marsh. After a cursory, unsuccessful look for a passageway to Gardiner Pond, we retreated from the south end to let the ducks feed undisturbed.

Tall trees surround the pond, with mostly deciduous trees on the west shore and many tall white pines along the east shore. Dense undergrowth extends down to the water and on the heavily vegetated islands. Pickerelweed and American eelgrass (*Vallisneria americana*), whose long leaves protrude up through and then lie flat on the surface, cover the water.

WOOD DUCK: BIRD WITH THE SPECTACULAR PLUMAGE

Of all our ducks, and perhaps of all our bird species, few approach the wood duck for sheer beauty, with its distinctive multicolored breeding plumage, iridescent in sunlight. Getting a close look at these extremely wary ducks, though, requires very quiet paddling. Look for them in marshy areas as you paddle around grassy islands and meandering inlet channels.

Along with its gorgeous plumage, the wood duck, *Aix sponsa*, has an unusual nesting habit. Unlike most ducks, the wood duck nests in trees, using abandoned woodpecker holes, cavities hollowed out by decay, and—more recently—artificial nesting boxes. Sharp, down-curved claws on the toes help the bird cling to tree trunks. The duck can also walk or run overland far better than most other ducks. We remember paddling on Umbagog Lake and being quite surprised to see a female wood duck with a string of chicks swim to the shore then run into the protective vegetation. When danger threatens, wood ducks can dive and swim underwater for a fair distance.

Wood ducks pair up in the Southeast, where they overwinter. During spring migration, the male follows the female—usually to the same pond where she was raised. The female selects a suitable nesting cavity from 4 to 50 feet up in the air and up to 1 mile from water.

The hen lays ten to fifteen eggs, and when the young hatch, all within a few hours of each other, they remain in the nest for only a day. After checking carefully for signs of danger, the mother flies down to the water or the ground below and calls. The chicks use their toe claws to climb up to the nest entrance and jump out without hesitation. Their short, stubby wings and

downy feathers slow the chicks' descent, and remarkably, even when jumping from a nest 50 feet above ground, they seldom get hurt.

Chicks can swim right away, but predators take many before they reach water. In the water, large fish (bass, northern pike, chain pickerel) and snapping turtles prey on the young. Wood duck chicks grow quickly during summer and can fly when eight to ten weeks old.

Wood ducks molt in summer, the male losing his beautiful breeding plumage until fall. In nonbreeding, or eclipse plumage, the male resembles the female. (The male retains his red eyes and bill; the female has distinct white eye-rings.) For a two- to three-week period during molting, the male cannot fly. The female goes through a molt a little later than the male, but her plumage does not change significantly in appearance.

In fall, wood ducks congregate in large numbers, especially in evening. Sometimes hundreds or even thousands of wood ducks fly to the same roosting pond each evening and leave at daybreak to feed on nearby ponds and streams. By mid-autumn, most wood ducks have migrated south, traveling in small, loosely aggregated flocks.

While wood duck populations remain relatively strong today, unregulated hunting nearly drove the species to extinction around 1900. Efforts began to protect it through state legislation after the U.S. Biological Survey reported in 1901 that wood ducks faced possible extinction. At that time, the newly formed National Audubon Society and a few other organizations began a long effort to get federal legislation enacted—considered necessary to ensure survival. The first national legislation protecting waterfowl, the Weeks-McLean Migratory Bird Act, passed in 1913 and signed into law in 1918, extended protection of wood ducks and other migrating birds to Canada, gave the federal government greater authority to regulate hunting, and prohibited the sale of wildfowl. The hunting season on wood ducks closed completely in the United States and Canada until 1941, when the species had recovered enough to open a limited fall season.

A 1938 hurricane, which blew down many old trees with nesting cavities, set back wood duck recovery in the Northeast. To provide more sites, biologists erected the first artificial nesting boxes in Great Meadows National Wildlife Refuge, in Massachusetts, and the idea soon spread around the country. Today, tens of thousands of wood duck nesting boxes appear nationwide.

Even so, the loss of suitable nesting habitat continues to threaten wood ducks and other cavity-nesting birds. Wood ducks need remote ponds and marshes to raise their young, and development increasingly threatens these areas. Keep your distance in the presence of ducks with young.

13 | Duckpuddle Pond and Pemaquid River

Duckpuddle Pond—and especially the connecting Pemaquid River, really a small stream—provides an outstanding quietwater paddling resource. Expect to see seas of aquatic vegetation, numerous shrubs including lots of swamp rose, and possibly loons, ospreys, and bald eagles. In the early morning or evening, you may see beavers in the connecting stream.

Location: Nobleboro, Waldoboro
Maps: *Maine Atlas & Gazetteer*, Map 7: A4 and Map 13: E4;
USGS Waldoboro West
Area/Length: 293 acres; stream length 2 miles one way
Time: 5 hours; shorter trips possible
Habitat Type: Shallow, marshy pond and long connecting stream
with shrub-lined shore

Fish: Smallmouth bass, white perch, chain pickerel (see fish advisories, Appendix A)

Take Note: Substantial boat traffic on Pemaquid Lake

GETTING THERE

From the junction of Routes 1 and 32 in Waldoboro, go 3.6 miles south on Route 1 and turn left on Winslow Hill Road. Go 0.4 mile (cumulative: 4 miles) and turn left on Duckpuddle Road. Go 1.3 miles (5.3 miles) and turn left on Bremen Road. Go 0.3 mile (5.6 miles) to the access on the left, just after the bridge. (44° 5.940′ N, 69° 26.346′ W)

WHAT YOU'LL SEE

As you paddle the narrow passageway from the access toward Duckpuddle Pond, a sea of waterlilies, alders, pickerelweed, rushes, grasses—and mosquitoes—greet you. On our first visit, a pond-wide algae bloom clouded the water. Given the pond's scattered development, we could not see the nutrient influx that caused it. We subsequently found that runoff from nearby roads and a dairy farm contributed to frequent algae blooms. The Knox-Lincoln County Soil and Water Conservation District has helped the dairy farm improve practices and worked with towns to upgrade ditches and culverts, significantly reducing nonpoint source pollution and helping the pond meet water quality standards.

Trees around this shallow pond include white pine, hemlock, birch, sugar and red maples, and red oak, with oak predominating along the north shore. Several marshy coves beg to be explored, but save time to paddle down the beautiful outlet stream—about a 4-mile round trip. Start east from the access and stay to the right around the peninsula, covered with large white pines, that separates the two lower bays.

In the marshy eastern bay, pickerelweed hides an inlet. Paddle right through the center of the pickerelweed, back into Beaverdam Brook, threading your way through the sweetgale and other marsh plants. Though a narrow passage, you can paddle in quite far, especially if you portage over the beaver dams of this appropriately named stream.

Portaging not your cup of tea? Paddle back to the access, go under the large culvert, and down the nearly 2 winding miles to Pemaquid Pond. The connecting stream usually does not require portages, and the vegetation and channel width change several times, making this a very quiet, interesting place to paddle.

In places, pickerelweed, yellow pondlily, and American white waterlily cover the wide channel, while in other areas, alder, sweetgale, buttonbush, and

TRIP 13: DUCKPUDDLE POND AND PEMAQUID RIVER

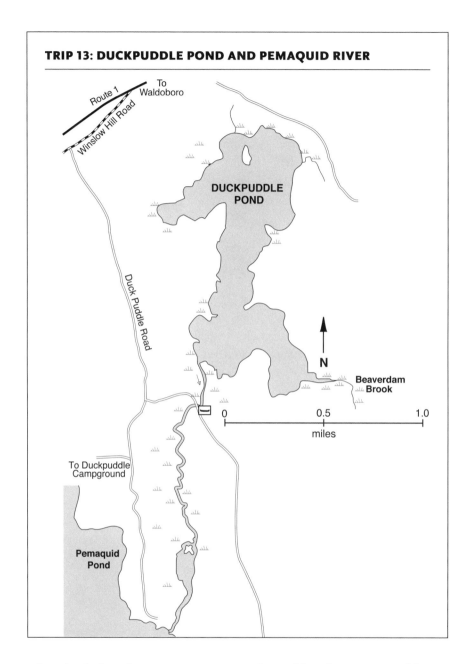

other shrubs line the narrower waterway. Beautiful pink swamp rose blooms everywhere, and a variety of songbirds calls from the undergrowth. Monster beaver lodges poke up here and there, some with tons of cuttings protruding up through the water surface, just in front of the lodge. The beavers seem barely able to keep the alders from closing the channel.

TRIP 13 : DUCKPUDDLE POND AND PEMAQUID RIVER   43

A 2-mile-long section of marshy Pemaquid Pond contains a large variety of plants, providing outstanding habitat for beavers, deer, and other wildlife.

The channel winds around the valley, drifting past many wood duck nesting boxes. In quieter stretches, note the patches of yellow-flowered bladderwort, a fully aquatic carnivorous plant whose bladders ingest microscopic organisms. The largest patch seems to be near Pemaquid Pond, just before a large grove of tamarack.

The outlet stream, with its great blue herons, ducks, and loads of other wildlife, provides a genuinely wild place to paddle, right in the middle of Midcoast Maine, one of the most heavily used recreational areas on the eastern seaboard.

Waterlilies

14 | Dyer Long Pond

Although it has some development, Dyer Long Pond is usually quiet and a great place to get exercise. Look for white pine, loons, swallows, ospreys, bald eagles, and beavers in the early morning and evening.

Location: Jefferson
Maps: *Maine Atlas & Gazetteer*, Map 13: D3; USGS North Whitefield
Area: 423 acres
Time: 4 hours
Habitat Type: Long, shallow pond with wooded shore
Fish: Smallmouth bass, largemouth bass (see fish advisories, Appendix A)
Take Note: Development but little boat traffic; hand-carry access

GETTING THERE

From Augusta, go east on Routes 17 and 32. From the Route 17/32 split, go 1 mile southeast on Route 32 and turn right on Route 215, jogging right, then left after 2.5 miles (cumulative: 3.5 miles). Continue on Route 215 for 1.7 miles (5.2 miles) and turn left on Hinks Road. Go 0.6 mile (5.8 miles) and turn right on the access road. (44° 11.142′ N, 69° 31.464′ W)

WHAT YOU'LL SEE

True to its name, long and narrow Dyer Long Pond extends in a northeast-southwest orientation. The marshy south and north ends and coves provide interesting areas to explore. Towering white pines that hide several cottages dominate the shoreline around the rest of the pond. Although the pond sees little boat traffic, paddling here is not a wilderness experience, but it's a great place to get exercise.

Granite boulders, deposited by glaciers 10,000 years ago as they gouged out the lake bed, cover much of the shoreline. Those just under the water's surface scrape the boat bottoms of unwary paddlers. Go slowly near the shoreline, especially where boulders jut out to form a point.

We saw an osprey, loons, and several beavers when we paddled here in the early evening. At the marshy southern end, the adjacent landowner had erected 30 songbird nesting boxes on poles out in the water. After a few minutes, we understood why. The owners obviously try to encourage tree swallows to feed their ever-hungry young with the ever-present hordes of mosquitoes.

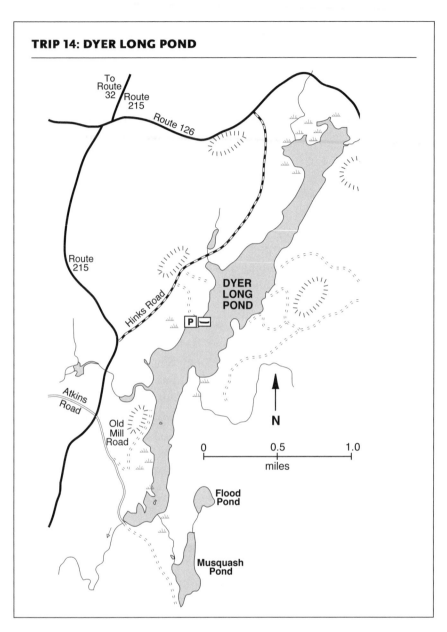

TRIP 14: DYER LONG POND

To Route 32
Route 215
Route 126
Route 215
Hinks Road
DYER LONG POND
Atkins Road
Old Mill Road
N
0   0.5   1.0
miles
Flood Pond
Musquash Pond

Unlike its purple martin cousin, the tree swallow typically does not nest in a colony. Instead, it chases other tree swallows away. To encourage bluebird nesting, people often put nesting boxes up in pairs. Tree swallows occupy the first box, leaving the second box free for bluebirds, which the swallows ignore. These tree swallows seem not to have heard of this theory, because every box had nesting tree swallows. Perhaps the sheer volume of pesky insects overwhelmed the swallows' aggressive territorial tendencies. If they spend all their time chasing insects, they have less time to chase each other.

15 | Jimmie Pond and Hutchinson Pond

These two small ponds offer great places to paddle. Jimmie Pond is readily accessible, Hutchinson Pond, not so much. Look for loons, ospreys, bald eagles, great blue herons, ducks, and beavers.

Location: Manchester, Farmingdale
Maps: *Maine Atlas & Gazetteer*, Map 12: C4; USGS Augusta, Winthrop
Area: Jimmie, 107 acres; Hutchinson, 100 acres
Time: 4 hours
Habitat Type: Jimmie is deeper, with wooded shore; Hutchinson is shallow and marshy, with a beaver-dammed connecting stream.
Fish: Jimmie, brook trout, splake, smallmouth bass, largemouth bass, chain pickerel (see fish advisories, Appendix A); Hutchinson, largemouth bass, chain pickerel.
Take Note: Little development; be careful portaging over Collins Road due to blind curves

GETTING THERE
In Hallowell at the junction of Route 201 and Central Street, go 1.7 miles west on Central Street and veer left on Shady Lane. Go 0.4 mile (cumulative: 2.1 miles) and turn right on Outlet Road in Manchester. Go 0.9 mile (3 miles) and veer right on Jamies Pond Road. Go 0.7 mile (3.7 miles) to the access. (44° 17.136′ N, 69° 51.120′ W)

WHAT YOU'LL SEE
You can access Jimmie Pond quite easily, whereas you have to work to get to Hutchinson Pond. These two quite different ponds used to supply water for the town of Hallowell. With the exception of the small southern arm, Jimmie lacks marshy areas and supports a coldwater fishery in the main pond, which reaches depths of up to 75 feet. In contrast, shallow, marshy Hutchinson Pond supports a warmwater fishery. The question becomes: How hard do you want to work to see the beautiful, seldom visited, wild Hutchinson Pond?

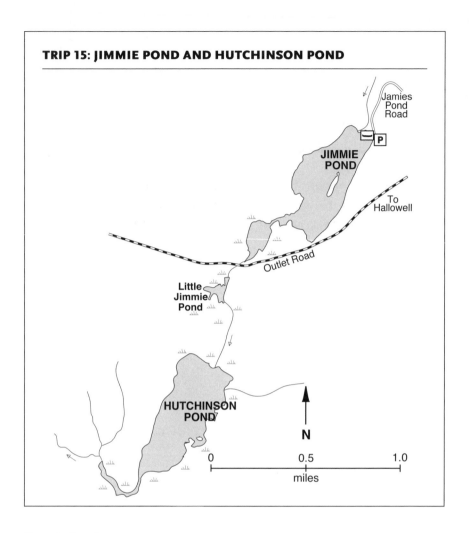

TRIP 15: JIMMIE POND AND HUTCHINSON POND

Jimmie Pond

Unless you're fishing, the larger body of Jimmie Pond does not hold a lot of interest. We spent most of our time in the small, southern arm. Ospreys nest here, competing with the anglers. Check the boggy areas for sundews and pitcher plants. Diverse species of bog plants inhabit this area, and shrubs dominate the shoreline, with large deciduous trees and a few scattered pines farther back. A beaver announced the displeasure of our company with a tail slap as we paddled by, and a loon swam before us in the channel between the two sections of Jimmie Pond.

The deeper main pond, in contrast, has almost no boggy areas. A tall mixed canopy marches down to the shoreline on all sides and, aside from one island,

Look for purple pitcher plants, *Sarracenia purpurea*, in the boggy areas of Jimmie Pond.

provides little to explore. It is still a picturesque little pond and well worth your visit, especially if you fish.

Hutchinson Pond

On the other hand, Hutchinson Pond attracts very little attention, thanks to its difficult access. Portage over the road from Jimmie Pond, watching carefully for cars careening around blind curves.

As you look down the narrow channel leading to Hutchinson, note the first of several beaver dams. It seemed as though all we did was portage over these amazing little engineering wonders when, in truth, we had to go over only six in 0.5 mile. Of course, the same six dams impeded our progress on the way back.

Vegetation crowds the beautiful channel after the last dam, and you have to thread your way through. Along the route, note the several lodges of the perhaps overly diligent waterway engineers. Extensive marshy areas occur on all sides of Hutchinson Pond, providing a lot to explore. On the northeast shore, look for the only bog-free area. A huge, beautiful granite boulder creeps up the shoreline. You get the impression you could spend a few days here and not see another soul.

Beware of leeches. We found three in the bottom of the boat that had dropped off our legs. At a gas station a half-hour later, we removed one tenacious little leech that had escaped detection under a sandal strap.

16 | Messalonskee Lake, Belgrade Stream, and Long Pond

This trip offers varied water, ranging from highly productive marshland to slow-flowing streams to large lakes. Messalonskee Lake is one of the few places in New England where you're likely to see nesting sandhill cranes and endangered black terns. Also expect to see bald eagles, loons, great blue herons, wood ducks, and huge numbers of marshland plants.

Location: Belgrade, Mount Vernon, Sidney
Maps: *Maine Atlas & Gazetteer*, Map 12: A3, A4, A5; USGS Belgrade, Readfield
Area/Length: Messalonskee Lake, 3,510 acres; Belgrade Stream, 6 miles one way; Long Pond, 2,714 acres
Time: All day; shorter trips possible
Habitat Type: Marshy lake and slow-flowing stream
Fish: Brown, brook, and lake trout; landlocked salmon; smallmouth bass; largemouth bass, white perch; chain pickerel (see fish advisories, Appendix A)
Take Note: A little development in places; some road noise; abundant invasive milfoil

GETTING THERE
Belgrade. From I-95, Exit 112B northbound, turn right on Routes 8, 11, and 27 and go 7.4 miles north to the access on the right. (44° 26.550′ N, 69° 49.860′ W)

Wings Mills. From the Belgrade access, go 0.3 mile north on Routes 8, 11, and 27 and turn left on Depot Road. Go 0.1 mile (cumulative: 0.4 mile) and turn left on Minot Hill Road. Go 1.1 miles (1.5 miles) and turn left on Route 135. Go 1.3 miles (2.8 miles) and turn right on Wings Mills Road. Go 2.4 miles (5.2 miles) to the access on the left above the dam in Mount Vernon. (44° 26.046′ N, 69° 54.234′ W)

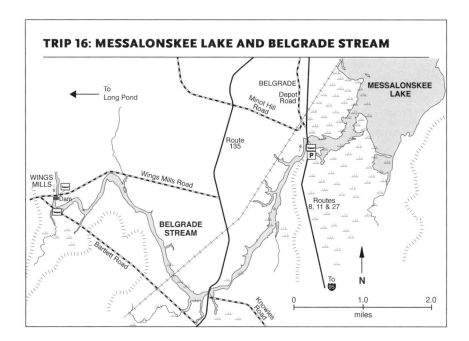

TRIP 16: MESSALONSKEE LAKE AND BELGRADE STREAM

Bartlett Road. Access is just around the corner from Wings Mills, on the left (also in Mount Vernon). (44° 25.902′ N, 69° 54.258′ W)

WHAT YOU'LL SEE
This trip offers several different types of water, but our favorite remains the marshy area at Messalonskee Lake's southern tip, an area that offers some of the best birding habitat in Maine.

Messalonskee Lake
From the access, paddle north and then east and south around the marsh for about 2 miles. In early spring, absent much of the emergent and floating vegetation, paddling into the marsh would be easier. Across the lake you will see some houses and docks with sizeable boats, but the south end's shallow water keeps most motorboats away.

Black terns live here, one of only a dozen places in the state where this endangered species nests. But we were totally taken by surprise to find sandhill cranes, one of very few places we have seen them in New England. We actually heard these birds—with their distinctive loud, rattling call—before we saw them. This tall, elegant bird only lately has begun nesting in Maine, with Messalonskee Lake's marshy habitat the first place in Maine (and New England) where they have nested in recent decades.

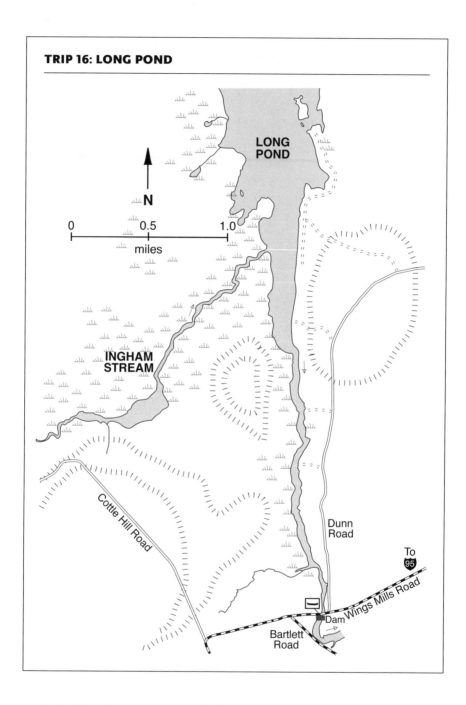

TRIP 16: LONG POND

LONG
POND

N

0   0.5   1.0
miles

INGHAM
STREAM

Cottle Hill Road

Dunn
Road

To
95

Wings Mills Road

Dam

Bartlett
Road

Pickerelweed dominates the shallows, but you also will see lots of yellow pondlily, American eelgrass, watershield, bur-reed, bulrush, cattail, and lesser amounts of American white waterlily. As you paddle along, look on the hillocks for northern pitcher plant and cranberry (with its tiny leaves and huge berries that ripen in fall). The hillocks also contain leatherleaf, sphagnum, marsh fern, royal fern, grasses, goldenrod, jewelweed, alder, and a few tamaracks and red maples trying to establish a footing on the higher ground. By late summer, you will see the distinctive seed heads of common cottongrass (*Eriophorum angustifolium*), which is actually in the sedge family.

Along with the huge sandhill cranes, we saw lots of wood ducks, great blue herons, and a pair of loons with chick out on the lake. Earlier in the year, this area would be a birder's paradise. If you're very lucky, you might see (or hear) the secretive least bittern, another endangered bird that nests here. We also saw dozens of painted turtles, but you'll see these on the ubiquitous half-submerged, sun-bleached logs and tree stumps only with quiet paddling.

Belgrade Stream

From the Belgrade access, head around to the left (west) under the Route 27 bridge. Paddling upstream on barely perceptible current, you'll see some houses—Loon Ridge Cabins on the left, where you can stay—along the shores of this wide, deep stream, but houses become less frequent farther upstream. Keep an eye out for an inlet brook on the right that you can explore for a short distance.

Farther upstream, another inlet on the right opens into a crescent-shaped section of water definitely worth exploring. We saw lots of wood ducks here, along with great blue herons and kingfishers arcing over the water with their rattling call. We also saw a muskrat and several active beaver lodges.

You also can launch a canoe or kayak farther upstream in Wings Mills. The entire area, unfortunately, is thick with invasive variable watermilfoil (*Myriophyllum heterophyllum*), so be sure to clean your boat well before launching on other waters.

Long Pond

Put in above the wooden Long Pond dam and paddle upstream, passing under Wings Mills Road. The low bridge should accommodate a large canoe if you duck.

The paddle up to Long Pond, initially a bit rocky, has a very different feel from Belgrade Stream at the other end. Watch out for boulders lurking just beneath the surface. You will pass a number of houses, most set back fairly far from the water, as is now required in Maine. Large motorboats and personal watercraft docked at these houses surprised us. On a busy summer weekend, it may not feel as tranquil as it did in early September.

From the boat access, you can see the marshy south end of Messalonskee Lake.

It's about a 2-mile paddle up to Long Pond on this widening channel. About 0.75 mile from the dam, pass under a small bridge that carries Spring Hill Road. A broader, marshy shore—covered mostly by bulrush—dominates as you move northward. Trees farther from shore include red oak, sugar maple, white birch, and white pine.

We saw lots more wood ducks and painted turtles here, as well as signs of beavers. The sandy bottom and mussel shells indicate fairly clean water, even though great quantities of milfoil infest shallower areas.

Long Pond itself has some development but offers pleasant paddling. Ingham Stream, which enters the western side 2.5 miles from the access, offers another opportunity for marshland exploration, undoubtedly with more solitude.

17 | Lower Togus Pond

This long, narrow pond—nearly devoid of development, despite lying within Augusta's city boundary—boasts acres of waterlilies, along with lots of bog vegetation. In the early morning or evening, look for beavers. If you're lucky, you might spy an otter. You should see loons, double-crested cormorants, great blue herons, and wood ducks.

Location: Augusta
Maps: *Maine Atlas & Gazetteer*, Map 13: C1, C2; USGS Togus Pond
Area: 515 acres
Time: 5 hours
Habitat Type: Long, shallow, marshy pond
Fish: Smallmouth bass, largemouth bass, white perch, chain pickerel (see fish advisories, Appendix A)
Take Note: Little development except on the very southern end

GETTING THERE

From Augusta, east of the Kennebec River on the rotary where Routes 202 and 105 divide, go east on Route 105 for 5.7 miles to the unmarked access along the roadway that separates Togus Pond from Lower Togus Pond. (44° 18.804′N, 69° 39.420′ W)

WHAT YOU'LL SEE

Quite a surprise awaits you on Route 105: first, the contrast between the development on Togus Pond and the lack of it across the road on Lower Togus Pond; second, and perhaps more surprising, that such a wild and beautiful place as Lower Togus Pond exists within the incorporated limits of Maine's capital city.

Long, narrow Lower Togus Pond has no development until you get to the very lowest section. Few boats ply these shallow, weedy waters. Several islands and lots of coves beg to be explored, but hundreds of acres of American white waterlily, especially in the extensive coves along the western shore, really draw one's attention. Some patches extend unbroken for 100 yards or more. Sundews and pitcher plants occur everywhere on the hummocks, and every native variety of bog vegetation certainly must be present.

In the spring, try to stay clear of the many wood duck nesting boxes as you thread your way back into the recesses of these coves. Big fish and beavers both

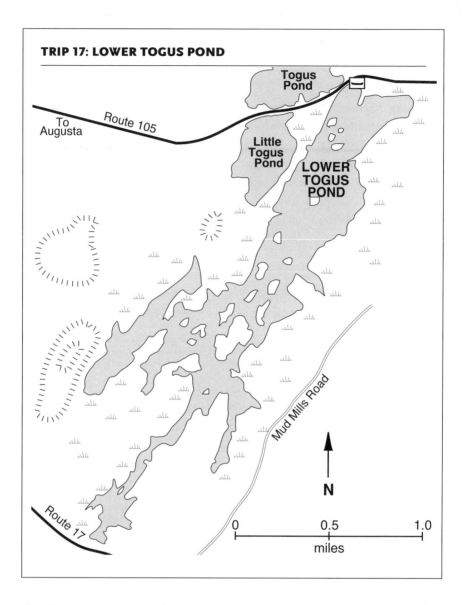

slap the water as you glide by, and two cormorants let us cruise close enough to catch the gleam in their eyes. We also saw several great blue herons fishing the shoreline and turtles sunning on nearly every log. Some beaver lodges extend 6 feet or more above the waterline.

It would take the better part of a day to fully explore this extraordinarily beautiful spot, a place you can paddle on windy days thanks to the waterlilies damping the swells and the numerous islands blocking the wind.

18 | Turner Pond

Elongated, shallow Turner Pond seems larger than its 193 acres. It has great spots for swimming and picnicking. Look for loons, ospreys, and ducks.

Location: Palermo, Somerville
Maps: *Maine Atlas & Gazetteer*, Map 13: B4, C4; USGS Razorville
Area: 193 acres
Time: 4 hours
Habitat Type: Shallow, marshy pond
Fish: Largemouth bass, chain pickerel (see fish advisories, Appendix A)
Take Note: No development; motors limited by access and shallow water

GETTING THERE

From Augusta, east of the Kennebec River on the rotary where Routes 202 and 105 divide, go east on Route 105 for 14.1 miles and turn left on Turner Ridge Road. Go 0.9 mile (cumulative: 15 miles) and turn left on Colby Road. Go 0.6 mile (15.6 miles) to the access on the right. (44° 19.692′ N, 69° 29.490′ W)

WHAT YOU'LL SEE

When we paddled here in the early 1990s, we found a rare, undeveloped gem with few visitors. More recently, the mill dam has begun to fail, exposing a few feet of muddy bank. Islands of all sizes dot the surface of this long, narrow pond, making it seem much larger than its 193 acres. One very smooth, gigantic boulder out in the middle just invites you to climb on it. Flat spots tucked

Mergansers

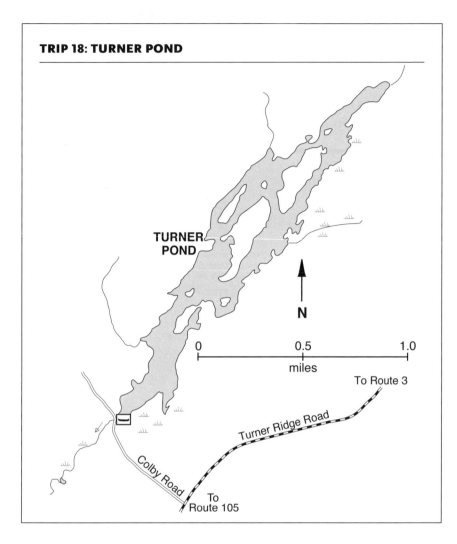

TRIP 18: TURNER POND

TURNER POND

N

0   0.5   1.0
miles

To Route 3

Turner Ridge Road

Colby Road

To
Route 105

up under the pines on both the mainland and the islands appear perfect for picnicking. We like two locations in particular: From the access, travel up the right shore, just past the first peninsula, to the right-hand shore opposite the large island. For the second: Go farther up the pond on the left-hand side, to a beautiful little spot on an island.

We saw a fuzzy, newborn baby loon swimming with its parents. The attentive parents called frequently as we tried to give them a wide berth, and they herded the little one between them. In contrast to the total chaos that erupts when one comes suddenly upon a mother merganser with a dozen babies in tow, the loons beat a much more dignified retreat. We had hoped to see one of the parents give the young loon a piggyback ride. They probably have the fish-

This large granite boulder in Turner Pond looks like a good rest stop or, perhaps, a good place to swim.

ing pretty much to themselves here. Although we didn't see any on our visits, this would be great place for ospreys, given the pond's maximum 7-foot depth.

Explore the numerous coves for wildlife and enjoy the waterlily-filled passages between islands. Marshy areas fill much of the shallow pond with typical bog vegetation. Many different tree species occur here, enhancing the pond's scenic quality. Due to the numerous coves and islands, it takes quite a bit of time to explore all of Turner Pond. Just when you think you have gotten to the end, you pass around yet another large island and emerge onto another stretch of open water.

19 | Stevens Pond

Although the town of Liberty maintains a park with swimming at this paddle's access point, the heavy-use area is screened from most of the pond by a large wooded island. The pond boasts acres of American white waterlily with sundew, pitcher plants, tree-covered islands, beavers, loons, great blue herons, and wood ducks.

Location: Liberty
Maps: *Maine Atlas & Gazetteer*, Map 14: B1; USGS Liberty, Washington
Area: 336 acres
Time: 4 hours
Habitat Type: Pond with many islands and a few marshy areas
Fish: Smallmouth bass, largemouth bass, chain pickerel (see fish advisories, Appendix A)
Take Note: Town park with swimming; 10 HP limit

GETTING THERE:

From Augusta, go east on Routes 3, 9, and 202. When they split, go 14.9 miles east on Route 3 and turn right on Route 220. Go 1 mile (cumulative: 15.9 miles) and continue straight on Route 173. Go 1.3 miles (17.2 miles) to the access on the right. (44° 22.902′ N, 69° 17.832′ W)

WHAT YOU'LL SEE

The town of Liberty maintains a park on Stevens Pond, so on warm summer days, especially weekends, bathers crowd the access near the outlet dam. Stevens Pond serves as a major tributary to the St. George River, and with popular Lake St. George just upstream, the motorboat traffic pretty much stays busy elsewhere. Most anglers here use canoes or rowboats; the occasional small outboard risks continual fouling from the ubiquitous aquatic vegetation. While others may intrude on your solitude occasionally, Stevens Pond provides a wonderful place to paddle, especially midweek.

Heading out from the access, stay left to explore the extensive marshes and to avoid development screened by the first large island. Beautiful granite boulders extend down into the water from the island.

Very tall white pines that thrive on the thin soil above the hard granite outcroppings dominate the shorelines of both the mainland and the large island.

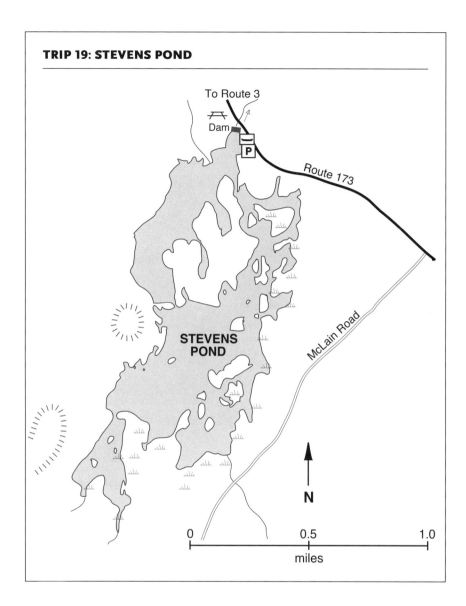

In contrast, hardwoods need more soil for their taproots, which generally go straight down. This explains, at least in part, the dearth of very large hardwoods along most of these granite-laden shorelines, as well as the presence of white pines and other conifers growing to great size. One wonders how such a thin layer of soil can support such towering trees. Perhaps they wedge their roots into the fissures in the underlying rocks.

Curving around left, you come to a boggy island with a sizable population of a rare pink orchid called dragon's mouth. Borne on 10-inch stalks, the delicate

Look for dragon's mouth, *Arethusa bulbosa*, a rare orchid in New England, growing along the boggy island in Stevens Pond.

pink flowers bloom in late June. Please be very careful not to injure these gorgeous flowers or any other orchids you might encounter.

You will see an unusually large number of pitcher plants in flower if you paddle here in early summer. Each tuft of sphagnum also seems to harbor a patch of tiny sundews, their sticky leaves waiting to latch onto unwary insects. Like the pitcher plant and other carnivorous plants, the sundew absorbs nitrogen and other nutrients from captured insects it dissolves with enzymes. For more on carnivorous plants, see "Carnivorous Plants: The Table is Turned," on page 108.

20 | Upper Mason Pond and Goose River

Serpentine Goose River offers hours of truly wild and wonderful marshland paddling. You'll see lots of birdlife here, along with aquatic plants and shoreline shrubs. Large numbers of great blue herons patrol the shoreline, and we saw many wood duck flocks gathering for fall migration.

Location: Belfast, Swanville
Maps: *Maine Atlas & Gazetteer*, Map 14: A4, A5; USGS Belfast, Searsport
Area/Length: 75 acres; river length, 6 miles one way
Time: 6 hours; shorter trips possible
Habitat Type: Shallow, marshy pond and meandering inlet stream
Fish: Smallmouth bass, largemouth bass, white perch (see fish advisories, Appendix A)
Take Note: Expect to get muddy at the access

TRIP 20: UPPER MASON AND GOOSE POND RIVER

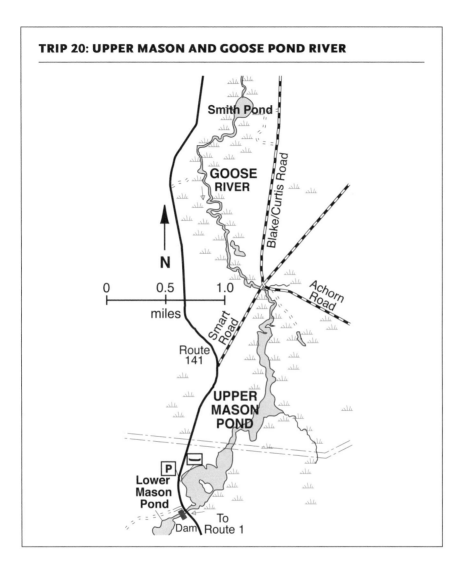

GETTING THERE

From Belfast, at the junction of Routes 1 and 141, go 1.9 miles north on Route 141 to the Belfast Canoe Launch on the right. (44° 27.642′ N, 69° 0.402′ W)

WHAT YOU'LL SEE

What a gem! We paddled more than a dozen miles—all the way to Smith Pond and back—and around the pond on a spectacular early-September Saturday, and we and the wildlife had the place to ourselves. The muddy access probably helps keep usage down.

Paddling on Goose River sometimes requires negotiating large patches of aquatic vegetation.

From the access, paddle northwest into Upper Mason Pond, a widened section of Goose River. By midsummer, emergent vegetation—principally pickerelweed—fairly chokes the pond, but you should be able to pick your way through these patches on reasonably open water.

If you head right from the access, you will get to the outlet. By paddling under a culvert from the outlet you can reach the dam. A few houses appear, but not many. The more interesting exploring, for most quiet-water enthusiasts, lies the other way: upstream on Goose River.

To explore upstream, head northeast from the access, aiming for the large power lines extending across the pond where it narrows to the river channel. As the inlet narrows, the channel deepens, providing relatively unimpeded paddling.

Along with the dominant pickerelweed, you'll see bur-reed, sedges, rushes, occasional patches of cattail, grasses (including some wild rice), and swamp milkweed, whose seedpods stick straight up in late summer.

Although we visited in September, we're confident this spot offers superb birding in spring and probably during fall migration. Almost everywhere we looked on the pond and along the river, we saw at least one great blue heron slowly flapping its broad wings. As we paddled along, flocks of wood ducks bolted into the air, usually long before we got a good look at them. On both our upstream paddle and our return, we saw an American bittern.

We paddled upstream through seemingly endless serpentine twists and bends, taking in the wild scenery. Although you are within a mile of a road most of the way, it feels far more remote.

If it isn't windy and the light is right (especially in the early morning), you will get a wonderful view into the water. Thick underwater vegetation undulates in the current in the beautifully clear water. If you watch for long, you will see largemouth bass and other fish. We also saw two snapping turtles underwater and one painted turtle.

About 2.5 miles from the access, a small, unnamed stream enters from the right, through a large culvert beneath Achorn Road. In a small boat, you could make it through—just barely. We paddled up the creek about 0.25 mile, spotting both painted and snapping turtles in the shallow water before alders and beaver dam remnants blocked our progress.

Back on the main channel, just around the bend, the river passes through two culverts beneath Smart Road. One can pull a boat out of the water on the left side, carry across the road, and put in on the other side, or the intrepid paddler can drop into the bottom of a canoe or lean over in a kayak and ease through—but not if you have a touch of arachnophobia! The roofs of the low culverts literally drip with spiders. We pushed through the left culvert, very glad to make it through without accumulating too many arachnids.

From the Smart Road culvert, you have another 3 or so miles of winding river up to Smith Pond, well worth the time. Along one stretch we saw quite a bit of a floating yellow flowers, water marigold (*Bidens beckii*), with finely divided underwater leaves (like fanwort) and entire leaves above water, with flowers about 1 inch across.

Smith Pond itself is not that exciting—a very small, roundish pond with a fully vegetated shoreline. We continued a short distance up Goose River but then headed back after a long morning. You also can paddle all the way to Swan Pond or do a one way trip, arranging to be dropped off or picked up at one end or the other.

21 | Sandy Pond

This shallow pond boasts lots of coves and some islands to explore, along with floating archipelagos of sphagnum that provides a habitat for sundew and pitcher plants. Look for loons, pickerelweed, and arrowhead in the water, and ospreys and kingfishers in the air.

Location: Freedom
Maps: *Maine Atlas & Gazetteer*, Map 22: E1; USGS Unity
Area: 430 acres
Time: 4 hours
Habitat Type: Shallow, marshy pond with floating and fixed islands
Fish: Largemouth bass, white perch, chain pickerel (see fish advisories, Appendix A)
Take Note: Limited development; few motors

GETTING THERE
From I-95, Exit 132, go 3.8 miles east on Route 139 and turn right on Fall Road, followed by a quick left on Albion/Benton Road. Go 7 miles (cumulative: 10.8 miles) and turn left on Routes 9/137/202. Go 2.1 miles (12.9 miles) and veer right on Route 137. Go 5.8 miles (18.7 miles) and turn right on Pleasant Street. Go 0.5 mile (19.2 miles) and turn right at the access sign (44° 31.422′ N, 69° 17.622′ W)

WHAT YOU'LL SEE
Anglers in small boats and canoes ply the waters of this nice little pond located right in the town of Freedom, but you should have it pretty much to yourself during the week. As you leave the access in the northeast cove, curve to the right into the extensive marshy area along the pond's north central section. The floating islands extend well out into the pond and will take a long time to explore fully. The rest of the shoreline lacks marshy areas, although aquatic vegetation occurs everywhere in this very shallow pond.

Acres of cattails, marsh grasses, and boggy islands provide extensive exploration opportunities. Protruding logs in various stages of decay drip with sphagnum, sundews, and basking turtles. Yellow pondlilies and pickerelweed fill the channels. When we paddled here, an osprey with a fish in its talons had better luck than the rod-and-reel set.

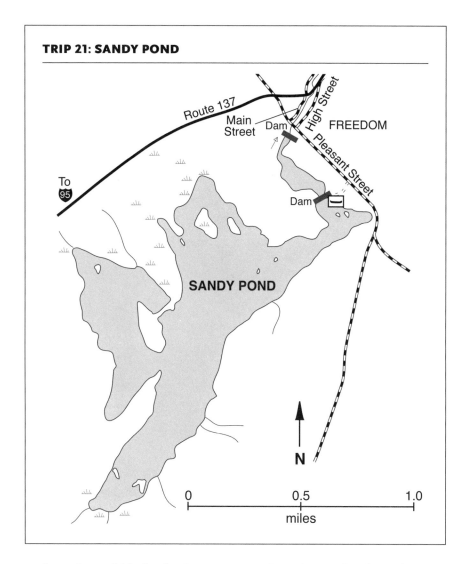

TRIP 21: SANDY POND

Route 137

Main Street

Dam

High Street

FREEDOM

Pleasant Street

To 95

Dam

SANDY POND

N

0   0.5   1.0
miles

Some beautiful little islands appear just where the pond widens, about 0.5 mile from the access, and the first one looks like a great spot for a picnic. Several herring gulls were ensconced on its shores, trying to keep out of the wind. We had much less success and had to use the islands and the marshy areas to shelter us from wind-driven swells.

When you reach the pond's west end, look for a stand of tamarack (*Larix laricina*), a bog-loving pioneer species that sometimes gets crowded out by later-growing black spruce. Needles of this pine relative grow in clusters but, unlike needles of pines and other conifers, turn yellow and drop in fall. Tamarack is the name given to the tree by the Algonquian.

Purple pickerelweed flowers lend color to summer and fall paddling.

Beautiful layered hillsides—now sporting three large windmills to the south-west—fade into the distance, and large trees dot the shoreline and cover the hills, making this a picturesque spot and an enjoyable place to paddle. The pond's far-southwest end has some development, more than when we published the first and second editions, and an Internet search reveals land for sale along the shore. As we paddled here previously, we listened to the ominous sound of chainsaws on surrounding hills. Paddle here now while this little gem remains relatively untrammeled.

22 | Carlton Pond and Carlton Bog

This wildlife management area has no development, making shallow Carlton Pond a great place to look for wildlife. Expect to see the rare black tern, ospreys, great blue herons, ducks, snapping turtles, muskrat, acres of marsh vegetation, and possibly moose and bald eagles.

Location: Troy
Maps: *Maine Atlas & Gazetteer,* Map 22: C1; USGS Unity Pond
Area: 430 acres; 1,055 acres in wildlife management area
Time: 4 hours
Habitat Type: Shallow, marshy pond with large amounts of aquatic vegetation
Fish: Smallmouth bass, largemouth bass, white perch, chain pickerel (see fish advisories, Appendix A)
Take Note: No development

GETTING THERE

From I-95, Exit 157 northbound, go 2.2 miles south on Routes 11 and 100, and turn left on Route 220. Go 9 miles (cumulative: 11.2 miles) and turn left on Bog Road. Go 0.4 mile (11.6 miles) to the access on the left; park on the right. (44° 41.748′ N, 60° 16.572′ W)

WHAT YOU'LL SEE

The U.S. Fish & Wildlife Service maintains Carlton Pond and Carlton Bog as a Waterfowl Production Area (WPA). We found it suitable not only for waterfowl but also for paddlers and for the rare black tern that nests here. Indeed, Carlton Pond remains one of our favorite places to explore. Because development has not intruded on the vast marshes here and to the immediate north, this is an excellent place to look for moose, although in the four times we paddled here we did not see any. In the spring and at other times of high water, one can paddle almost the entire bog area, including the sinewy channel on the other side of the road, and it would take most of a day to explore every nook and cranny. With a maximum water depth of only 8 feet, nearly every species of aquatic vegetation found in this area—including the slender blue flag (*Iris prismatica*), a threatened species in Maine—covers the pond's surface, except for a few narrow channels.

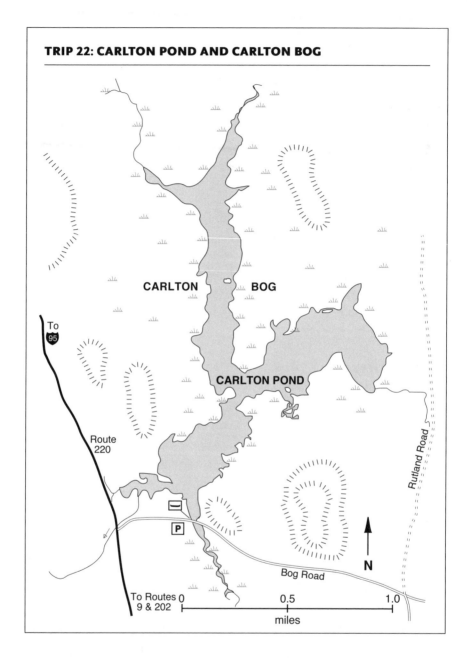

TRIP 22: CARLTON POND AND CARLTON BOG

CARLTON   BOG

CARLTON POND

To
95

Route
220

Rutland Road

P

Bog Road

N

To Routes
9 & 202

0   0.5   1.0

miles

Typical bog vegetation covers the higher ground in and around this gigantic marsh. Hummocks covered with sweetgale, rhodora, blueberries, sheep laurel, and lots more seem to float everywhere. Pitcher plant, sundew, and sphagnum abound. The sphagnum provides habitat for rose pogonia, an orchid that blooms in large numbers in late June.

Sphagnum provides more than a soft, mossy pad for sundews, pitcher plants, and orchids. It exchanges some of its hydrogen ions for waterborne metal ions, thereby acidifying its immediate vicinity. This process makes the habitat unsuitable for most other plants that might crowd it out, except those that can tolerate an acid environment. When many layers of sphagnum accumulate, the bottom layers become devoid of oxygen and cannot decay much; as a result, peat develops.

When we paddled here, we saw hundreds of waterfowl but no loons, cormorants, or diving ducks, probably due to the shallow water, but we did see dozens of dabbling ducks bobbing on the surface, occasionally dipping for a mouthful of aquatic vegetation. We tried not to get too close, but when we did, the ducks would leap into the air with a single wing beat, helicopter style. This takeoff contrasts with the way heavier loons and cormorants run across the water's surface to get up enough speed to become airborne.

When you see a duck on land, note its horizontal profile, in contrast to the vertical profile of a perching cormorant. The feet of cormorants and loons are set well back on their bodies, enhancing their underwater swimming capabilities as they chase fish. Their resulting streamlined profile in the water, along with their heavy bodies, makes it difficult for them to achieve vertical liftoff. On the other hand, the legs of puddle ducks, which only bob their heads and necks underwater to gobble up plants, are set at midbody. Consequently, they just stretch their necks upward to get vertical.

You might have to share this bog with a few mosquitoes. Fortunately, few make it out onto the water. Back on land, though, we must have set a record for getting the boat loaded up.

23 | Canaan Bog, Carrabassett Stream, and Black Stream

These three streams sandwiching Sibley Pond offer wonderful marshland paddling, although road noise impinges on Carrabassett Stream. Besides a wide assortment of wetland plants, look for loons and beavers in the evening.

Location: Canaan, Pittsfield
Maps: *Maine Atlas & Gazetteer*, Map 21: B3; USGS Belfast, Searsport
Area/Length: 380 acres; stream length, 7 miles one way

Time: 6 hours, longer if portaging over beaver dams; shorter trips possible
Habitat Type: Shallow, marshy pond and meandering inlet and outlet streams
Fish: Smallmouth bass, largemouth bass, white perch, chain pickerel (see fish advisories, Appendix A)
Take Note: Development on Sibley Pond; road noise on Carrabassett Stream

GETTING THERE
From I-95, Exit 150 northbound, go 0.8 mile west on Somerset Avenue and turn right on Phillips Corner Road. Go 2.6 miles (cumulative: 3.4 miles) and turn left on Route 2. Go 3.9 miles (7.3 miles) to the access on the left, just before the bridge. (44° 47.310′ N, 69° 30.828′ W)

WHAT YOU'LL SEE
Canaan Bog
Though not technically a bog, Canaan Bog is definitely worth exploring. From the access below the looming Route 2 bridge, head away from the bridge to explore the 2-plus miles of winding, secluded stream channel. Although wetland shrubs and emergent vegetation, especially pickerelweed, crowd the margins, the fairly deep stream does not support much floating vegetation that would impede paddling. Most floating aquatic plants cannot take root in more than about 4 feet of water.

Buttonbush, with its distinctive round, white, buttonlike flowers followed by seedpods, grows in profusion here. At the base of these bushes look for cranberry, with its long stems and tiny 0.75-inch-long leaves. By September, you should see the disproportionately large red berries. Although the commercial industry has bred cranberries to increase productivity, these are essentially the same fruit you buy at Thanksgiving for cranberry sauce.

Paddling generally south, head upstream on an almost imperceptible current. In fact, we weren't confident about flow direction until we reached several beaver dams about 2 miles upstream. We portaged up and over one dam but turned around at a second. We suspect you could continue farther if you don't mind periodic portaging.

Carrabassett Stream and Black Stream
Paddle out onto Sibley Pond and around the point to the left to access the pond's outlet, Carrabassett Stream. You could explore Sibley Pond, but development makes that less appealing. Judging from boats we saw at the many docks and a marked waterskiing course, we suspect that, on a nice summer

TRIP 23: CANAAN BOG, CARRABASSETT STREAM, AND BLACK STREAM

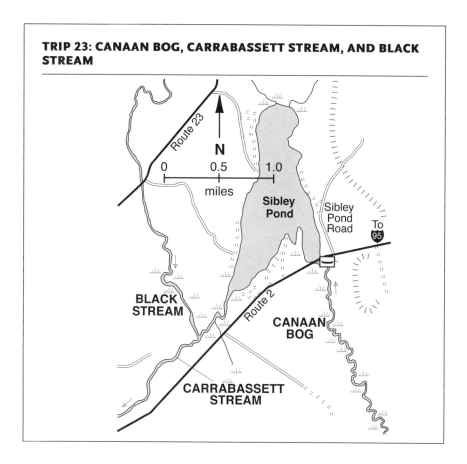

weekend, paddling Sibley Pond would be far from a quietwater experience.

If you do explore Sibley Pond, you will find the north end and part of the western shoreline more interesting. Incredibly, given the heavy recreation, loons have nested here, as evidenced by the adult and nearly grown chick we saw, and we watched an osprey near the pond's north end.

Like Canaan Bog, Carrabassett Stream also has a nearly imperceptible current. Submerged vegetation barely moves in the current; without maps, we would have had trouble confirming it does indeed flow out of Sibley Pond.

Unfortunately, Carrabassett Stream runs roughly parallel to Route 2, so you hear road noise the entire way. We paddled a little over 2 miles downstream to the west before heading back. Close to our turnaround spot, northern white cedar, including some quite large trees, grew thickly along both banks. Crush some of the leaves to get that distinctive, fresh scent.

You also will see gray birch, yellow birch, ash, alder, and silky dogwood

We often portage over beaver dams to reach upstream waters.

here, the latter with distinctive clusters of bluish berries. In fall, you also may see winterberry, a member of the holly family with many red berries clustered along its stems.

Not too far from the start of Carrabassett Stream as you paddle southwest, Black Stream flows in from the right. We loved exploring this channel, as it took us away from Route 2 noise.

Black Stream carries a lot of water; it seemed almost as wide and deep as Carrabassett Stream. Like Carrabassett and Canaan Bog, the edges grow thick with pickerelweed, bur-reed, and assorted grasses, sedges, and rushes.

Beavers had been busy on the stream. About 0.5 mile north from the confluence with Carrabassett Stream, we reached the largest beaver dam we've come across in this part of Maine. We estimate this dam raised the water level by a full 2 feet across the 25-foot channel. Portaging beyond the dam opened up lots of additional stream channel to explore.

Look for a sizable American elm near the dam. We saw other dead elms along here, but this one, so far, has weathered Dutch elm disease—knock on wood!

24 | Douglas Pond and Sebasticook River

Douglas Pond is a great place to paddle if you enjoy marshlands. You can also paddle miles up the Sebasticook River, which is relatively free of development. Expect to see the regular marsh species of plants and animals, as well as the rare black tern.

Location: Palmyra, Pittsfield
Maps: *Maine Atlas & Gazetteer*, Map 21: A4, A5, B5; USGS Pittsfield
Area/Length: 566 acres; stream length 2 miles one way
Time: 4 hours for pond, 1 to several hours for river; shorter trips possible
Habitat Type: Marshy pond and slow-flowing inlet river
Fish: Smallmouth bass, white perch, chain pickerel (see fish advisories, Appendix A)
Take Note: No development; road noise from I-95

GETTING THERE

From I-90, Exit 150 northbound, turn right, go 0.8 mile east, and turn left on Route 152/Hartland Avenue. Go 0.7 mile (cumulative: 1.5 miles) and turn right on Waverly Avenue in Pittsfield. Go 0.1 mile (1.6 miles) to the access on the left before the bridge. (44° 47.436′ N, 69° 23.147′ W)

WHAT YOU'LL SEE

Douglas Pond, a natural body of water enhanced by a small dam on the Sebasticook River, forms part of the Madawaska Marsh Game Management Area, set aside primarily as a duck-breeding and fish-breeding habitat. Because of its popularity with anglers, you may not paddle alone here, but few people travel back into the marsh itself, where you will find acres of solitude.

From the access, paddle left, going under the interstate. Large deciduous trees, including red and sugar maples, elm, red oak, and mature paper birch, line the banks of this narrow section of river. Look for the drooping branches of a hemlock grove hanging out over the water on the left. As the channel widens, an alder swamp appears on both sides. Notice the large beaver lodges just past the interstate.

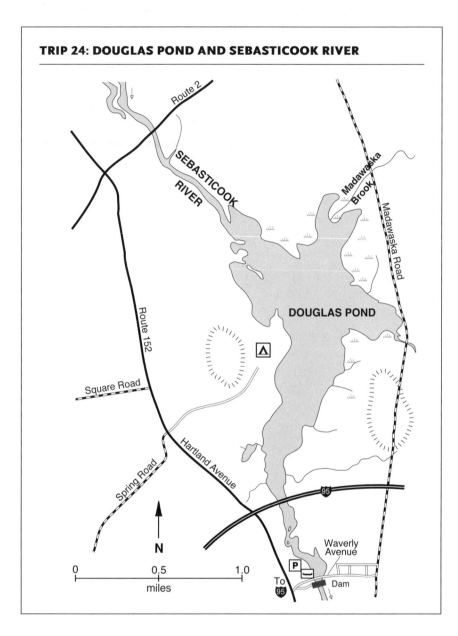

TRIP 24: DOUGLAS POND AND SEBASTICOOK RIVER

Route 2

SEBASTICOOK RIVER

Madawaska Brook

Madawaska Road

Route 152

Square Road

Spring Road

Hartland Avenue

DOUGLAS POND

95

N

0   0.5   1.0
miles

Waverly Avenue

P

To 95

Dam

Acres and acres of cattails, rushes, and pickerelweed greet you as the channel broadens out into the shallow pond. Except perhaps in late summer, you should be able to paddle way back into the marsh, where you should see wood ducks, muskrats, pickerelweed, arrowhead, great blue herons, and red-winged blackbirds—to mention only a few. It's one of a handful of places in Maine with a breeding population of black tern.

As you enter the marsh, interstate noise gradually fades into the distance as your focus turns to the sounds of birds, insects, and frogs, while your eyes feast on the vast beauty of Madawaska Marsh. It is hard to believe that such a wonderful place, teeming with fish and wildlife, exists right under the road whisking trailered boats to more popular destinations.

If you crave exercise, paddle up the Sebasticook River. Except during flood stages, the river flows with a current ranging from modest to nearly undetectable. We paddled about 1 mile above the Route 2 bridge and saw Canada geese, kingfishers, great blue herons, green herons, two loons, and many other birds.

3 | DOWNEAST

A maritime term, "downeast" refers to sailing downwind in an easterly direction. From southern New England, where in summer the wind blows roughly south to north along the coast, sailing downeast takes you to the northeastern Maine coast. Here, ocean meets land along scenic rocky shores and cliffs, but the region's inland landscape and waters can be just as dramatic. Acadia, one of the most popular and spectacular national parks, covers large portions of Mount Desert Island along the Downeast coast. This rocky and mountainous island boasts 100 miles of hiking trails through thriving forests; freshwater streams, ponds, and lakes; and 17 mountains, including Cadillac Mountain, at 1,530 feet the highest point on the East Coast north of Rio de Janeiro. In this section, we cover Acadia's Long, Seal Cove, and Jordan ponds and Eagle Lake (Trip 28), giving paddlers a taste of the park's inland waters. For more Downeast trips, including hikes, bikes, and paddles, see AMC's *Outdoor Adventures: Acadia National Park* (formerly *Discover Acadia National Park*), by Jerry and Marcy Monkman (AMC Books, 2017) and find more coastal paddles in *AMC's Best Sea Kayaking in New England*, by Michael Daugherty (AMC Books, 2016).

Outside of Acadia, this section includes 26 great destinations and some of the best paddling available in Maine. Featured trips include Scammon Pond (Trip 31), which lies in the center of R. Lyle Frost Wildlife Management Area; Bog Brook Flowage (Trip 32), which takes you through an undeveloped, seldom-visited wetland bursting with wildlife; the Rocky Lakes (Trips 35 and 36), two great, close-by locations with the same name; and the Machias Lakes (Trips 44 and 45), great places to look for moose and beavers. If you crave multiday trips on bigger water, by all means visit Pocumcus, Junior, and Sysladobsis lakes (Trip 47), perhaps with a side trip into Scraggly and Pleasant lakes (Trip 48). New to this edition are Fields Pond (Trip 25), just south of Bangor, and Orange River (Trip 37), a newly developed canoe trail in the Orange River Wildlife Management Area.

25 | Fields Pond

Fields Pond, a few miles south of Bangor, provides marshland habitat and a good place to see loons, ospreys, and bald eagles.

Location: Orrington
Maps: *Maine Atlas & Gazetteer*, Map 23: C2, C3; USGS Brewer Lake, Hampden
Area: 182 acres
Time: 3 hours
Habitat Type: Marshy pond and stream
Fish: Brook trout, smallmouth bass, white perch, chain pickerel (see fish advisories, Appendix A)
Information: Fields Pond Audubon Center, maineaudubon.org/find-us/fields-pond/ or 207-989-2591
Take Note: Some noise from nearby airport; development along northern shore

GETTING THERE
From I-95, Exit 182, go east on I-395 to Exit 5. Go 0.4 mile to Parkway South. Turn right, go 0.3 mile (cumulative: 0.7 mile), and turn right on Dirigo Drive. Go 0.6 mile (1.3 miles) and turn right on Green Point Road. Go 0.9 mile (2.2 miles) and turn left on Wiswell Road. Go 1.6 miles (3.8 miles) and turn right

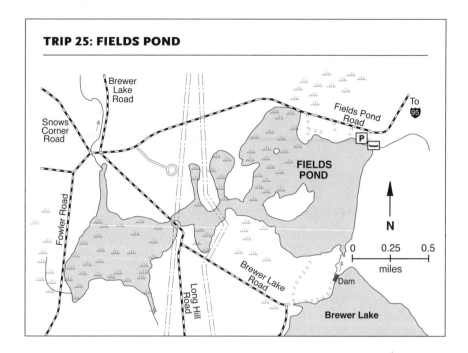

TRIP 25: FIELDS POND

on Fields Pond Road. Go 1.2 miles (5 miles), passing the entrance to Fields Pond Audubon Sanctuary, and turn left at the access road. (44° 44.202′ N, 68° 43.926′ W)

WHAT YOU'LL SEE

Fields Pond, just a few minutes from downtown Bangor, offers several hours of exploration, with plenty of wildlife and interesting vegetation. Although jets flying into or out of Bangor International Airport 5 miles to the northwest sometimes mar the solitude (the single runway is exactly lined up with the pond), we found the pond to be a great place to paddle.

In summer, impenetrable emergent vegetation—including bulrush, pickerelweed, cattail, and arrowhead—makes much of the shoreline inaccessible. In spring, it may be possible to paddle a significantly greater area, both in Fields Pond and in the marshy extension to the west, after paddling under Brewer Lake Road.

In some coves, you'll find American white waterlily and yellow pondlily and, if you look carefully, the much smaller leaves of little floating heart. We also saw lots of American eelgrass, with its long, narrow leaves floating on the surface. In a few places, we saw large stands of buttonbush growing in the shallows or just above water level.

We get ready to paddle the clear waters of Fields Pond.

On higher shorelines, including the island, you'll find red oak, grey birch, hemlock, white pine, and red maple, among other species. There are a few places where you could pull up on shore for a picnic lunch.

Paddling around the shoreline and along the sinewy, slow-flowing outlet that extends west and under Brewer Lake Road, we saw both an adult and an immature bald eagle, suggesting they nest nearby, and we watched a hovering osprey. We were pleased to see a loon with a nearly grown chick on our early August visit.

Beneath the surface, we saw lots of sunfish and minnows in the shallows. Amid the outlet's submerged vegetation, we caught a brief glimpse of a painted turtle.

At Fields Pond's south end, we tried to paddle down into Brewer Lake via a small connecting stream. We didn't succeed, although we did make it in 200 yards, and it's possible that in early spring a channel would be passable.

The western-outlet stream is wide, deep, and easy to paddle. The winding stream passes beneath a massive series of power distribution lines. This is one of the most concentrated collections of power lines we've seen, reminding us we're not in the wilderness here—not that you're likely to forget with the airplane traffic!

Part of Fields Pond's shoreline is an Audubon sanctuary. You can explore trails here and perhaps spend some time in the visitor's center.

26 | Silver Lake

Silver Lake provides an outstanding, but relatively untrammeled, paddling resource. Look for loons, ospreys, bald eagles, ducks, muskrat, and beavers in the evening or early morning. We saw deer here midday.

Location: Bucksport
Maps: *Maine Atlas & Gazetteer*, Map 23: D2; USGS Bucksport
Area: 630 acres
Time: 5 hours
Habitat Type: Pond dotted with islands
Fish: Smallmouth bass, white perch, chain pickerel (see fish advisories, Appendix A)
Take Note: Limited development; motorboats

GETTING THERE

From I-395, Exit 4 at Bangor, go 8.9 miles south on Route 15 and turn left on Millvale/Hincks Road. Go 2.6 miles (cumulative: 11.5 miles) and veer right on Silver Lake Road. Go 3.4 miles (14.9 miles) to the access on the left. (44° 36.078′ N, 68° 47.616′ W)

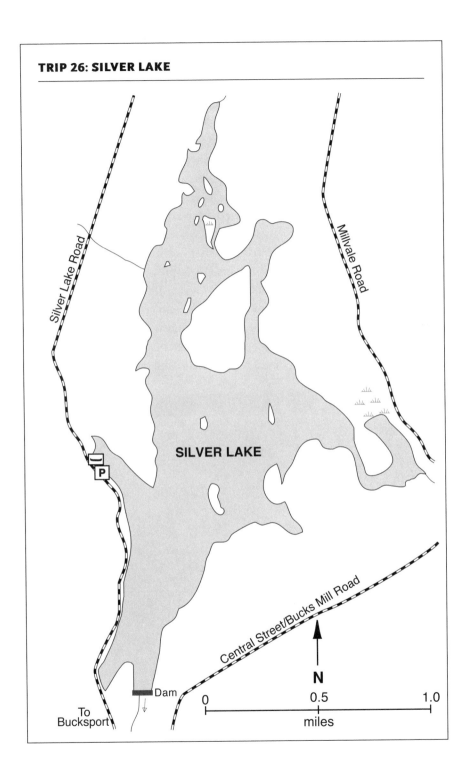

Silver Lake Road

Millvale Road

SILVER LAKE

Central Street/Bucks Mill Road

N

Dam

To
Bucksport

| 0 | 0.5 | 1.0 |

miles

WHAT YOU'LL SEE

Even though Silver Lake lies in close proximity both to Bangor and to the vacation destinations of Acadia, Blue Hill, and Camden, it remains relatively untrammeled and, as far as we could tell, seldom visited. When we paddled here on a warm, sunny Sunday in August, we saw only one other canoe, which is surprising, given the natural wonders we found.

We saw at least three and probably four bald eagles at close range: two immature, which superficially resemble golden eagles, and one or two different adults with their characteristic white heads and tails. A group of seven loons swam together, and the far eastern cove harbored dozens of feeding wood ducks. Right at high noon, when you would least expect it, a doe and her spotted fawn came down to the northern arm's shore to take a lengthy drink, seemingly oblivious to our presence, while two adult and one juvenile ospreys took serious exception to our presence within 50 yards of their nest on a utility pole.

We saw muskrat swimming out to harvest aquatic plants; young, ungainly great blue herons learning to fish the shallows; and several beaver lodges with masses of fresh cuttings. Most grassy areas near shore harbored large numbers of frogs, and we found piles of mussel shells where raccoons frequent the

The northern leopard frog, *Rana pipiens*, is one of several frog species you could see on Silver Lake.

shoreline on nightly feeding forays. A power line cuts diagonally along the northwestern shore, providing aeries for two osprey pairs. Look for an excellent camping spot along the northwest shore, under a grove of large conifers. An elegant hand-carved sign contains the plea: Please carry in, carry out. Cut no live trees.

Marshy coves sport luxuriant growths of pickerelweed, cattail, bulrush, arrowhead, horsetail, bladderwort, and bur-reed. Shrubs grow densely along the shoreline, while white pine, aspen, birch, red maple, and red spruce dominate the canopy. The northern reaches harbor dozens of islands, ranging from a few feet to 0.5 mile in length. Sphagnum, sundew, and pitcher plant cover a few smaller, floating islands, while sweetgale, bog rosemary, stands of tamarack, and other typical marsh plants cover the rest. The intricate pattern of islands and waterways can lead to hours of paddling in quiet seclusion.

BALD EAGLE: OUR NATIONAL BIRD, BACK FROM THE BRINK

The bald eagle, with its unmistakable white head and tail, flies over the nation's waterways on powerful wings. In flight, its large size stands out: It soars on wings that span up to 8 feet. From beak to tip of tail, an eagle measures 34 to 43 inches; males weigh 8 to 9 pounds, while the larger females weigh 10 to 14 pounds. Belying the moniker "light as a feather," feathers can contribute up to 15 percent of the bird's body weight.

A bald eagle attains its distinctive plumage only after four or five years. Until then, it resembles the dark brown golden eagle, except with some white mottling on the underside and tail. As it matures, the bird's head and tail become progressively whiter. At close range, the adult's large yellow beak and piercing yellow eyes convey a fierce strength. Our country's founders evidently felt this image symbolized what our young nation stood for, selecting *Haliaeetus leucocephalus* as our national symbol. Appropriately, this is the only eagle found exclusively in North America.

The bald eagle ranges throughout Maine. Eagles generally locate their nests in trees at the water's edge. Pairs return to the same nest for years, adding to it annually. An old eagle nest can easily measure 6 feet in diameter, 8 feet deep, and weigh more than a ton. The largest nest ever found measured 9.5 feet in diameter and 20 feet deep. Because eagles often build nests in dead trees, an old nest's huge mass may eventually topple the tree.

Bald eagles usually lay two eggs several days apart. Incubation lasts 30 to 36 days, during which the male and female share nesting duties. The young hatch several days apart, a strategy that improves the chances of fledging at least one chick. If food is scarce, the earlier-born chick might outcompete its younger sibling for food, and the younger chick would die. Because eagles live long lives, as long as 30 years in captivity but usually much less in the wild, they really only need to fledge a few chicks to replace themselves, thus maintaining a stable population.

After ten to twelve weeks of a diet consisting mostly of fish, chicks fledge and begin to fly. For the next seven or eight weeks, they increasingly gain independence, eventually leaving the nest to migrate to coastal areas and to outfalls below dams, where the water does not freeze. In years past, they congregated in great numbers off both coasts and in the Mississippi drainage each fall. Eagles still congregate by the thousands in mid-November along a 10-mile stretch of the Chilkat River in Alaska to feed on hordes of dead and dying salmon.

While bald eagles occur frequently in Maine today, just a few years ago only a few remained. Maine's eagle population plummeted to a low of 21 breeding pairs in 1967, producing just six chicks. In the late 1960s and early 1970s, long-lasting chlorinated hydrocarbons—such as DDT and its break-down product DDE, left over from mosquito-control projects—reached high concentrations in eagles, peregrine falcons, and other species at the top of the food chain and caused eggshells to break during incubation. Eagle populations have rebounded to about 10,000 nesting pairs (up from 4,000 in 1993; 8,000 in 2003) in the United States outside Alaska, with more than 400 of them in Maine (150 in 1993; 300 in 2003)—the greatest concentration around remote lakes in the eastern and northern regions. Despite the gains, Maine's annual nesting success rate had remained below one fledged chick per nest. Some pairs had fledged two chicks, which means that many failed to produce a single surviving chick. Since the last edition of this book, however, the fledge rate has returned to more than one per nest. Indeed, one nest recently fledged four young, a first for Maine in modern times.

Maine's Department of Inland Fisheries & Wildlife had blamed the low nesting success rate on various toxins in the eagle's food chain: mercury, mostly from coal-burning power plants in the Midwest, deposited in Maine by rain; DDE, a breakdown product from DDT that still remains in Maine's environment, more than 40 years after the DDT ban; dioxins, released by the paper industry; and PCBs, released from various industrial operations and

found in older electrical transformers. These toxins have started to decrease, which may explain the increasing fledging success.

Because eagle populations rose during the 23 years after DDT's ban, aided by reintroductions in many areas in the country, the U.S. Fish and Wildlife Service removed the bald eagle from the Endangered Species List in 1995, placing it on the Threatened List.

We feel privileged to paddle on lakes with bald eagles. Some accuse them of being opportunists, and indeed we have watched a few chase smaller ospreys, laboring with heavy fish, circling to gain altitude before flying off to their aeries. In one case, after the osprey dropped its hard-won catch, a bald eagle snatched it and flew off. This is not a case of good and evil; instead, it represents the triumph of bald eagle adaptation, ensuring its survival.

Humans still shoot eagles on occasion and build high-voltage lines that electrocute them, although designs and devices exist that reduce eagle mortality, and many eagles die from flying into human-made structures (power lines, towers, smokestacks, and buildings). But the biggest threat to the eagle's continued survival comes from an expanding human population, one that spews forth toxic chemicals into the environment and continues to develop shorelines. If we wish to continue to enjoy this majestic creature as it patrols America's waterways—and to keep it from returning to the Endangered Species List—we must take steps to keep some of its habitat undeveloped and unadulterated by the toxic wastes of a consumer society. The eagle represents an enduring wildness that we must protect for future generations to enjoy.

27 | Wight Pond

With a shoreline protected by Blue Hill Heritage Trust, this is a great place to look for wildlife, especially birds. Expect to see loons, ospreys, kingfishers, mallards, and lots more. We saw a bittern here in the marsh on the north end.

Location: Penobscot
Maps: *Maine Atlas & Gazetteer*, Map 15: A3; USGS Bucksport
Area: 135 acres
Time: 2 hours
Habitat Type: Long, narrow pond rimmed with boulders; marshy inlet stream
Fish: Largemouth bass, white perch, chain pickerel (see fish advisories, Appendix A)
Information: Blue Hill Heritage Trust, bluehillheritagetrust.org
Take Note: No development

GETTING THERE

From the junction of Route 177 and Routes 15, 172, and 176 in Blue Hill, go 5.6 miles northwest on Route 177 to the easy-to-miss access road on the right, just after an S-curve sign. (44° 27.042′ N, 68° 40.434′ W)

WHAT YOU'LL SEE

Amazingly, given its close proximity to Penobscot Bay and millions of tourists, Wight Pond has no development along its shoreline. In 2013, Blue Hill Heritage Trust purchased 106 acres on Wight Pond, along with conservation easements on an additional 35 acres. The trust previously had purchased easements on the remaining abutting property.

The long, narrow pond has much to offer. If you paddle here in late summer, check out the outlet stream for cardinal flower, a brilliant-red member of the lobelia family. Years ago we visited here with a New England Wildflower Society naturalist who said this was the largest and most spectacular concentration of cardinal flowers she had seen. (Because that was a long time ago, cardinal flowers, which often sprout up in disturbed areas, may no longer bloom here. If you go, shoot us a note and let us know what you see.)

TRIP 27: WIGHT POND

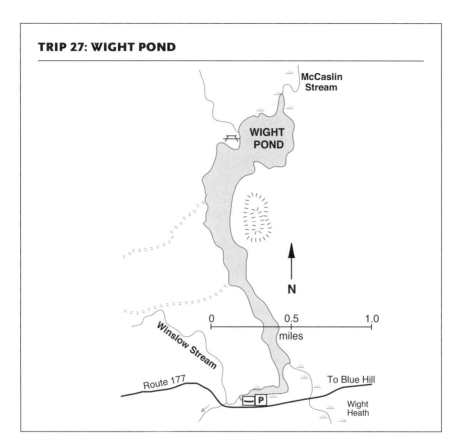

Paddling out from the access, you pass through acres of aquatic vegetation, including pickerelweed, arrowhead, yellow pondlily, American white waterlily, bulrush, bur-reed, and eastern purple bladderwort. Passing into the main lake, aquatic vegetation disappears as large rocks take over the shoreline. A large variety of trees, shrubs, and ferns lines the shore; predominant tree species include white pine, red oak, red spruce, red maple, and balsam fir.

We managed to paddle right up to a painted turtle that was out sunning on a log. Uncharacteristically, it never moved as we floated on by. Seemingly everywhere, we found piles of empty mussel shells, indicating the dining locations of otters or raccoons. Look for a great picnic spot for humans at the north end of the pond, on the left.

At the pond's northeast corner, an inlet weaves back through the marsh for about 0.5 mile. We scared black ducks and a bittern from the reeds. Besides the wildlife and two anglers, we had this pond to ourselves on a beautiful Saturday in mid-August.

28 | Mount Desert Island: Long Pond, Seal Cove Pond, Eagle Lake, and Jordan Pond

Mount Desert Island and Acadia National Park provide truly abundant recreational opportunities, including paddling on glacier-carved deep lakes and ponds. We include four bodies of water here, each with great scenic value. Due to very high summer visitation, we recommend paddling here in spring and fall.

Location: Bar Harbor, Mount Desert Island, Southwest Harbor, Tremont
Maps: *AMC's Acadia National Park Map, Maine Atlas & Gazetteer*, Map 16: B2, B3, B4, C2, C3; USGS
Bar Harbor, Bartlett Island, Eagle Lake, Salsbury Cove, Seal Harbor, Southwest Harbor
Area: Long Pond, 897 acres; Seal Cove Pond, 283 acres; Eagle Lake, 436 acres; Jordan Pond, 187 acres
Time: Long Pond, 5 hours; Seal Cove Pond, 3 hours; Eagle Lake, 3 hours; Jordan Pond, 1 hour
Habitat Type: Long, narrow, deep lakes
Fish: Long Pond, brook trout, landlocked salmon; Seal Cove Pond, brown trout, brook trout, smallmouth bass, white perch; Eagle Lake and Jordan Pond, brook trout, lake trout, landlocked salmon (see fish advisories, Appendix A)
Camping: Reservations essential; visit recreation.gov or call 877-444-6777
Information: Acadia National Park, nps.gov/acad/index.htm; see also Jerry and Marcy Monkman's *Outdoor Adventures: Acadia National Park* (AMC Books, 2017; outdoors.org/amcstore)
Take Note: 10 HP limit on Eagle Lake, Jordan Pond, and Seal Cove Pond

GETTING THERE
Long Pond North Access. From the end of the causeway at the junction of Route 3 and Routes 102 and 198, go 1.9 miles south on Routes 102/198 and turn right on Indian Point Road/Oak Hill Road. Go 2.7 miles (cumulative: 4.6 miles) and turn right on Whitney Farm Road. Go 1 mile (5.6 miles) and turn right on Route 102. Access is immediately on the left. (44° 21.282′ N, 68° 21.798′ W).

    Long Pond South Access. From the end of the causeway at the junction of Route 3 and Routes 102 and 198, go 10 miles south on Route 102 and turn right on Seal Cove Road. Go 0.6 mile (cumulative: 10.6 miles) and turn right

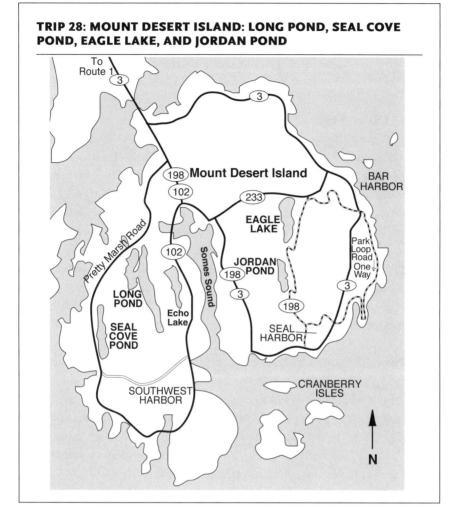

on Long Pond Road. Go 1.2 miles (11.8 miles) to the access. (44° 18.018′ N, 68° 20.994′ W)

Seal Cove Pond. From the Long Pond North Access, go 6.1 miles west on Route 102 and turn left on Seal Cove Road. Go 0.5 mile (cumulative: 6.6 miles) and turn left on Western Mountain Road. Go 0.7 mile (7.3 miles) and turn left on Seal Cove Pond Road. Go 0.6 mile (7.9 miles) to the access. (44° 17.502′ N, 68° 23.544′ W)

Eagle Lake. From the end of the causeway at the junction of Route 3 and Routes 102 and 198, go 4.3 miles south on Routes 102/198 and turn left on Routes 3/198. Go 1.4 miles (cumulative: 5.7 miles) and turn left on Route 233. Go 3.6 miles (9.3 miles) to the access on the right. (44° 22.578′ N, 68° 15.006′ W)

Jordan Pond. From the Eagle Lake access, go 0.9 mile east on Route 233, turn left and loop around, veering left, for 0.1 mile (cumulative: 1 mile) on Paradise Hill Road. Continue 4.9 miles (5.9 miles) south on Paradise Hill Road, which joins Park Loop Road, to the access on the right. (44° 19.392′ N, 68° 15.216′ W)

WHAT YOU'LL SEE

Known primarily for its craggy shorelines, deep harbors, sailboats, tide pools, lobsters, and coastal vacationing, Mount Desert Island also offers some surprisingly pleasant freshwater lake and pond paddling. The island, Maine's most popular vacation spot, extends roughly 15 miles north to south and 12 miles east to west. Acadia National Park—the oldest national park east of the Mississippi and the second most visited, with about three million visitors per year—makes up about half of this rocky island. Four freshwater lakes and ponds that we highly recommend nestle among the island's majestic granite peaks.

One can paddle at least five lakes and ponds on the island. We've paddled four: Eagle Lake and Long, Seal Cove, and Jordan ponds. We didn't paddle Echo Lake, as busy Route 102 runs along the eastern shore.

Long Pond. The largest freshwater lake on the island, Long Pond stretches for about 4.5 miles. Quite a bit of development exists at the north end, so on a nice summer weekend you will share the pond with motorboats, water-skiers, and anglers. Lots of people paddle here, as well, but personal watercraft are excluded. Across the road from the access, a concessionaire rents canoes and kayaks. Acadia National Park covers nearly the entire western shore of the lake, as well as the eastern shore near the lake's southern tip.

Long Pond runs generally north-south, with the north end divided into eastern and western sections by Northern Neck. The pond's eastern arm suffers from more development than the western arm, which has some surprisingly isolated and wild coves where you can get away from most activity. We passed a few northern fens here, with sphagnum, pitcher plant, sundew, tamarack, cranberry, leatherleaf, and other species more commonly seen farther north.

The long, narrow, southern half of Long Pond suffers from winds that commonly blow south to north, making the water quite rough. And yet, the south end provides dramatic views, with mountains rising to either side; tall rock cliffs overlooking the water; and jagged, wind-sculpted pines perched here and there. Numerous trails radiate out from the pond's southern end.

TRIP 28: MOUNT DESERT ISLAND: LONG POND

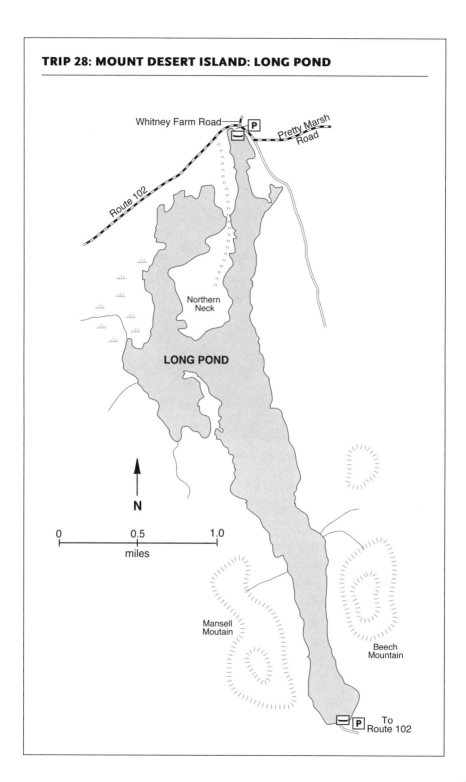

Whitney Farm Road

P

Pretty Marsh Road

Route 102

Northern Neck

LONG POND

N

0   0.5   1.0
miles

Mansell Moutain

Beech Mountain

P

To Route 102

Mansell Mountain rises over Long Pond in Acadia National Park. Photo: Jerry and Marcy Monkman/Ecophotography

Seal Cove Pond. Much smaller and more remote than Long Pond, Seal Cove Pond also differs ecologically. Most of the shallow pond grows thick with American white waterlily, bulrush, horsetail, and pickerelweed, providing superb wildlife habitat. We saw wood ducks, cormorants, loons, great blue herons, and a mature bald eagle. You can see a few houses along Route 102, but the pond's entire eastern shore lies within the park.

Eagle Lake. Eagle Lake, the second largest freshwater body on Mount Desert Island, remains undeveloped and very attractive, serving as a water supply for the island, with the northeastern tip off-limits and no swimming. Spectacular vistas of 1,248-foot Pemetic Mountain to the south and 1,530-foot Cadillac Mountain to the east await as you paddle Eagle Lake. Carriage roads and trails extend around the lake and connect to Jordan Pond, the West Face Trail up Cadillac Mountain, and a beautiful area between Eagle Lake and Jordan Pond known as The Bubbles.

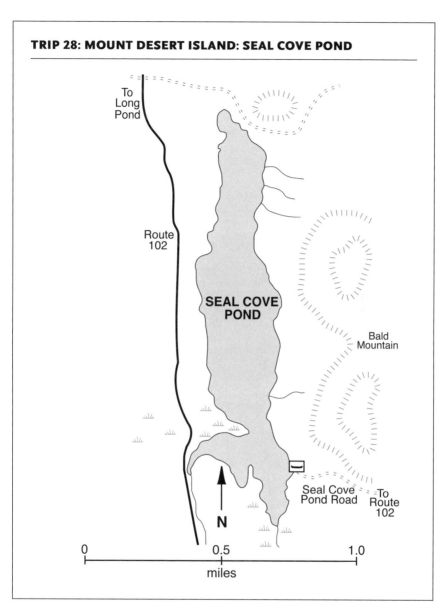

To
Long
Pond

Route
102

**SEAL COVE
POND**

Bald
Mountain

Seal Cove
Pond Road

To
Route
102

N

0   0.5   1.0
miles

In places, massive slabs of characteristic pink granite extend down into the water. Along other sections, coarse, chunky gravel—stones that could cut deep scratches in your boat—populates the shoreline. A few marshy areas occur along the western shore, where you'll see pickerelweed, bulrush, and a few other wetland plants, but mostly this is a biologically unproductive, or oligotrophic, lake. You'll see conifers where they have succeeded in gaining a foothold in the rocky soil: white pine, red pine, cedar, spruce, and balsam fir.

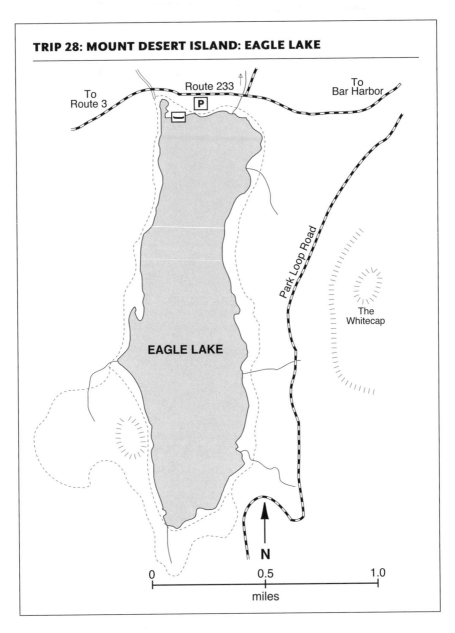

To
Route 3

Route 233

To
Bar Harbor

P

Park Loop Road

The
Whitecap

EAGLE LAKE

N

0   0.5   1.0

miles

Jordan Pond. Despite its small size, Jordan Pond is probably the best known pond on Mount Desert Island. The dramatic scenery around the pond, the trail and carriage road network, and—probably most significantly—the Jordan Pond House restaurant at the southern end all contribute to its reputation. The original house on this site dated to 1847, when the Jordan family of Seal Harbor built a mill close to the pond's outlet. The house

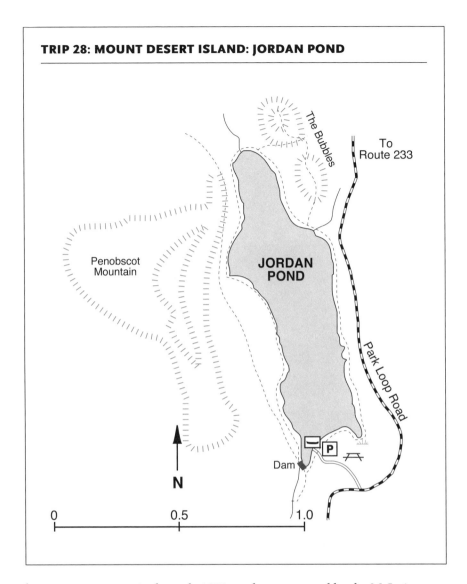

became a restaurant in the early 1870s and was operated by the McIntire family for more than 50 years starting in 1895. John D. Rockefeller Jr. purchased the property and gave it to the National Park Service to ensure its continuation. In June 1979, the original house burned but was rebuilt. From the restaurant you can enjoy elegant dining in sight of the spectacular pond.

Because the pond serves as a public water supply, the park restricts boats at the south end to a narrow strip up the pond's center. Paddling along the shore provides beautiful views but no coves or marshy areas to explore. On the plus side, the park restricts motors to 10 HP here.

Jordan Pond's bottom drops off to more than 100 feet just a few yards from shore, with a maximum depth of 150 feet. The cold, well-oxygenated waters provide fairly good habitat for coldwater fish. A picnic area near the access, as well as the easy 0.5-mile Jordan Pond Nature Trail, provide extra enticements for a visit.

Kayaks await on the shore of Acadia National Park's Jordan Pond. Photo: Jerry and Marcy Monkman/Ecophotography

GEOLOGIC HISTORY OF MOUNT DESERT ISLAND

Several important geologic events have shaped Mount Desert Island. Volcanic activity deep underground 350 to 400 million years ago extruded lava, creating thick layers of rock that had originally formed as sea-bottom sediment. This magma bubble did not erupt as a volcano but instead cooled underground. Because the rock (technically a pluton) cooled slowly, it formed distinctive, coarse, pink granite crystals. Then the entire region uplifted as North America collided with Europe and Africa.

Over the next few hundred million years, overlying rock gradually eroded away, exposing the pink granite below. Finally, during the last millennium, glaciation scoured the granite, rounding off mountain peaks and gouging deep valleys and cliffs so characteristic of the island. The last glacier melted off Mount Desert Island only 13,000 years ago—a mere wink of an eye in geologic time. Deep glacier-carved troughs of Somes Sound connect with the ocean, making it the only true fjord in the United States, outside of Alaska. Its steep rock faces extend deep into the salt water. Several other glacial troughs, sealed off from the sea, form freshwater lakes and ponds.

Sunset silhouettes The Bubbles rising behind Jordan Pond. Photo: Jerry and Marcy Monkman/Ecophotography

29 | Jones Pond

If you find yourself in the Bar Harbor area and are looking for a little less traffic, visit Jones Pond. While you won't encounter wilderness, you will encounter wildlife. Expect to see loons, cormorants, gulls, Canada geese, kingfishers—and beavers in the evening.

Location: Gouldsboro
Maps: *Maine Atlas & Gazetteer*, Map 16: A5 and Map 17: A1; USGS Winter Harbor
Area: 467 acres
Time: 3 hours
Habitat Type: Pond with several islands
Fish: Brown, brook, and rainbow trout; landlocked salmon; smallmouth bass; chain pickerel (see fish advisories, Appendix A)
Take Note: Development; motorboats

GETTING THERE
From Ellsworth at the junction of Routes 1 and 3, go 18.4 miles east on Route 1 and turn right on Route 195. Go 0.4 mile (cumulative: 18.8 miles), turn right on Recreation Road, and go 0.3 mile (19.1 miles), veering right on Balsam Drive, to the access. (44° 27.762′ N, 68° 4.716′ W)

WHAT YOU'LL SEE
Just a few miles, as the gull flies, from Mount Desert Island lies much less well-known Jones Pond. The town of Gouldsboro maintains a heavily used recreation area on the pond, and on a nice summer weekend, you can expect to see a lot of people. In addition, scattered houses intrude on the shoreline. Although paddling here will not be a wilderness experience, you can enjoy wildlife in the early morning, or before or after the main summer season. Nesting loons we saw here suggest the pond never gets too crowded, as repeated human disturbance drives loons away.

Several attractive islands add scenic character, and beautiful mosses and lichens festoon the far shore's huge granite boulders. A mature mixed canopy with a well-developed understory surrounds the pond. Although the understory exhibits good diversity, sweetgale, with its pungent leaves, dominates the shoreline.

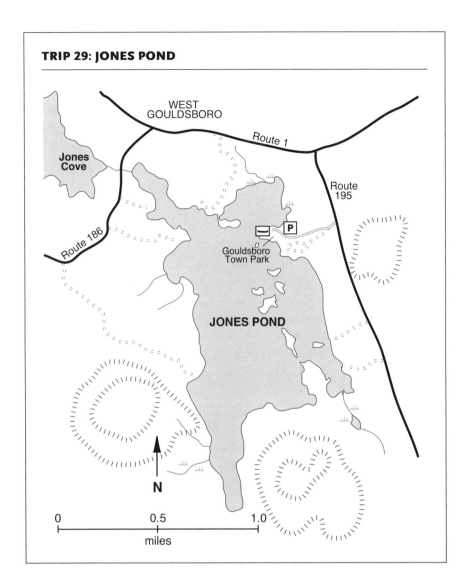

WEST GOULDSBORO

Jones Cove

Route 1

Route 195

Route 186

P

Gouldsboro Town Park

JONES POND

N

0   0.5   1.0
miles

According to local anglers, some huge brown trout lurk in Jones Pond's depths, as well as a healthy smallmouth bass population. Because of the pond's close proximity to salt water, large numbers of herring and great black-backed gulls appear, along with double-crested cormorants, great blue herons, and belted kingfishers. We saw yellow and chestnut-sided warblers, American redstarts, and song sparrows. Look for beavers at the base of the southeast arm.

The town park has several picnic tables, grills, and a small building with bathrooms, screens, and a wood stove. Spring wildflowers bloom in profusion in the vicinity.

30 | Donnell Pond

Because the state now owns much of the land surrounding Donnell Pond, this is a great place for a multiday visit. You can camp, paddle, and hike here among scenic peaks. Look for loons, ospreys, and bald eagles.

Location: Franklin, T9 SD
Maps: *Maine Atlas & Gazetteer*, Map 24: D4, D5; USGS Sullivan
Area: 1,120 acres
Time: All day
Habitat Type: Large, irregularly shaped pond with several islands
Fish: Brook trout, lake trout, landlocked salmon, white perch, chain pickerel (see fish advisories, Appendix A)
Camping: Several campsites available on a first-come, first-served basis
Take Note: Development on west end; motors, but personal watercraft prohibited

GETTING THERE
From Ellsworth at the junction of Routes 1 and 3, go 4.8 miles east on Route 1 and turn left on Route 182. Go 7.5 miles (cumulative: 12.3 miles) and turn right on Donnell Pond Road. Go 0.2 mile (12.5 miles) and veer right. Go 1.4 miles (13.9 miles) and turn right at the access. (44° 35.772′ N, 68° 10.734′ W)

WHAT YOU'LL SEE
Don't be too discouraged by the development along the western arm. Past Little Island, largely undeveloped Donnell Pond offers superb paddling on all but the busiest summer weekends, when motorboats and water-skiers can be oppressive. To enjoy the pond's full beauty, paddle here on weekdays or after Labor Day, when most people have departed with the bugs.

The state recently purchased 14,000 acres in the area, setting it aside as Donnell Pond Public Reserved Land. That includes about two-thirds of the shoreline.

This deep, rocky pond has low biological productivity, which keeps the water exceptionally clear. Granite boulders, bedrock, and sand beaches define much of the shoreline, with thick woodland extending back from the water. The pond nestles beneath several mountains that rise up a thousand feet from

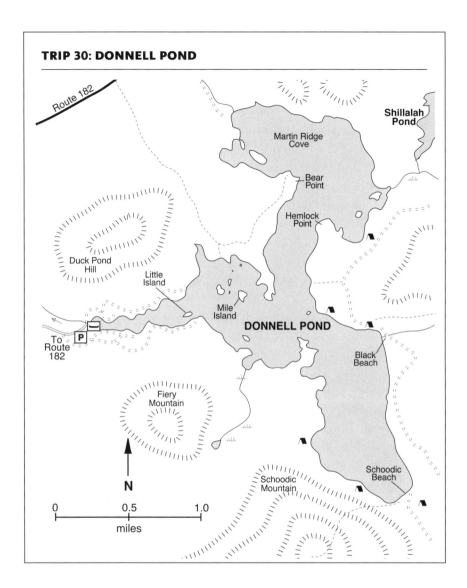

the water's surface. About a mile east of the access you will come to a cluster of islands. Great slabs of exposed granite bedrock extend down into the water, the largest of these—appropriately named Mile Island—is a superb picnic spot.

Geologically, Donnell Pond lies in the center of a massive granitic intrusion extending more than 70 square miles. The granite, rich in quartz and feldspar, weathers into a coarse, well-drained, acidic soil, leading to generally dry conditions and fire-prone vegetation. Researchers believe that fires contributed to the exposed bald peaks on nearby Schoodic and Black mountains. A number of plant species reach the northern limit of their ranges here, including bayberry, common juniper, golden heather, and highbush blueberry. The Schoodic and Black mountain balds support a number of rare plant species.

Several loon pairs nest here, and ospreys have nested in a dead spruce along the pond in recent years. We frequently see bald eagles. For anglers, Donnell Pond's deep, clear waters offer coldwater fishing opportunities.

Schoodic Bay and the day-use area—with picnic tables, outhouses, and camping—lie at the pond's south end, roughly 3 miles from the access. Coarse, pebbly granite sand makes up this broad, natural beach. Schoodic Mountain (1,069 feet) rises from the pond's south end; a trail extends up the mountain from the day-use area. Black Beach, an equally nice beach and camping area, perches along the east side, where Redman Brook flows in.

The pond has an interesting recent history. A land speculator, Patten Corporation, purchased much of the surrounding land in the late 1980s and planned to develop it with hundreds (or thousands) of vacation homes. Fortunately, conservation groups and the state of Maine got wind of the impending loss, and in 1988 the state acquired approximately 7,000 acres around the pond, including roughly two-thirds of the shoreline, starting near the middle of Martin Ridge Cove's northern shore and moving clockwise all the way around to Little Island.

The parcel includes land to the east and south, acquired through a complex five-way land swap; the state now owns more than 14,000 acres in the area. This land transaction helped catalyze the formation of the Northern Forest campaign by several environmental and outdoors organizations in the Northeast, including the Appalachian Mountain Club.

While Donnell Pond narrowly escaped large-scale development that would have ruined its beauty and tranquility, any warm, sunny, summer weekend will remind paddlers that the pond still sees heavy use by motorboaters. To remain relatively pristine, Donnell Pond needs an initiative to restrict motorboat access. The state has banned personal watercraft, but carry-in boats only would be even better, and a 10 HP restriction would be a great step forward.

Hiking opportunities abound at Donnell Pond. As noted previously, a trail to Schoodic Mountain begins at Schoodic Beach, at the pond's south end, and a network of trails from Black Beach on the east shore leads to Black Mountain and Wizard Pond, which harbors a 21-acre stand of old-growth red spruce. In addition to these maintained trails, many old logging roads crisscross public lands to the east.

31 | Scammon Pond

The state protects Scammon Pond from development, making this a good place to look for solitude. At times, it can be a challenge to paddle here due to aquatic vegetation, barely submerged stumps and boulders, and beaver dams, but it's a great place to look for wildlife. Expect to see great blue herons, ospreys, ducks, muskrat, and possibly bald eagles and moose.

Location: Eastbrook
Maps: *Maine Atlas & Gazetteer*, Map 24: C3, C4, D4, D5; USGS Eastbrook, Molasses Pond
Area: 396 acres; 1,421 acres in wildlife management area, including 658 acres of wetland
Time: 3 hours
Habitat Type: Shallow, weed-choked pond
Fish: Chain pickerel (see fish advisories, Appendix A)
Take Note: No development; watch for stumps and boulders on west end; obstacles and shallow water limit motors

GETTING THERE

From Ellsworth at the junction of Routes 1 and 3, go 4.8 miles east on Route 1 and turn left on Route 182. Go 5.1 miles (cumulative: 9.9 miles) and turn left on Route 200. Go 6.7 miles (16.6 miles) and turn right on Molasses Pond Road. Go 0.3 mile (16.9 miles) to the access on the right. (44° 40.896′ N, 68° 15.738′ W)

WHAT YOU'LL SEE

Scammon Pond, a beautiful place to paddle and well worth exploring, lies in the center of the R. Lyle Frost Wildlife Management Area. Some huge granite boulders—actually glacial erratics deposited here in a previous ice age—line the shore, and you should expect to run into an occasional submerged stump or granite boulder. We recommend you go slowly and enjoy the birds, plants, and animals of this quiet and scenic spot.

A few enormous, flat-topped boulders protruding from the water make great picnic spots. On hot, sunny days, a better picnic spot would be under the pines on either shore where the pond narrows, about 1 mile from the access.

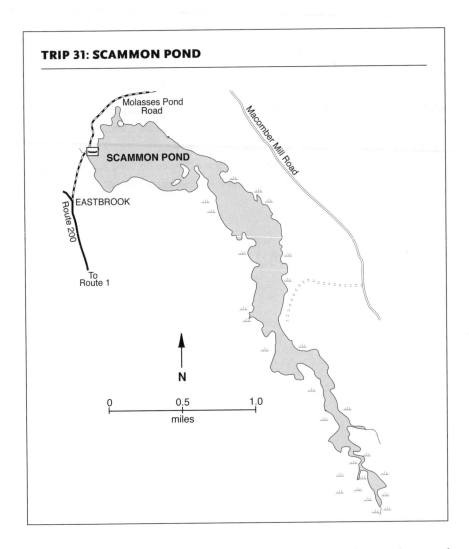

Many tree species and a dense understory line the shore. Along with acres of American white waterlily, we found lots of sundew growing on exposed stumps and hummocks. This boggy area provides ideal habitat for carnivorous plants, including many pitcher plants.

Although the pitcher plant digests unlucky insects that enter its water-filled, tubular leaves, for some mysterious reason it does not digest the larvae of one species of mosquito. Why does this mosquito lay its eggs in pitcher plants, when every conceivable location in Maine harbors stagnant or slow-moving water? Probably because no dragonfly—or other predacious insect larvae or small fish or bladderwort—inhabits the pitcher. In the competition for space, this mos-

Aquatic vegetation, stumps, and granite boulders keep motorboats out of Scammon Pond.

quito seems to have done well. So have the 38 or more species of damselflies and dragonflies that inhabit these waters.

We found ducks everywhere, feeding among the aquatic plants, and we saw several ospreys fishing. Ravens, cedar waxwings, and swallows cavorted over the water, while several great blue herons fished the shoreline. We thought we heard young birds calling from a great blue heron rookery, but we could not locate the nests among the dense rows of trees lining the shore. You may find bald eagles here as well.

Several mammoth beaver lodges perch along the pond's upper end. Keep an eye out for muskrat harvesting grasses in the shallows. The pond's upper reaches narrow considerably, and you have to wend your way through meandering channels filled with pickerelweed and dense patches of waterlily. After paddling about three-quarters of the way to the pond's end, you would have to portage over a beaver dam to gain access to the rest. This would be a good place to look for moose.

CARNIVOROUS PLANTS: THE TABLE IS TURNED

Carnivorous plants thrive in New England's marshes, and their meat-eating adaptations make them one of nature's true wonders. Carnivory in plants apparently resulted from convergent evolution: the development of similar traits among unrelated species. Plant families on nearly every continent include some carnivorous species, with two common characteristics: They live in mineral-poor soils, supplementing soil nutrients with those from animals, and they use modified leaves to trap food.

Two capture strategies have evolved, active and passive. The Venus flytrap, which grows in sandy soils along the Carolina coast, uses an active capture strategy. A few others have adopted active strategies, including bladderworts (genus *Utricularia*), which form dense mats in shallow marshes. Bladderwort leaves consist of minute bladders that ingest and digest insect larvae and other organisms.

Passive capture strategies have taken two main paths. The pitcher plant (*Sarracenia purpurea*) collects rainwater in funnel-shaped leaves, and enzymes digest insects that fall into those leaves. Sundews (genus *Drosera*) form sticky pads that digest insects with enzymes.

Although each plant—bladderwort, pitcher plant, and sundew—captures prey in a different way, they all have the same reason for doing so. In nutrient-poor marshes, absorbing minerals from insects and other prey gives them a selective advantage over other plants. Tea-colored bog water, laden with organic acids from decaying vegetation, washes out minerals. Although carbon dioxide and water remain plentiful, nitrogen, phosphorus, potassium, and other important elements get leached out or bound up in underlying layers of sphagnum and peat.

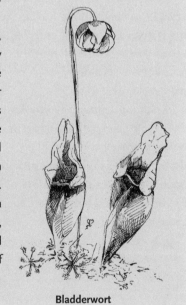

Bladderwort

Bladderwort

Bladderwort grows in shallow waters or in shoreline muck. Look for small yellow or purple snapdragonlike flowers, leading on short stalks to carnivorous underwater bladders that form dense, feathery mats. These mats bear hundreds of tiny (0.02- to 0.1-inch-long), bulbous traps that form the plant's leaves. Bladders have two concave sides and a trapdoor. When a small organism bumps into the door's guard hairs, the bladder's sides pop out and the door swings open, sucking in the hapless critter. This occurs in 0.002 second, followed by slow digestion by plant enzymes.

Mosquito larvae form the bulk of the bladderwort's diet, but the plant also ingests other larvae, rotifers, protozoans, and small crustaceans. With large prey, such as a tiny tadpole, the door closes around the organism, and the plant digests only part of it. The next time the hairs get triggered, the plant ingests more of the organism, eventually sucking it all in.

Several bladderwort species grow in New England; two species have purple flowers, and as many as ten species have yellow flowers. We usually notice these plants when we see their snapdragonlike flowers protruding a few inches above the water's surface.

Pitcher Plant

The northern pitcher plant, *Sarracenia purpurea*, grows from British Columbia to Nova Scotia, southward through the Great Lakes region, and down the eastern coastal plain, crossing the Florida panhandle to the Mississippi River. Its pitcher-shaped leaves, initially green in spring, turn purple in fall

Pitcher plants

and return to green the next spring. Flowering occurs in June and July, and single reddish flowers, borne on stout stalks, tower a foot or more above the pitcher cluster.

The curved pitchers recline, allowing rain to fall into the open hood. Stiff, downward-pointing hairs in the plant's throat keep insects from climbing back out, and the narrow funnel leaves littleroom for airborne escape. Upper pitcher walls sport a waxy coating, making for slippery footing. A combination of plant and bacterial enzymes degrades the unlucky insects, and their nutrients pass easily through the lower pitcher's unwaxed surface.

Sundew

Sundew grows mainly in sphagnum bogs from Alaska to northern California, across the Canadian Rockies and plains, through the Great Lakes, north throughout Labrador, south to Chesapeake Bay, and down through the Appalachians. The same plant grows in Europe, and four species occur in New England, including roundleaf sundew (*Drosera rotundifolia*), the most common.

Sundew plants average about 3 inches across and 1 inch tall, with leaves modified into flattened oval pads covered with red, stalked glands. Longer glands secrete a sticky fluid, while shorter glands secrete digestive enzymes. Attracted to nectarlike secretions, insects become trapped and then digested by plant enzymes. The usually white flowers hover well above the plant's leaves, borne on slender stalks. To find sundew, look for tiny glistening drops on their traps. Look carefully on sphagnum mats for reddish rosettes. You should also see several small insects in various stages of digestion.

Sundew

32 | Bog Brook Flowage

You will have a real wilderness experience when you paddle this shallow, irregularly shaped pond. Expect to see loons, ospreys, bald eagles ducks, and turtles, as well as beavers in the evening and possibly moose.

Location: Beddington, Deblois
Maps: *Maine Atlas & Gazetteer*, Map 25: B2; USGS Lead Mountain, Northeast Bluff
Area: 625 acres; 1,602 acres in wildlife management area
Time: 6 hours
Habitat Type: Shallow pond and marshland
Fish: Chain pickerel (see fish advisories, Appendix A)
Take Note: No development; steer clear of osprey nests

GETTING THERE

From Airline Highway/Route 9 east of Bangor at the junction with Route 193, go 1.2 miles east on Route 9 and turn right on East Beddington Lake Road, just after crossing the Narraguagus River. Go 2 miles (cumulative: 3.2 miles), and stay right. Go 3.6 miles (6.8 miles) to the access on the left, just after crossing Bog Brook bridge in Beddington. (44° 47.322′ N, 68° 0.252′ W)

The Flynn Pond access is exceedingly difficult to find and requires driving through miles of blueberry fields in Deblois. (44° 46.038′ N, 67° 57.042′ W)

WHAT YOU'LL SEE

Bog Brook Flowage can be described only with superlatives. Completely undeveloped, seldom visited, and maintained as a Maine Wildlife Management Area, it would take an entire day to explore every nook and cranny of this small, 3-mile-long lake. Numerous side channels and coves extend, seemingly in every direction, away from the main channel's open water.

True to the area's name, bog shrubbery dominates the shoreline, including bog rosemary, sweetgale, rhodora, cranberry, leatherleaf, and Labrador tea. While exploring the coves, you will have to thread your way through numerous small islands covered with these plants. Large patches of yellow pondlilies and other aquatic vegetation poke up through shallow water. Keep an eye out for small yellow, snapdragonlike bladderwort flowers, leading on short stalks

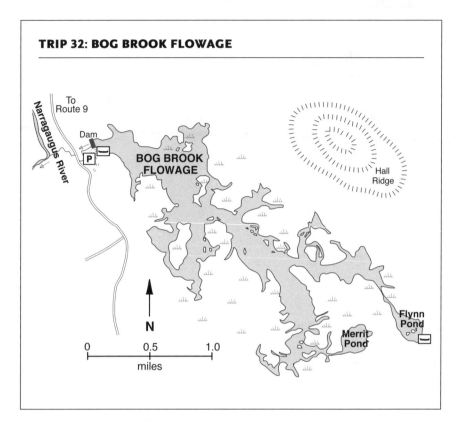

TRIP 32: BOG BROOK FLOWAGE

to carnivorous underwater bladders that suck in and digest—all too few—mosquito larvae. (For more on bladderwort feeding habits, see "Carnivorous Plants: The Table is Turned" on page 108.

As you paddle up the flowage's left side, look for osprey nests next to the water. Bald eagles nest nearby as well. A great blue heron rookery occupies another extensive patch of dead trees. If you paddle here in the spring or early summer, enjoy these wonders with binoculars, as paddling too close may interfere with nesting or interrupt parents feeding their young. Large numbers of black ducks and wood ducks feed in the shallows. A couple of loon pairs nest here as well.

In the boggy areas, keep an eye out for bobolinks, one of the few birds that is black underneath and brightly colored on the back—in this case yellow and white. The black tern, another rare marsh bird, also black underneath, inhabits these wetlands as well. We also saw upland sandpipers, increasingly rare in the Northeast, strolling about the blueberry fields. Northern harriers cruise these same fields, tilting back and forth, patiently waiting to pounce on rodents that do not have the good sense to be under cover midday.

33 | Great Pond and Dead Stream

We come to Great Pond for its scenic views and, especially, to paddle up Dead Stream in search of beavers. Also spotted: loons and bald eagles.

Location: Great Pond
Maps: *Maine Atlas & Gazetteer*, Map 34: E2, E3; USGS Great Pond
Area/Length: 679 acres; Dead Stream, 1 mile one way
Time: 4 hours
Habitat Type: Scenic pond and meandering, marshy stream
Fish: Brown trout, brook trout, landlocked salmon, smallmouth bass, chain pickerel (see fish advisories, Appendix A)
Take Note: Camping allowed when not in use by military personnel; 10 HP limit

GETTING THERE

From Airline Highway/Route 9 east of Bangor at the junction with Route 179, go 1.5 miles east on Route 9, turn left, go 0.1 mile (cumulative: 1.6 miles), and turn right on Great Pond Road. Go 7 miles (8.6 miles) to the access on the left. (44° 57.216′ N, 68° 16.914′ W).

WHAT YOU'LL SEE

Although this is the site of the Navy's Outdoor Adventure Center, we saw few other visitors the two times that we paddled here: the Saturday of Labor Day weekend and later in September. Great Pond marks the beginning of the West Branch of the Union River trip. The West Branch starts just around a bend, to the left from the access. If you paddle down this stream, you will not be able to paddle back up against the substantial current at the pond's outlet. We hear the river turns to flat water shortly after leaving the pond but have not yet done this reconnaissance.

Deciduous vegetation covers the hillsides and islands here, with only a few scattered pines, making us wonder about the recreation area's former name, Dow Pines. It is a scenic spot, with two nice tree-covered islands. Unless you get caught up watching the antics of the resident beaver population, it should not take more than a few hours to explore all of Great Pond.

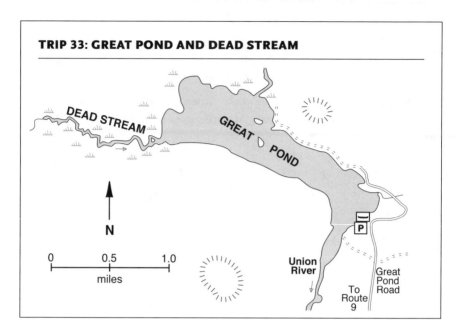

TRIP 33: GREAT POND AND DEAD STREAM

DEAD STREAM

GREAT POND

N

0   0.5   1.0
miles

Union
River

Great
Pond
Road

To
Route
9

P

We recommend paddling here in the evening or the very early morning, especially up the Dead Stream inlet at the lake's west end. At nearly every bend in the meandering stream we came across beavers that protested our presence with loud tail slaps. Several waited until we got right up to them before sounding the alarm and diving for cover, splashing us with water. We had such a good time that we waited until well after sunset to paddle back, our way lighted by alpenglow on the hillsides.

You should see loons and great blue herons here. If you're lucky, you also may spot a bald eagle or two.

34 | Mopang Lake and Second Mopang Lake

Mopang Lake, surrounded by forest, is an out-of-the-way place to paddle. Look for nesting common and black terns along with loons, ospreys, and bald eagles. You could see moose here.

Location: Devereaux Township, T30 MD BPP
Maps: *Maine Atlas & Gazetteer*, Map 25: A1, A2 and Map 35: E1, E2; USGS Peaked Mountain, Quillpig Mountain

Area: Mopang Lake, 1,487 acres; Second Mopang Lake, 145 acres
Time: 5 hours
Habitat Type: Large lakes with islands, coves, marshy entrance stream
Fish: Brook trout, splake, landlocked salmon, white perch, chain pickerel (see fish advisories, Appendix A)
Take Note: Campfire permit required, 207-827-1800

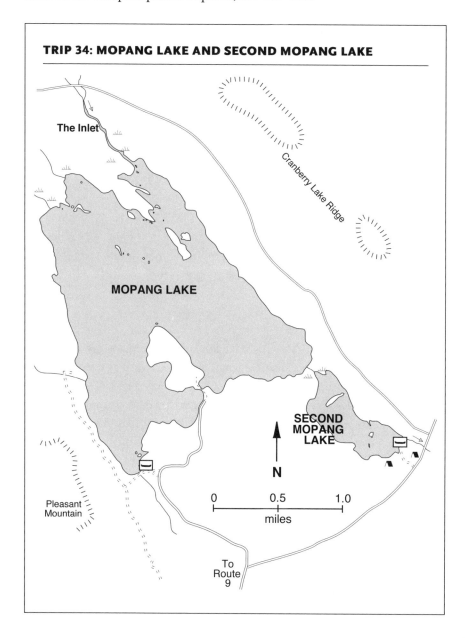

TRIP 34: MOPANG LAKE AND SECOND MOPANG LAKE

The Inlet

Cranberry Lake Ridge

MOPANG LAKE

SECOND MOPANG LAKE

N

Pleasant Mountain

0   0.5   1.0
miles

To Route 9

Common tern

GETTING THERE

Mopang Lake. From Airline Highway/Route 9 east of Bangor at the junction with Route 193, go 6.6 miles east on Route 9 and turn left. Go 1.3 miles (cumulative: 7.9 miles), and veer left. Go 1.2 miles (9.1 miles) and veer left. Go 0.1 mile (9.2 miles) through a hemlock corridor to the access on the right in North Washington (Devereaux Township). (44° 53.970′ N, 68° 0.270′ W)

   Second Mopang Lake. Proceed as above, except veer right at 7.9 miles. Go 1.7 miles (9.6 miles), and turn left on an unmaintained, high-clearance road. Go 0.3 mile (9.9 miles) to the access; stay right at fork in North Washington (Devereaux Township). (44° 54.144′ N, 67° 57.840′ W)

WHAT YOU'LL SEE

Mopang Lake and Second Mopang Lake are among the many great paddling lakes in Washington County, also known as Sunrise County, as it feels the sun's morning rays before anywhere else in the United States. The larger, somewhat bell-shaped lake harbors a sizable peninsula near the south end and numerous islands and large boulders near the north end. Typical Maine trees populate the shore: red spruce, northern white cedar, white pine, hemlock, some red pine, paper birch, and maple. The shore overflows with sweetgale, leatherleaf, rhodora, alder, and highbush blueberry. Second Mopang Lake resembles its larger neighbor but has a more remote feel.

   In spring, one can paddle a small boat upstream from Second Mopang into Mopang. Pick your way carefully among the rocks as you paddle up the briskly flowing, small connecting creek. We only paddled in one direction; going downstream, the current would carry you into rocks. Alternatively, you can carry your boat either through the water or through the brush and trees. Several very nice campsites hide along the southeastern end of Second Mopang Lake.

We watched two species of terns here: the more prevalent common tern, though no longer very common over most of its range; and the distinctive black tern, nearly solid black with a white undertail patch and dark, silvery wings. The common tern nests in small colonies on some of the large protruding boulders on the lake's northern half. During nesting season, keep your distance from nesting terns. At the north end's marshy inlet, you may see wood ducks, mergansers, and other waterfowl. We noticed at least three loon pairs on the two lakes, and this is a good place to see ospreys and bald eagles.

A coarse pegmatite granite—mostly black-and-white with large crystals of biotite mica, feldspar, and quartz—dominates the rocky shoreline. The large crystal size indicates that the granite formed deep underground, where molten magma cooled very slowly.

For camping, we prefer the neck connecting the large peninsula near the southern end of Second Mopang. Sandy coves occur on both sides of this neck, with pleasant tenting sites under the tall conifers and several trails for exploring the area and observing numerous wildflowers, including painted trillium, pink lady's slipper, wild sarsaparilla, and bunchberry.

35 | Rocky Lake, Rocky Lake Stream, East Machias River, and Second Lake

Under the right weather conditions, mainly little wind, Rocky Lake and Rocky Lake Stream can provide a daylong trip into the wilderness, in the heart of the 11,000-acre Rocky Lake Public Reserved Lands. Expect to see loons, ospreys, bald eagles, moose, and lots more.

Location: Berry Township
Maps: *Maine Atlas & Gazetteer*, Map 26: A2, A3; USGS Bog Lake, Lake Cathance, Hadley Lake, Round Lake
Area/Length: Rocky Lake, 1,555 acres; Round Lake, 352 acres; stream length, 6 miles one way to Second Lake
Time: All day
Habitat Type: Large lake with many islands, coves; entrance stream leads to Round Lake
Fish: Brook trout, smallmouth bass, white perch, chain pickerel (see fish advisories, Appendix A)
Take Note: Campfire permit required, 207-827-1800

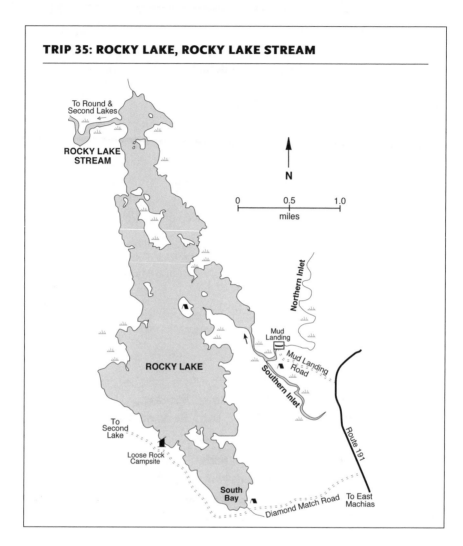

TRIP 35: ROCKY LAKE, ROCKY LAKE STREAM

To Round & Second Lakes

ROCKY LAKE STREAM

N

0   0.5   1.0
miles

Northern Inlet

Mud Landing

Mud Landing Road

Southern Inlet

ROCKY LAKE

Route 191

To Second Lake

Loose Rock Campsite

South Bay

Diamond Match Road   To East Machias

GETTING THERE

Rocky Lake, Mud Landing. From East Machias at the junction of Routes 1 and 191, go north on Route 191 for 8.4 miles, turn left at the blue sign, and go 0.7 mile (cumulative: 9.1 miles) to the access and campsite. (44° 51.684′ N, 67° 26.322′ W)

Rocky Lake, South Bay. From East Machias, go north on Route 191 for 7.3 miles and turn left at the blue sign. Go 1.4 miles (8.7 miles) on Diamond Lake Road to a campsite and access on the right. (44° 50.286′ N, 67° 26.982′ W)

Second Lake. Diamond Match Road continues to Second Lake, ending in a small parking area with a portage of several hundred feet down to the lake. (44° 51.060′ N, 67° 29.652′ W)

WHAT YOU'LL SEE

Which one of these lakes you choose to paddle depends on what type of trip you have in mind—and on the weather. Rocky Lake and its inlet and outlet streams include lots of interesting water to paddle. Although we did not paddle Second Lake, we include a short description here because the state owns the southern four-fifths and has no development. About the same percentage of Rocky Lake, again the southern portion, is included in the Rocky Lake Public Reserved Lands.

Rocky Lake

The state owns the southern portion of this lake, up to and including the large, 59-acre island (see map), of this 4.5-mile-long lake. Several access points allow flexibility in planning a trip—an important factor when north or south winds roll deep swells and whitecaps up or down this north-south oriented lake. In calm or modest wind conditions, by all means paddle Rocky Lake.

We prefer the main access at Mud Landing. As you leave the inlet, the southeast shore sports an extensive stand of white cedar that provides an important wintering yard for deer. Quite shallow, the lake remains true to its name, with rocks everywhere: lining the shore, protruding from the water, lurking just beneath the surface, effectively keeping down the number of high-speed boats. Generally, you will see only other paddlers and a few anglers with small outboards. One can still have a true wilderness experience here in a great location for looking at plants and wildlife.

You can camp at both access points: Mud Landing and South Bay. Along the southwestern shore at Loose Rock, you will find a third official campsite with a picnic table, outhouse, and lean-to. In addition to official campsites, several informal campsites exist on islands and at various points along the shore.

If you have enough time, explore Rocky Lake Stream at the lake's northwest end. Paddling down Rocky Lake Stream, you will come to Northern Stream entering from the right (north). Take a side trip up Northern Stream or continue downstream to the East Machias River, where you can turn left and paddle downstream to Second Lake or turn right and paddle upstream to Round Lake.

We paddled on Rocky Lake in May, July, and September. In May, a severe wind and driving rain kept us from leaving the inlet at the end of Mud Landing. In July, the wind barely rippled the water, but in September the whitecaps broke over the bow as we dipped through 2-foot swells that almost—and should have—kept us off the lake. If the wind keeps you off the main lake or if you want solitude, by all means paddle from Mud Landing to the right up Northern Inlet or to the left up the southern inlet, taking you into remote,

TRIP 35: ROCKY LAKE STREAM, EAST MACHIAS RIVER, AND SECOND LAKE

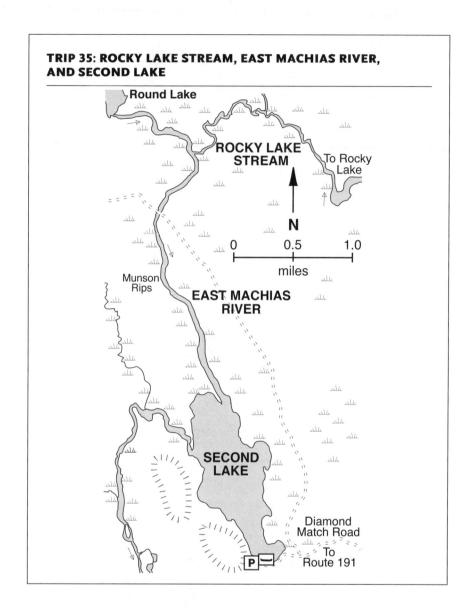

marshy areas filled with plants and wildlife.

In the southern inlet, you will have to portage over a beaver dam almost immediately. After we crossed the dam, we had smooth sailing up the meandering stream—although, as you know, other dams may appear. This quite boggy area, mainly filled with shrubs, also contains occasional stands of dwarf red maple and some good-size tamarack. Alder, birch, aspen, and red maple dominate the shoreline farther back, and white pine, spruce, and many other tree species appear back in the woods. We paddled more than a mile into the marsh until a second beaver dam blocked our way; you certainly could go farther.

We also paddled up Northern Inlet some distance, until we reached the first beaver dam. We leave it to you to explore this area more fully.

If the wind blows from the south, as it often does during the summer, you could launch from South Bay and stick to that area. Alternatively, you could paddle Second Lake or put in at Round Lake (see *Maine Atlas* for directions) on the East Machias River and paddle to Rocky Lake or Second Lake on streams generally unaffected by wind.

Second Lake

You can paddle from Rocky Lake to Second Lake, a distance of about 9 miles from Mud Landing. Not having paddled all the way to Second Lake, we can't comment about water conditions, especially at Munson Rips; paddling back upstream may be difficult. If, however, you leave a car at Second Lake, you could make this a one way trip. With one vehicle, you could also walk on Diamond Match Road back to the Rocky Lake southern access, retrieve your vehicle, and drive back to Second Lake to get your boat. Bald eagles have nested over the years just above Second Lake.

36 | Rocky Lake II

Paddle this spot in the spring or in wet summers; shallow water will hamper your progress in dry times. We saw an osprey catch a fish here. It's a great place to look for loons, ospreys, bald eagles, beavers, and moose.

Location: Edmund Township, Marion Township, Whiting
Maps: *Maine Atlas & Gazetteer*, Map 26: B5 and Map 27: B1;
USGS Long Lake, Whiting
Area: 1,126 acres
Time: 6 hours
Habitat Type: Large, shallow lake with several islands and deep coves
Fish: Brown trout, brook trout (see fish advisories, Appendix A)
Take Note: Campfire permit required, 207-827-1800

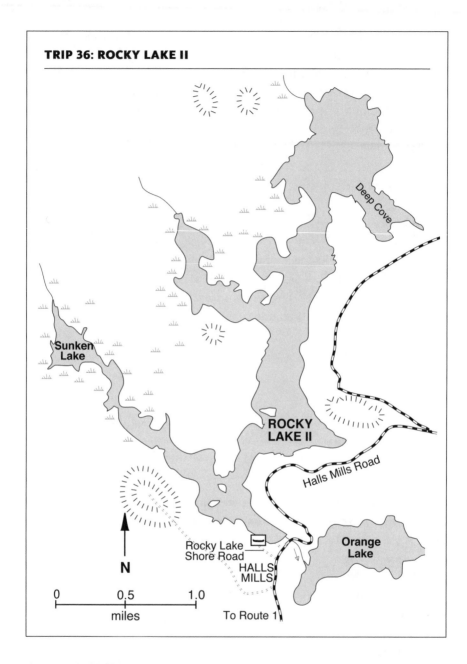

TRIP 36: ROCKY LAKE II

Deep Cove

Sunken Lake

ROCKY LAKE II

Halls Mills Road

Orange Lake

N

0   0.5   1.0
miles

Rocky Lake Shore Road

HALLS MILLS

To Route 1

GETTING THERE

From East Machias at the junction of Routes 1 and 191, go east on Route 1 for 7.4 miles and turn left on Halls Mills Road. Go 1.6 miles (cumulative: 9 miles), turn left on Rocky Lake Shore Road, and go 0.1 mile (9.1 miles) to the access. (44° 46.290′ N, 67° 16.050′ W)

WHAT YOU'LL SEE

Why would two large lakes within 8 miles of each other both carry the name Rocky Lake? To keep them separate, we affectionately call them Rocky I and Rocky II. Perhaps affection does not really describe our feeling toward these lakes, given the large number of submerged rocks and the generally shallow character of both. This lake, Rocky II, lies east of Machias, while Rocky I lies north of Machias (see Trip 35).

As we paddled up the southern arm from the access, albeit during a dry summer, almost every single paddle stroke struck the mud bottom of this heavily vegetated, marshy lake. We tried to paddle up the northwestern arm to Sunken Lake but had to turn back around the halfway point due to shallow water. With repairs to the dams and resultant deeper water, it would be well worth the trip up this most interesting arm of the lake.

As you look up the waterway with binoculars, you will see among the lily pads and pickerelweed a series of evenly spaced beaver lodges and evidence of beaver cuttings everywhere. Back up in this remote area would be a good place to look for moose. We saw ospreys fishing here, one with a fish in its talons, and a pair of Canada geese with a raft of downy goslings.

As you go up the main section of Rocky II, much deeper water accommodates at least one pair of nesting loons. The shallow coves, however, particularly the large one on the left, grow thick with aquatic vegetation. A few scattered cottages dot this part of the lake, but one gets the impression Rocky II does not see much traffic. We hope it stays that way!

---

37 | Orange River

The Down East Coastal Conservancy has developed a wonderful water trail with a wilderness feel, encompassed by the Orange River Wildlife Management Area. Look for wading birds and waterfowl, along with ospreys, bald eagles, beavers, and muskrat.

Location: Whiting
Maps: *Maine Atlas & Gazetteer*, Map 27: B1; USGS Whiting
Length: 5 miles one way from Orange Lake outlet to Whiting Bay; additional paddling on Reynolds Brook and other feeder streams
Time: 5 hours; shorter trips possible

Habitat Type: Small lake and marshy stream within wildlife management area

Fish: Brook trout (see fish advisories, Appendix A)

Take Note: Accesses owned by Down East Coastal Conservancy, which also provides three picnic areas along the water trail

GETTING THERE

Landing Road Access. From East Machias at the junction of Routes 1 and 191 north, go 11.8 miles east on Route 1 and turn left on Playhouse Lane. Go 0.1 mile (cumulative: 11.9 miles) and turn left on Landing Road, which ends at the access. (44° 47.148′ N, 67° 11.556′ W)

    Reynolds Marsh Access. From East Machias at the junction of Routes 1 and 191 north, go 10.3 miles east on Route 1, and turn left on Old U.S. Route 1. Go 0.1 mile (10.4 miles) to the access by the bridge. Drop your boat, and park off Route 1, just before the turnoff. (44° 45.954′ N, 67° 12.186′ W)

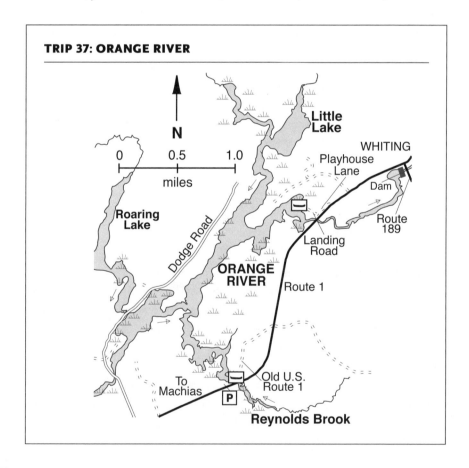

WHAT YOU'LL SEE

The Orange River Wildlife Management Area completely surrounds the Orange River Reservoir and Little Lake, included here. You can paddle from either access for miles along Orange River and Reynolds Brook channels. The area has a wild feel to it, with little development until you near Orange Lake, although you do hear some road noise from Route 1. Ruins from a long-abandoned, steam-powered watermill sit just south of the Landing Road access.

Aquatic plants fill these shallow waters and adjacent marshes, providing a good location for studying aquatic vegetation. American white waterlily, American eelgrass with its narrow floating leaves, pickerelweed, and lots more will be your constant companions as you paddle along meandering channels. Except for the shores of Little Lake on the north, trees stand well back from where you paddle.

Besides being a major waterfowl and wading bird production area, Orange River also harbors bald eagles and ospreys. The rare and elusive least bittern is found here, along with other hard-to-see species, such as sora (a type of rail), Virginia rail, and common snipes. Also look for great blue herons, green herons, common moorhen, glossy ibis, pied-billed grebe, and ring-necked ducks.

When paddling here, you may have to portage over a few beaver dams. You could also see muskrat, deer, otters, or moose.

---

38 | First, Second, and Third Chain Lakes

The north end of Chain Lakes provides an excellent spot for wilderness camping and wildlife viewing. You can get exercise here because the water extends for about 8 miles in one direction. Look for loons, great blue herons, ducks, beavers in the evening, and possibly moose.

Location: Day Block Township, T26 ED BPP, T37 ED BPP, Wesley
Maps: *Maine Atlas & Gazetteer*, Map 35: D5, E5; USGS Clifford Lake, Wesley
Area: First Chain Lake, 336 acres; Second Chain Lake, 589 acres; Third Chain Lake, 157 acres
Time: 5 hours; shorter trips possible
Habitat Type: Long, connected lakes
Fish: Brook trout, white perch, chain pickerel (see fish advisories, Appendix A)

Take Note: Some development, particularly on First Chain Lake; campfire permit required, 207-827-1800

GETTING THERE

From Machias at the junction of Routes 1A and 192 (Broadway Street), go 20 miles north on Route 192 and turn left on Route 9. Go 3.1 miles (cumulative: 23.1 miles) and turn right on Old Mill Road. Go 0.4 mile (23.5 miles) and veer right on Chain Lake Boulevard. Go 1.4 miles (24.9 miles) and turn right. Go 0.4 mile (25.3 miles) to the access on the right. (44° 57.924′ N, 67° 43.398′ W)

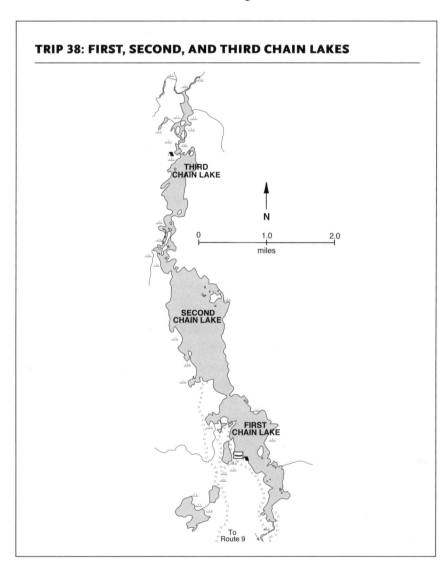

TRIP 38: FIRST, SECOND, AND THIRD CHAIN LAKES

WHAT YOU'LL SEE

First, Second, and Third Chain lakes provide very good paddling, particularly the northern sections between Second and Third Chain lakes and above Third Lake. Because the best areas lie 6 or 7 miles from the access, we recommend this trip primarily for paddlers seeking exercise or planning to camp. From the access, we would head north into Second Chain Lake, although if you have time you might want to explore the southern part. A few houses stand near the outlet, but some interesting islands also beg to be explored, and the shallow water discourages most motorboaters.

In Second Chain Lake's marshy coves, look for great blue herons, wood ducks, moose, and beavers. For more of a wilderness feel, paddle through Second Lake into the boggy channel between Second and Third lakes. Although it is only about a mile in length, if you paddle around the islands and explore all of the inlets and coves, you could easily paddle two or three times that distance. Watch for pitcher plants and the many different heaths that grow here: rhodora, bog laurel, bog rosemary, leatherleaf, highbush blueberry, and lowbush blueberry.

The few rustic cabins along the southwest shore of Third Chain Lake do not spoil its beauty. Farther north, some absolutely gorgeous lichen- and moss-covered boulders extend down into the water. A beautiful campsite perches on a large boulder at the lake's north end. You can also paddle the slowly meandering Chain Brook Stream, which you can explore for another mile or so.

---

39 | Clifford Lake and Silver Pug Lake

Clifford Lake and the attached Silver Pug Lake make for a remote, beautiful spot with scenic hillsides. This is a great place to see loons. Also look for bald eagles, ospreys, great blue herons, a variety of ducks, and possibly moose.

Location: Greenlaw Chopping Township, T26 ED BPP
Maps: *Maine Atlas & Gazetteer*, Map 35: D5; USGS Clifford Lake
Area: Clifford Lake, 954 acres; Silver Pug Lake, 198 acres
Time: 6 hours; shorter trips possible
Habitat Type: Lake with large peninsula, many coves, and islands
Fish: Smallmouth bass, white perch, chain pickerel (see fish advisories, Appendix A)

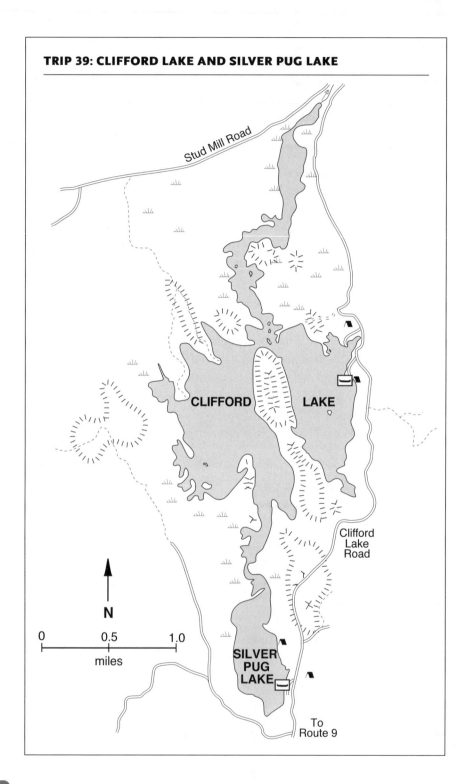

TRIP 39: CLIFFORD LAKE AND SILVER PUG LAKE

Stud Mill Road

CLIFFORD LAKE

N

0   0.5   1.0
miles

Clifford
Lake
Road

SILVER
PUG
LAKE

To
Route 9

Take Note: No personal watercraft; campfire permit required, 207-827-1800; some authorized sites do not require permits

GETTING THERE

Clifford Lake. From Machias at the junction of Routes 1A and 192 (Broadway Street), go 20 miles north on Route 192 and turn right on Route 9. Go 3 miles (cumulative: 23 miles), and turn left on Clifford Lake Road. Go 8.2 miles (31.2 miles) to the access on the left. (45° 3.918´ N, 67° 40.902´ W)

   Silver Pug Lake. Access is on the left after 5 miles (28 miles). (45° 1.716´N, 67° 41.556´ W)

WHAT YOU'LL SEE

Clifford Lake is a beautiful spot: remote, undeveloped, and small enough that you don't feel too exposed in an open boat. The west arm of the lake's horseshoe configuration connects by stream to Silver Pug Lake. Many attractive islands and shoreline granite boulders dot Clifford Lake's surface. During our first ten minutes on the east arm, we saw five loons; traveling about, we saw several more. You may see eagles here. They routinely return to the same nest year after year, enlarging it each spring.

Cormorant

Wood ducks can be seen in and around Clifford and Silver Pug Lakes. Photo: Photographybymichael.net

Both fairly shallow, Clifford and Silver Pug lakes harbor warmwater fish species, primarily some large smallmouth bass that hide out among the numerous rocks. Lacy hemlock branches drape out over the water, and lime-green lichens festoon the dead trees along shore. A variety of conifers, including spruce, red and white pines, and hemlock, cover the surrounding hillsides. Occasional maples and other deciduous trees break the monotony of thick conifer canopy.

We saw several cormorants; ring-necked, wood, and black ducks; great blue herons; and lots of songbirds. Numerous coves, begging for exploration, line the shore, and you can paddle all the way up to the small dam at the lake's north end. This wild place seems to get few visitors and will provide hours of paddling in solitude.

40 | Bearce Lake

Bearce Lake lies in the Baring Wilderness Area of Moosehorn National Wildlife Refuge. This out-of-the-way pond and surrounding refuge provide a good location to look for woodcocks, bald eagles, ospreys, wood ducks, river otters, and moose. On sphagnum mats, look for pitcher plants, along with rose pogonia and grass pink orchids.

Location: Baring PLT, Meddybemps
Maps: *Maine Atlas & Gazetteer*, Map 36: C5, D5; USGS Meddybemps Lake East
Area: 275 acres; 17,200 acres in National Wildlife Refuge
Time: 2 hours
Habitat Type: Small, shallow lake in wildlife refuge; wooded hillsides
Fish: Smallmouth bass, yellow perch, chain pickerel (see fish advisories, Appendix A)
Information: Moosehorn National Wildlife Refuge, fws.gov/refuge/moosehorn
Take Note: No motors, no development

GETTING THERE

Bearce from East Machias. At the junction of Routes 1 and 191, go 30 miles north on Route 191 to the access on the right in Baileyville. (45° 4.200′ N, 67° 19.560′ W)

Bearce from Calais. At the junction of Route 1 and South Street, go 4.2 miles south(!) on Route 1 North and turn left on Route 191. Go 4 miles (cumulative: 8.2 miles) to the access on the left.

Visitor Center. From the access road, go 3.1 miles north on Route 191 and turn right. Go 0.2 mile (cumulative: 3.3 miles) and turn right. Go 2.2 miles (5.5 miles) to the visitor center on the left in Baring PLT. We watched a porcupine wandering around the headquarters grounds. (45° 6.864′ N, 67° 16.854′ W)

WHAT YOU'LL SEE

Bearce Lake—a long way from anywhere, unless you happen to live in Calais, on the New Brunswick border—provides a great place to paddle. It lies wholly

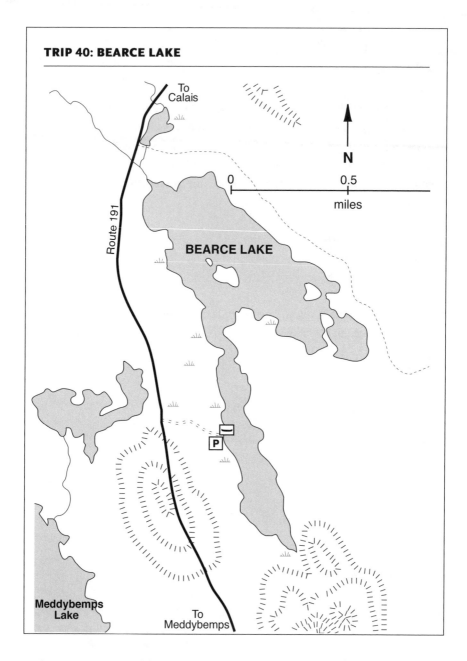

To
Calais

N

0   0.5
            miles

Route 191

BEARCE LAKE

P

Meddybemps
Lake

To
Meddybemps

within a 4,680-acre wilderness section of Moosehorn National Wildlife Refuge.

The refuge provides unspoiled habitat for the American woodcock, a strange-looking bird (but perhaps not to other woodcocks) with an inordinately long bill that probes the mud of alder swamps and other wetlands for whatever

A porcupine munches balsam fir bark at the visitors center near Bearce Lake.

wiggles. Perhaps more interesting to most visitors, however, are the nesting bald eagles. As many as three pairs have nested at a time on the refuge. Since 1991, a pair has nested on a small platform within 200 feet of the main highway, a few miles from Bearce Lake, apparently oblivious to the steady stream of cars. Several osprey pairs nest nearby, as well.

Northern boreal forest, consisting mostly of conifers, forms part of the refuge and harbors such species as the spruce grouse, boreal chickadees, Cape May warbler, gray jay, red and white-winged crossbills, and black-backed and three-toed woodpeckers.

Many different types of trees border this beautiful lake. We noted white birch, spruce, white pine, northern white cedar, tamarack, hemlock, red maple, and gray birch. A well-developed understory and several marshy areas contribute to the high plant-species diversity, which includes pitcher plants, sundew, and rose pogonia and grass pink orchids. Look here for beavers, moose, wood ducks, and black ducks. When we visited, a huge flock of bank swallows darted continually over the water, trying its best to reduce the flying-insect population, also huge.

Granite boulders lining the shore and poking up from the water add another dimension to Bearce Lake. Be careful paddling here, because the barely submerged boulders contain jagged, protruding quartz crystals, the kind that produce deep gouges in passing hulls.

41 | Crawford Lake, Pocomoonshine Lake, and Mud Lake

These connected lakes are best visited on a multiday trip, possibly including a one way jaunt down the Maine and East Machias rivers. Multiple coves, meandering inlet streams, and marshlands provide much to explore.

Location: Alexander, Big Lake Township, Crawford, Princeton
Maps: *Maine Atlas & Gazetteer*, Map 36: C2, D1, D2; USGS Crawford Lake, Princeton
Area: Crawford Lake, 1,677 acres; Pocomoonshine Lake, 2,464 acres; Mud Lake, 100 acres
Time: All day or multiday; shorter trips possible
Habitat Type: Shallow lakes with many islands; boggy connector streams; 4,200-acre peatlands, among the largest in Maine, and bog ecosystems abound
Fish: Smallmouth bass, white perch, chain pickerel (see fish advisories, Appendix A)
Information: Sunrise Expeditions, sunrise-exp.com; *AMC River Guide: Maine*, by John Fiske (AMC Books, 2008; outdoors.org/amcstore)
Take Note: Wind can make paddling hazardous; campfire permit required, 207-827-1800

GETTING THERE

Pocomoonshine Lake has three access points:

East Machias River. Start at the southeast access. With wind from the south and using the southeast access, circle around to the west and head down to the Mud lakes and Crawford Lake. With wind from the north, use one of the two northern access points.

Northeast. From Calais at the junction of Route 1 and South Street, go 9.2 miles south(!) on Route 1 North and turn left on South Princeton/Woodland roads. Go 4.4 miles (cumulative: 13.6 miles) then go 0.4 mile (14 miles) straight to the access in Princeton. (45° 8.766′ N, 67° 30.672′ W)

Northwest. From the junction of South Princeton and Woodland roads (near northeast access), go 3.2 miles north and turn left on Pocomoonshine Mountain Road. Go 3.6 miles (cumulative: 6.8 miles) and turn left at the access and campsite road in Princeton. (45° 9.630′ N, 67° 33.534′ W)

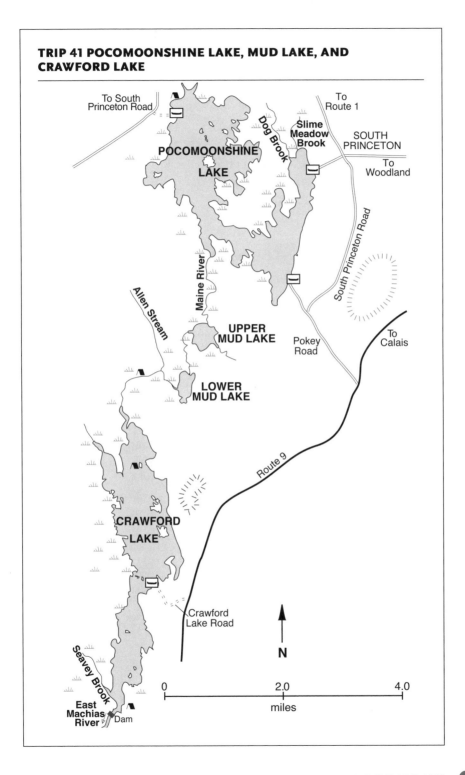

TRIP 41 POCOMOONSHINE LAKE, MUD LAKE, AND CRAWFORD LAKE

To South Princeton Road

To Route 1

Dog Brook

Slime Meadow Brook

SOUTH PRINCETON

To Woodland

POCOMOONSHINE LAKE

South Princeton Road

Maine River

Allen Stream

UPPER MUD LAKE

Pokey Road

To Calais

LOWER MUD LAKE

Route 9

CRAWFORD LAKE

Crawford Lake Road

N

Seavey Brook

East Machias River

Dam

0   2.0   4.0
miles

Southeast. From the junction of Routes 1N and 9, go 8.1 miles south on Route 9 and turn right on South Princeton Road. Go 1.1 mile (cumulative: 9.2 miles) and veer left on Pokey Road. Go 1.2 miles (10.4 miles) to the access. (45° 7.080′ N, 67° 31.272′ W)

Crawford Lake East. From the junction of Routes 1N/9, go 12.5 miles south on Route 9 and turn right on Crawford Lake/Crawford Landing Road. Go 0.8 mile (cumulative: 13.3 miles) to the access. (45° 2.682′ N, 67° 34.146′ W)

Crawford Lake South. As above but go 16.7 miles on Route 9 and turn right on Pokey Dam Road. Go 0.9 mile (cumulative: 17.6 miles) to the access at the dam. (45° 0.732′ N, 67° 35.160′ W)

WHAT YOU'LL SEE
East Machias River Trip and Crawford Lake

We've paddled Pocomoonshine in July and August. The southeast access marks the start of the East Machias River trip: down the Maine River, through Upper and Lower Mud lakes, Crawford Lake, and into the East Machias River. You can take out on Crawford or Round lakes; you can continue on Rocky Lake Stream, taking out in Rocky Lake; or you can continue down the East Machias River through Second Lake, taking out at Hadley Lake or East Machias. During July in a dry year, we opted for a long two-day, middle-distance trip, taking out at Rocky Lake (Trip 35).

We would avoid the river trip in late summer or during low water. Below Crawford Lake, we walked our boats for about 3 miles through boulder-laden riffles, seriously scratching our shins and boats to about the same degree. In the spring, during higher water, you supposedly can sail right through this stretch. According to the *AMC River Guide,* even those with limited whitewater experience can navigate the modest rapids. If you have questions about water conditions, contact Sunrise Expeditions, which can also arrange a car-ferrying service.

From the southeast access, paddle across to the far southwestern cove and head south, staying left. Pocomoonshine's forested shoreline gives way to the slowly meandering Maine River. After traveling a mile or so through typical bog and floating-plant vegetation, the stream widens out, twice in quick succession, into Upper and Lower Mud lakes. Following the channel through these weed-choked waterways presents a challenge. We stayed to the right and battled our way through rushes, sedges, and pickerelweed until we found the west-leading outlets of each lake. In Lower Mud Lake, stay in the more open water until well down the lake; then look for an obvious channel leading to the right (west). Dabbling ducks love these shallow lakes, and we tried our best not to disturb their foraging.

As you head west out of Lower Mud Lake, after about 200 yards Allen Stream enters from the right; you can paddle up this marshy stream quite a distance. Look for a campsite on the left where Allen Stream flows in and another on one of the northernmost islands as you enter Crawford Lake, just off a peninsula jutting out from the left shore. A sloping granite boulder off the southwestern shore provides the best take-out.

Crawford Lake, 5 miles long and narrow, funnels wind and churns up swells and whitecaps whenever the wind blows north or south. At the lake's southern end, besides finding a dam, campsite, and access, you can double back up the meandering, marshy Seavey Brook; it looks to be a truly wild place, perfect for moose watching.

At the end of Crawford Lake, you have come more than 11 miles, and with any wind, you will not be able to paddle this round trip in just one day. It makes an ideal two-day trip, allowing time for side-channel exploration.

Crawford Lake is renowned for its smallmouth bass fishing.

Pocomoonshine Lake

With wind from the north, we would explore Pocomoonshine's northern arms. From the South Princeton access, Dog Brook presents a beautiful paddle up a meandering, wide, slow-flowing inlet. Conifers dominate the shoreline, set quite far back from the channel.

White pine, tamarack, spruce, and hemlock grow in profusion. Dwarf red maples grow out from the shore; grasses and low-growing bog vegetation lead down to the stream channel, covered with yellow pondlily, American white waterlily, pickerelweed, and other aquatic vegetation. After about 1 mile, the channel narrows and gets quite rocky. If you pick your way back through the rocks for another 0.25 mile, a series of beaver dams appears. We did not portage above the dams, leaving further exploration for another visit.

If you paddle the northeast arm, check out Slime Meadow Brook. Beavers have opened a narrow channel, allowing you to paddle quite a way back in. Of course, when you try to turn your boat around, that's when you get slimed.

Putting in on the northwest arm, a relatively large open expanse of lake dotted with a few islands faces you. The seemingly never-ending series of marshy coves, starting directly across from the access and extending south down the large peninsula separating the northern arms, provides the most interesting areas to explore.

42 | Big Lake, Clifford Stream, Little River, and Little Musquash Stream

This trip includes the southwest section of enormous Big Lake and three pristine marshy inlet streams. You will see bald eagles, ospreys, loons, bobolinks, muskrat, and possibly beavers, otters, and moose.

Location: Big Lake Township, Grand Lake Stream PLT, Greenlaw Chopping Township, Indian Township
Maps: *Maine Atlas & Gazetteer*, Map 35: B5, C5 and Map 36: B1, C1; USGS Big Lake, Clifford Lake, Grand Lake Stream, Princeton
Area/Length: 10,305 acres; 9 miles one way
Time: All day or multiday; shorter trips possible
Habitat Type: Large, shallow lake with many islands and marshy coves; rivers through marshlands
Fish: Landlocked salmon, smallmouth bass, white perch, chain pickerel (see fish advisories, Appendix A)
Information: 370,000 acres preserved by Down East Lakes Land Trust, downeastlakes.org
Take Note: Wind can make paddling hazardous; campfire permit required, 207-827-1800

GETTING THERE

From the junction of Routes 1 and 9 west of Calais, go 15.5 miles north on Route 1 and turn left on Grand Lake Stream/Milford roads. Go 10.1 miles (cumulative: 25.6 miles) and turn left on Water Street/Big Lake Landing Road. Go 2.9 miles (28.5 miles) to the access. (45° 9.918′ N, 67° 43.464′ W)

WHAT YOU'LL SEE

We include this section not so much for Big Lake but for the several marshy streams that flow into it. Paddling Little River, Little Musquash Stream, and Clifford Stream provides a great opportunity to see the region's wildlife. If you spend any amount of time here, you should see bald eagles, ospreys, bobolinks, red-winged blackbirds, yellowthroats, yellow warblers, other typical marshland birds, moose, muskrat, beavers, and snapping and painted turtles. In addition to the muskrat you see swimming, keep a lookout for otters.

Big Lake, although huge at more than 10,000 acres, seems much smaller due to the large number of islands that populate its waters. We would stick to the

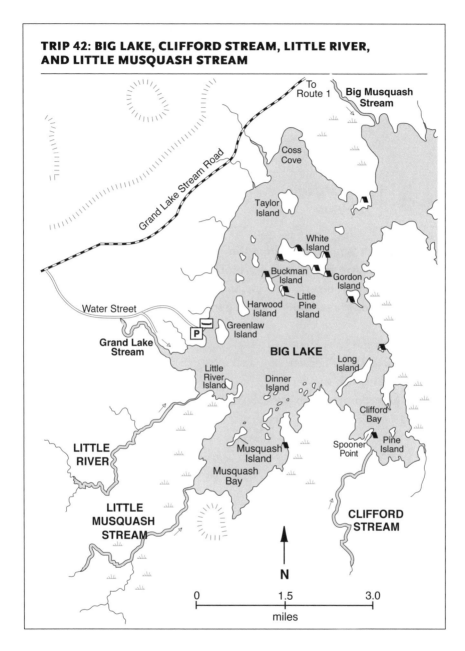

TRIP 42: BIG LAKE, CLIFFORD STREAM, LITTLE RIVER, AND LITTLE MUSQUASH STREAM

lake's west end near the access, which suffers least from winds. When winds blow from the northwest, you should be able to paddle down the west shore and into the feeder streams.

Because marshlands abound around the lake, we would camp on the islands, where you need a permit to build a fire. It takes a couple of days to explore thoroughly the lake's west end, islands, and inlet streams. Down East Lakes Land Trust purchased the land or acquired conservation easements that include all streams included here, as well as most of Big Lake's shore.

On the lake you should see ospreys, bald eagles, loons, and ducks. This is also a good place to look for moose. Paddle here in the spring or later in the season, after the ubiquitous black flies and mosquitoes have abated.

43 | Big Musquash Stream

Big Musquash Stream meanders through a broad, treeless valley. Paddling here, we saw bobolinks, black ducks, ring-necked ducks, great blue herons, otters, weasels, muskrat, and moose. You could see beavers in the side streams and headwaters.

Location: Grand Lake Stream PLT
Maps: *Maine Atlas & Gazetteer*, Map 35: A1, B1; USGS Big Lake, Waite
Length: 6 miles one way
Time: 5 hours; shorter trips possible
Habitat Type: Slowly meandering, marshy stream, flowing through a broad, treeless valley
Fish: Smallmouth bass, chain pickerel (see fish advisories, Appendix A)
Information: 370,000 acres preserved by Down East Lakes Land Trust, downeastlakes.org
Take Note: Paddle here when wind makes lake paddling treacherous

GETTING THERE
From the junction of Routes 1 and 9 west of Calais, go 15.5 miles north on Route 1 and turn left on Grand Lake Stream/Milford roads. Go 4.1 miles (cumulative: 19.6 miles) to the access on the right, just before the bridge. (45° 13.656′ N, 67° 40.866′ W)

WHAT YOU'LL SEE
Big Musquash Stream, at least 100 feet across for much of its length, flows several miles through a broad, treeless valley. Down East Lakes Land Trust protects the stream's west side; the Passamaquoddy tribe, the east side.

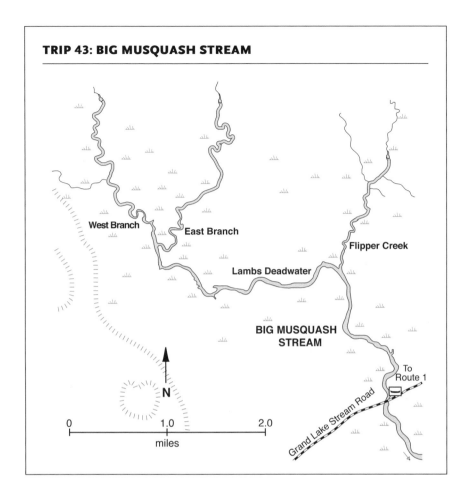

TRIP 43: BIG MUSQUASH STREAM

West Branch

East Branch

Flipper Creek

Lambs Deadwater

BIG MUSQUASH
STREAM

To
Route 1

N

Grand Lake Stream Road

0   1.0   2.0
miles

Pointed firs of the northern boreal forest border the meadow. A few white birch, aspen, and red maple mix in among the conifers. Some shrubby alders border the water in places, along with bog rosemary, leatherleaf, and sweetgale that were blooming when we paddled here.

We spotted a weasel hunting for mice along the shore and found piles of mussel shells left by feeding otters. In addition to the common yellowthroats and yellow warblers that graced the shores, we saw many bobolinks—a ground-nesting oriole and one of the few birds with a light back and dark belly.

As you return back up the valley, you also can paddle into some of the feeder streams a ways. Although a good place at any time, this is an especially nice paddle when winds keep you off larger lakes. We suspect the stream sees little traffic, making it a great spot to look for moose in early morning and evening.

BLACK FLIES AND MOSQUITOES: SCOURGES OF THE NORTH

Anyone who has spent any time at all in the North Country knows these insects all too well. They can detract from outdoor fun in summer and can make most of June virtually off-limits to outdoor recreation in northern Maine. Although it won't take away the itch, understanding these insects may help us accept them as part of the ecosystem we enjoy.

Black Flies

Black flies belong to the family *Simuliidae*, and most species of concern belong to the genus *Simulium*. Scientists have identified more than 1,500 species of black flies, including 300 in North America. Only 10 to 15 percent of black fly species suck blood from humans or domestic animals.

In parts of northern North America, black flies cause considerable livestock difficulties. Mostly, they cause weight loss because cattle do not eat well when tormented by flies, but black flies can actually kill cattle. In parts of Alberta, Canada, mortality rates from black flies range from 1 to 4 percent. Researchers have collected as many as 10,000 feeding black flies from a single cow. Black fly problems in North America, however, pale compared to those in Africa and Central America, where the aptly named species *Simulium damnosum* has infected an estimated 20 million people with onchocerciasis, or river blindness, a disease caused by roundworms transmitted by the fly.

Black flies begin their lifecycle in streams and rivers. Females deposit eggs in the water, and emerging larvae attach to rocks, plants, and other surfaces. Larvae use two tiny, fanlike structures to sweep food particles into their mouths. Black fly larvae can become so dense that they form a slippery, mosslike mat. A several-hundred-foot stretch of a narrow stream can support more than 1 million larvae. In a river, the population can number in the multibillions per mile.

After a period of days or weeks, each larva builds a pupal case in which it metamorphoses into an adult black fly. When ready to emerge, it splits the case open and rides to the water's surface in a bubble of oxygen that had collected in the case.

Adult black flies have one primary goal: to make more black flies. Female black flies seek the nourishing blood meal that they need to lay eggs. Only females bite (actually, they puncture and suck); pacifist males sip nectar from

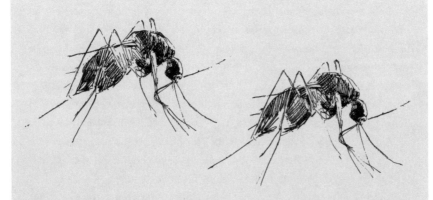

flowers and may be important blueberry pollinators. Black flies rely heavily on eyesight to find prey, so they are active almost exclusively during daylight and at temperatures above 50° F. Some black flies range more than 50 miles in search of blood meals.

No black fly species preys exclusively on humans. We are too new on the evolutionary chain to be a specific host to black flies, which arose 180 million years ago during the Jurassic period. An estimated 30 to 45 species in North America feed on humans. One species (*Simulium euryadminiculum*) feeds only on loons.

Mosquitoes

Another insect nemesis is the ubiquitous mosquito. Mosquitoes, members of the *Culicidae* family, number more than 3,400 species worldwide, including 170 in North America. Three-quarters of the mosquito species in the United States and Canada belong to three genera: *Aedes* (78 species), *Culex* (29 species), and *Anopheles* (16 species).

As with black flies, mosquito larvae live an aquatic life. Unlike black flies, most have adapted to still water. In any bog or salt marsh, you can find mosquito larvae wriggling about, ingesting algae and other organic matter they filter out of the water with brushlike appendages. Larvae molt several times as they grow and develop into pupae. Both larvae and pupae breathe through air tubes at the water's surface.

Adult mosquitoes live short lives: females about a month and males about a week. The high-pitched buzz comes from beating their wings at about 1,000 beats per second. Females generate a higher-pitched whine that helps males locate mates. You can recognize males with a hand lens; look for their bushier antennae.

Both sexes feed on plant nectar as their primary energy source, but females of most mosquito species also require a blood meal to fuel egg production. As with the black fly, a mosquito does not really bite. Rather, she stabs through the victim's skin with six sharp stylets that form the proboscis center. Saliva flows into the puncture to keep the blood from coagulating. Most people have an allergic reaction to the saliva that involves swelling and itching. Upon repeated exposure to bites, one gradually builds immunity.

Although really just a nuisance in the Northeast, mosquitoes cause more deaths in the tropics than any other animal. They carry more than 100 different diseases, including malaria, yellow fever, encephalitis, filariasis, dengue, and West Nile virus. The most destructive of these, malaria, kills about 1 million people a year, mostly children, and as many as 200 million people carry the disease. More recently, Zika virus has become a human scourge in the tropics and the southern United States, which harbor populations of host mosquitoes, *Aedes aegypti* and *Aedes albopictus*.

Southern latitudes have far greater mosquito-species diversity (tropical areas can harbor as many as 150 different species in 1 square mile), but the numbers of individuals generally increase farther north. In the Arctic, with fewer than a dozen species, adult mosquitoes can be so thick they literally blacken the skies. In one experiment, several rugged Canadian researchers bared their torsos, arms, and legs to Arctic mosquitoes and reported as many as 9,000 bites per minute! At this rate, an unprotected person could lose half of his or her blood in two hours.

So, you see, we really don't have it so bad in Maine. Most mosquitoes don't carry deadly diseases (despite occasional cases of mosquito-borne encephalitis and West Nile virus), and even in northern Maine in June, we have found it rare to get more than 1,000 bites per minute.

Black Fly and Mosquito Control

Humans have tried many different control strategies. For mosquito control, we drained thousands of square miles of salt marsh during the 1930s and 1940s by building long, straight drainage ditches—many still visible. As much as half of U.S. wetland area has been lost during the last 200 years, partly for mosquito control and partly for development and agriculture. Along with eliminating habitat, we have used thousands of tons of pesticides in the battle against mosquitoes. DDT remained the chemical of choice for decades due to its supposed safety—a claim that proved tragically untrue. Since banning DDT and other deadly chlorinated-hydrocarbon pesticides in 1973, ospreys, bald eagles, peregrine falcons, and other important bird species have made a comeback in the Northeast.

Today, most attention focuses on biological control of these insects, relying on natural enemies: viruses, protozoa, bacteria, fungi, and parasites. A bacterium generally known as Bti (*Bacillus thuringiensis* subspecies *israelensis*), discovered in 1977 in Negev Desert sand, has exhibited the most successful control. Gardeners use another variety of this bacterium for controlling cabbage loopers, European corn borers, and other garden pests, and foresters use it for gypsy moth control. Bti bacteria produce protein crystals that react with other chemicals in the insects' stomachs, yielding a poison that kills larvae.

Although Bti currently enjoys high success rates, hidden problems could arise, just as with DDT, especially as bioengineers incorporate the Bti gene into plants. This widespread and indiscriminate spreading of the Bti protein easily could lead to pest resistance. Conservation biologists also worry that monarch butterflies, on their 1,000-plus-mile migrations to their wintering grounds in Mexico, will suffer huge mortality rates from Bti-engineered corn.

Protecting Yourself from Biting Insects

To protect yourself from biting insects, you could stay out of the woods, buy a good book on paddling and read it in the comfort of your home. As Thoreau said in his book *The Maine Woods*, "I was fortunate also in the season of the year, for in the summer myriads of black flies, mosquitoes, and midges, or, as the Indians call them, 'no-see-ums,' make traveling in the woods almost impossible; but now their reign was nearly over."

Staying home might be a good choice in June, when clouds of black flies and mosquitoes might stick in your mind as the most memorable part of an outing. Largely due to biting insects, autumn and May—during that narrow window between ice-out and the black fly hatch—remain our favorite times for paddling the North Country. During all but the height of the black fly season in June, however, these insects should not spoil your trip. Out on the water, where breezes blow, paddlers can often escape insects.

Proper clothing forms the most important line of defense. During black fly season, wear long-sleeved, tight-knit shirts and pants with elastic cuffs, or tuck your pant legs into oversized socks. Black flies land on your clothing and search for openings, such as wrists, ankles, and necks. A mosquito-cloth head net works well, but with a collared shirt, black flies will usually find a route in. Cotton gloves can help, too.

Mosquitoes can penetrate soft clothing better than black flies can, so more rugged materials work well for shirts and pants. Wearing two light shirts also works. Tight cuffs are not as important because mosquitoes usually fly directly to their dining table.

Insect repellents generally repel mosquitoes better than black flies. DEET (N,N-Diethyl meta-toluamide) remains the chemical of choice in the North Country. Fortunately, one of our co-authors, a chemist, can actually pronounce this name. Unfortunately, he also knows enough about its chemical structure to be concerned about potential long-term toxicity to humans. Most repellents work by evaporating into the nearby air to clog insects' odor receptors, but because you have to keep slathering it on, we recommend clothing as the primary defensive strategy.

Due to Zika's penetration into the United States, *Consumer Reports* released to the public in 2016 the results of its research on repelling *Aedes* and *Culex* mosquitoes, found in the northern United States and Canada). Here are the results, in hours of effectiveness, for the eight highest-rated products.

Product	Active Ingredients	Hours against *Aedes*	Hours against *Culex*	Hours against deer ticks
Sawyer Picaridin	Picaridin 20%	8	8	8.5
Ben's 30% Deet Tick & Insect Wilderness	DEET 30%	7.5	8	8.5
Repel Lemon Eucalyptus	Oil of Lemon; Eucalyptus 30%	7	8	7
Repel Scented Family	DEET 15%	5	8	8.5
Natrapel 8 Hour	Picaridin 20%	8	8	6
Off! Deepwoods	DEET 25%	8	8	5
Coleman SkinSmart	IR3535	3	6	8
Avon Skin-So-Soft Bug Guard plus	Picaridin 10%	3	8	7

For information on chemical toxicity, see ewg.org/research/ewgs-guide-bug-repellents/repellent-chemicals.

Is There Anything Good about Black Flies and Mosquitoes?

In reviewing all of the problems with black flies and mosquitoes, one wonders what might possibly be good about the little beasts. The answer lies in the role they play in aquatic ecosystems, where they provide a vital food source for a wide variety of animals. Many game fish rely on black fly and mosquito larvae for part of their diets. One study found that black fly larvae constitute as much as 25 percent of the brook trout diet. Even if black fly and mosquito larvae do not provide a direct food source for our favorite game fish and waterfowl, chances are pretty good they form a vital part of the food chain upon which these animals rely. If we appreciate angling for brook trout, listening to the call of the loon, or watching the stately great blue heron, we should recognize these species might not be here without black flies and mosquitoes.

44 | Third Machias Lake

Third Machias Lake, protected by the state, is part of the 75-mile-long Machias River. It has several official campsites, making it a good place for a multiday trip. Expect to see loons, bald eagles, red-breasted mergansers, ring-necked ducks, moose, and beavers in the stream.

Location: T42 MD BPP, T43 MD BPP
Maps: *Maine Atlas & Gazetteer*, Map 35: C2, C3; USGS Dark Cove Mountain, Fletcher Peak, Monroe Lake
Area: 2,778 acres
Time: All day; shorter trips possible; good location for multiday trip
Habitat Type: Long, shallow lake with marshy inlet stream
Fish: Smallmouth bass, white perch, chain pickerel (see fish advisories, Appendix A)
Information: Machias River corridor, including Third Machias Lake, protected by State of Maine, maine.gov
Take Note: Campfire permit required, 207-827-1800

GETTING THERE
From Grand Lake Stream. At the junction of Milford Street, Water Street, and Little River Road in North Washington (T42 MD BPP), go 8 miles southwest

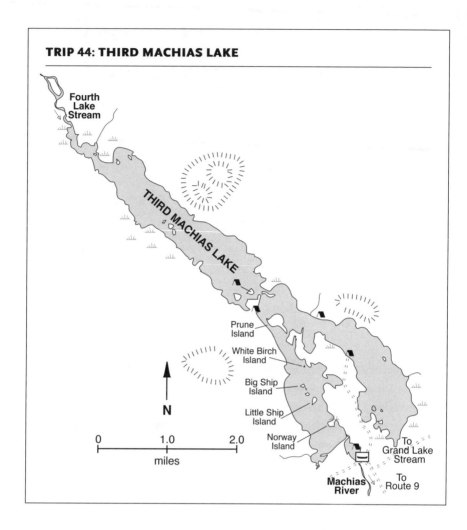

TRIP 44: THIRD MACHIAS LAKE

Fourth Lake Stream

THIRD MACHIAS LAKE

Prune Island

White Birch Island

Big Ship Island

N

Little Ship Island

0   1.0   2.0

miles

Norway Island

To Grand Lake Stream

Machias River

To Route 9

on Little River Road and veer right. Go 1.2 miles (cumulative: 9.2 miles) and turn right. Go 0.1 mile (9.3 miles), veering left at the fork, to the access on the right. (45° 5.352′ N, 67° 51.798′ W)

From north of Machias. At the junction of Routes 9 and 192, go 10.3 miles west on Route 9 and turn right on CCC Road. Go 8.7 miles (cumulative: 19 miles) and turn right. Go 0.1 mile (19.1 miles), veering right on Stud Mill Road, and turn left on Little River Road. Go 4.2 miles (23.3 miles) and turn left. Go 0.7 mile (24 miles) and turn left. Go 0.1 mile (24.1 miles) to the access on the right.

WHAT YOU'LL SEE

Paddling out from the access and indeed throughout most of the southwest arm, notice the beautiful, enormous granite boulders deposited at random by retreating glaciers. Many of them protrude well out into the lake, making this a very picturesque spot. Conifers cover most of the shoreline and retreat up the hillsides into the distance. A well-developed understory right at the water's edge consists of small birches, red maples, and a variety of shrubs.

Staying to the right as you leave the small arm at the access, note the extensive sand beach around to the left. Paddling out among the boulders and islands, you may notice that Little Ship Island is indeed bigger than Big Ship Island and that red pines cover White Birch Island. Tons of large granite boulders guard the large cove off to the right, just after Norway Island. A small amount of marshland gives way to scrub vegetation on the shore, followed by a uniform stand of pines on higher ground.

After threading our way through the islands at the top of the southwest arm, we turned right (south) into the east arm and paddled down to campsite 6 on the west shore. A road leads to this spot, but we liked the other campsites better, particularly those on the island and peninsula that separate the lake's north and south ends.

If you have time, check out the inlet, Fourth Lake Stream, in the far northwest that drains Fourth Machias Lake. You can paddle back almost a mile before boulders and riffles block your way. Beaver lodges and recent cuttings fill this peaceful, marshy area. Although we did not see any moose here in midafternoon, this would be a good place to look for them. Indeed, we did watch a cow moose feeding in a similar marshy area on Fourth Machias Lake. In spring, you can paddle down from Fourth Machias Lake, through Third Machias Lake, all the way to the town of Machias.

While paddling here, we saw few other people and lots of red-breasted mergansers, ring-necked ducks, loons, and other birds. In the early morning and evening, you should have no trouble finding beavers willing to slap their tails on the water as they dive out of sight. One could easily spend several days exploring this beautiful, wild place.

45 | Fourth Machias Lake

Fourth Machias Lake represents the essence of eastern Maine's wild lake country. Paddle here for a long day or a multiday trip. Look for loons, bald eagles, the rare black tern, Canada geese, and moose.

Location: Sakom Township, T42 MD BPP
Maps: *Maine Atlas & Gazetteer*, Map 35: B2, C1, C2; USGS Dark Cove Mountain, Duck Lake, Fletcher Peak, Gassabias Lake
Area: 1,539 acres
Time: 6 hours; shorter trips possible; good location for multiday trip
Habitat Type: Shallow lake with marshy inlet stream
Fish: Smallmouth bass, white perch, chain pickerel (see fish advisories, Appendix A)
Information: Machias River corridor, including Fourth Machias Lake, protected by State of Maine, maine.gov
Take Note: Campfire permit required, 207-827-1800

GETTING THERE

From Grand Lake Stream at the end of Milford Street pavement, go 0.3 mile then go right on Fourth Lake Road/Wabassus Road. Go 11.2 miles (cumulative: 11.5 miles) and stay left (right goes to the Pines, Sysladobsis Lake). Go 0.9 mile (12.4 miles), turn left, and go 0.2 mile (12.6 miles) to the access. (45° 10.164' N, 67° 59.550' W)

WHAT YOU'LL SEE

Fourth Machias Lake is quintessential wild lake country. Remote, marshy, nestled beneath gentle mountains, and filled with wildlife, it receives few visitors. One could explore the whole lake and its tributaries in one long day, but a leisurely two-day exploration would allow more time to absorb the beauty of this setting and to enjoy its abundant wildlife.

In evening and early morning, explore for moose in the extensive marshes surrounding the five inlet streams. The largest expanse of marsh surrounds Dead Stream, which flows northwest into the lake's upper arm. Occasional tamaracks dot this broad valley's otherwise flat terrain. When we paddled here in mid-June, we went back in about 1 mile, past Canada geese with their fluffy yellow goslings, to find a cow moose wallowing in the water, buried up to her

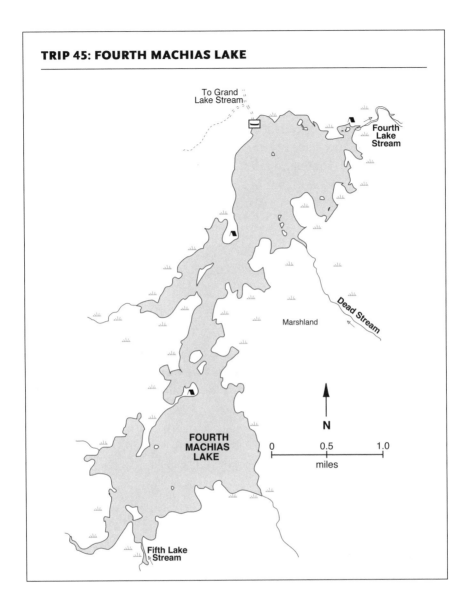

To Grand
Lake Stream

Fourth
Lake
Stream

Dead Stream

Marshland

N

0   0.5   1.0
miles

FOURTH
MACHIAS
LAKE

Fifth Lake
Stream

nose. We watched her long ears bat away hordes of black flies. We even forgot for a moment the accumulating bites on the backs of our own necks as we glided silently past the cavorting moose.

On higher ground, away from the huge expanses of marshland, you will find large stands of white and red pines, with a few spruce thrown in. Birch and red maple grow along the shore, along with scattered hemlock. Tamarack, black spruce, northern white cedar, and red maple grow on the swamp's higher hummocks.

Extensive marshes surround Fourth Machias Lake, affording little high ground to support campsites. We found suitable sites on peninsulas on the right-hand side at the beginning and end of the connector, between the lake's upper and lower arms, and at the mouth of Fourth Lake Stream. Of course, if you want to enjoy a respite from the bugs, you can stay at The Pines, a lodge a short way back down the road on Sysladobsis Lake.

In spring, you can paddle Fourth Lake Stream down to Third Machias Lake. From there, you can continue on the Machias River trip eventually taking out at Machias. In the middle of June in a high-water year, the water did not quite cover the rocks. In a low-water year in September, the stream was down to a trickle.

46 | Nicatous Lake

The many island coves of Nicatous, one of the largest lakes in this book, can be a great place to paddle, but we would avoid it under windy conditions. Expect to see many loons, along with ospreys, bald eagles, and possibly moose.

Location: T3ND, T40 MD, T41 MD
Maps: *Maine Atlas & Gazetteer*, Map 34: C4, C5; D5; USGS Gassabias Lake, Spring Lake, West Lake
Area: 5,165 acres
Time: All day; shorter trips possible; good location for multiday trip
Habitat Type: Huge lake with dozens of islands, most owned by the state
Fish: Brown and brook trout, landlocked salmon, smallmouth bass, white perch, chain pickerel (see fish advisories, Appendix A)
Take Note: Under windy conditions, Nicatous Lake can be treacherous; no personal watercraft; some development; much of shoreline preserved; state maintains six permitted campsites on a first-come, first-served basis (no campfire permits required)

GETTING THERE
From I-95, Exit 217 northbound, go 28.3 miles east on Routes 155 and 188, turning right on Route 188 when Route 155 goes left, to the access in East Hancock (follow access signs). (45° 7.974′ N, 68° 11.934′W)

TRIP 46: NICATOUS LAKE

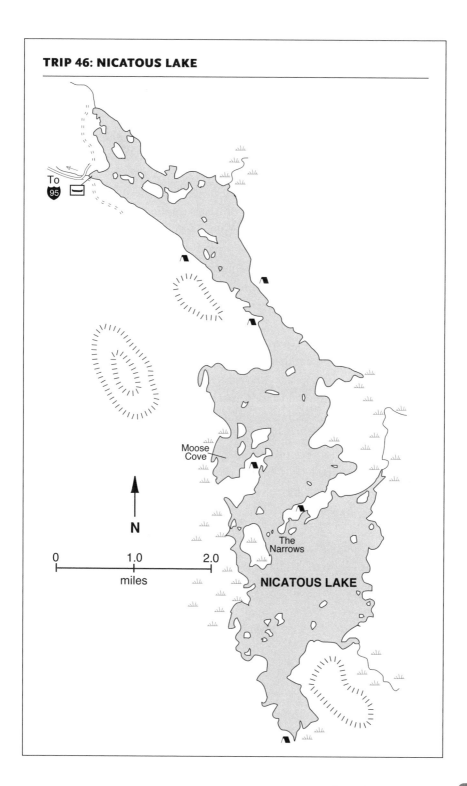

To 95

Moose Cove

N

0   1.0   2.0
miles

The Narrows

NICATOUS LAKE

WHAT YOU'LL SEE

Nicatous Lake, much more accessible than many of eastern Maine's large lakes, suffers from the same drawback: Because glaciers crept down out of the north in this region, most large lakes point north-south, meaning that wind blowing strongly from the north or south causes treacherous waves. Under these conditions, retreat to the nearby smaller bodies of water, such as Great Pond (Trip 33); Bearce Lake (Trip 40); Folsom, Crooked, and Upper ponds (Trip 50); or Bog Brook Flowage (Trip 32).

Northern and middle sections of Nicatous Lake, the most interesting to paddle, contain many islands, several campsites, and little development away from the access. In contrast, the southern end below The Narrows widens out and consequently has more open water—and more development. It would take a few days to explore the entire shoreline and all of the islands in this 9-mile-long lake. One gets the feeling, in this beautiful setting with forested hillsides all around, that the lake does not see much motorboat traffic, especially on the north end.

Paddling out from the access, we were struck by the granite boulders and white cedars that dominate the shoreline. Lots of sugar maples grow here, as well as birch, hemlock, spruce, and white and red pines. Tall, mature trees populate the heavily forested islands, most dominated by conifers, some with dense stands of red pine, with a few birch and red maple thrown in.

In addition to exploring the islands, paddle quietly down into Moose Cove, featuring the lake's most extensive marshy area, to look for wildlife. One of the nicest campsites on the lake is located on a little peninsula on the west shore, just above the Nicatous Club. Sparse vegetation should allow the breeze in, keeping the bugs down.

In 2000, the Trust for Public Land, Forest Society of Maine, and Maine Coast Heritage Trust obtained a 20,767-acre conservation easement—at the time the largest in Maine—working with the owner, Robbins Lumber, that includes large parts of Nicatous Lake. In addition, the state bought 76 of the lake's 98 islands.

47 | Pocumcus Lake, Junior Lake, and Sysladobsis Lake

This is a multiday trip on big, scenic lakes that provide great opportunities to see loons, bald eagles, ospreys, otters, and moose. If you plan a trip here, you may find calm conditions, but make sure you're prepared for wind-driven waves.

Location: Lakeville, Pukakon Township, Sakom Township, T6 ND BPP, T6 R1 NBPP
Maps: *Maine Atlas & Gazetteer*, Map 34: A5 and Map 35: A1, A2; B1, B2, B3; USGS Bottle Lake, Dark Cove Mountain, Duck Lake, Scraggly Lake
Area: Pocumcus Lake, 2,201 acres; Junior Lake, 3,866 acres; Sysladobsis Lake, 5,376 acres
Time: Multiday trip
Habitat Type: Large lakes with many marshy coves
Fish: Brook and lake trout, landlocked salmon, smallmouth bass, white perch, chain pickerel (see fish advisories, Appendix A)
Information: 370,000 acres, including most of Sysladobsis Lake, preserved by Down East Lakes Land Trust, downeastlakes.org
Take Note: These lakes can be treacherous under windy conditions; campfire permit required, 207-827-1800

GETTING THERE
From Grand Lake Stream at the end of Milford Street pavement, go 0.3 mile then go right on Fourth Lake Road/Wabassus Road. Go 6.1 miles (cumulative: 6.4 miles) and turn right at the sign for Elsemore Landing in North Washington. Go 0.8 mile (7.2 miles) and bear right toward the water at the state campground. (45° 10.836′ N, 67° 53.760′ W)

WHAT YOU'LL SEE
Pocumcus, Junior, and Sysladobsis lakes, in the heart of eastern Maine's lake country, offer one of the best extended quietwater loop trips in the state, especially when one detours for a few days into Scraggly Lake (Trip 48). These lakes flow into the St. Croix River, which forms the southeastern border between Maine and New Brunswick. Because you can end up where you started, the trip requires just one vehicle.

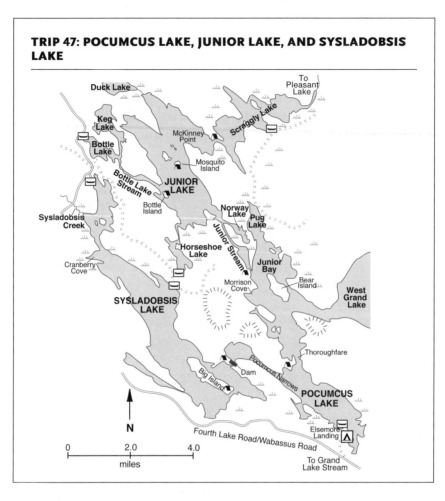

TRIP 47: POCUMCUS LAKE, JUNIOR LAKE, AND SYSLADOBSIS LAKE

The ease of this trip depends on water levels. With relatively high levels, usually until midsummer, you can paddle from Junior Lake into Sysladobsis Lake via Bottle Lake Stream, Bottle Lake, and a 0.5-mile carry into Sysladobsis. With lower water levels, the Bottle Lake take-out may be inaccessible. In that case, the carry would require either disembarking on someone's yard (heavy development on Bottle Lake) or making a much longer carry from the state access at the north end. So from midsummer through fall, you might want to plan an up-and-back trip, rather than making a loop trip. The loop trip described here takes anywhere from three to five days or longer.

Elsemore Landing on Pocumcus Lake to Junior Lake. Elsmore Landing, near the south end of Pocumcus Lake (pronounced po-COM-ses, locally known as Compass Lake), has a state-run campground with boat access. The campground can be rowdy on popular summer weekends.

Pocumcus Lake, 1 mile across at its widest point, stretches about 5 miles in length. Make sure you explore the boggy islands of Deer Brook Cove, about 2 miles up on the left. We watched a cow moose grazing on underwater vegetation near the cove's north end, observed lots of beaver activity, and paddled by a week-old loon chick riding on its parent's back. On sphagnum islands and floating logs, look for small, reddish sundew leaves. On a windy day, this cove provides a nice respite from the main lake.

To reach Junior Lake, paddle north through the Thoroughfare, and after clearing it, you can explore several interesting islands and a deep cove along the west shore. To the east, you will see the 0.25-mile-wide outlet into West Grand Lake, too big to paddle enjoyably except in very calm conditions. Head north between Morrison Cove and Bear Island into Junior Bay.

Near Bear Island's north end on the western shore, Junior Stream drains Junior Lake. You'll find a great campsite here (no fire permit required), with picnic tables, outhouses, and plenty of tent locations. If you camp here, spend a few hours around daybreak looking for moose that frequent marshy coves of Junior Bay, Pug Lake, Junior Stream, and Norway Lake. Also watch for otters, deer, loons, and bald eagles.

With favorable weather, you can make the Junior Stream campsite a lunch stop and continue on to Junior Lake, where you will find some island campsites. We chose to continue on—and regretted it. Most of the morning we had paddled with a light tail wind, but by early afternoon, when we got out onto Junior Lake, the wind had picked up. Our two laden canoes (with precious cargo of four- and seven-year-old daughters) bobbed in the increasingly rough water as we made our way for an island campsite near the lake's center. We got there all right, but just in time, as the wind-driven waves rose to 2 feet.

We camped on the aptly named Mosquito Island; two stagnant lagoons, one at each end, bred a healthy crop of mosquitoes that became all too present when the wind eventually died down. Bottle Island, where we also camped, farther to the south and a bit west, had far fewer mosquitoes. McKinney Point hosts another campsite. On one of the islands just north of McKinney Point, a bald eagle nest perches in a tall white pine; be careful not to get too close.

The McKinney Point island area has a very wild and remote feel to it. Huge granite boulders dot the undeveloped shoreline. Watch for more boulders lurking just beneath the water's surface. From the eastern arm of Junior Lake, you can make a wonderful trip into Scraggly Lake, to the east (Trip 48). Deep coves extending to the north and Duck Lake to the northwest offer hours—and miles—of exploration.

You can take another interesting side trip from Junior Lake's southwest shore into Horseshoe Lake. The channel narrows to just a few yards across in places, and a few spots were swarming with mosquitoes, but we loved this out-of-the-way alcove. On the west shore, just before the channel widens into the lake, look for a floating bog. The thick, floating sphagnum mat harbors pitcher plants, sundew, bog laurel, leatherleaf, and two species of orchid: rose pogonia and *Calopogon*, both in full bloom at the beginning of July. We watched a deer drink, and it looked like a great area for moose.

Junior Lake to Sysladobsis Lake. From Bottle Island, paddle northwest up Bottle Lake Stream into Bottle Lake, where you can portage into Sysladobsis. The 2-mile marshy stream abounds with cattail, pickerelweed, yellow pondlily, and many tree stumps, along with some development. As part of a 1979 land settlement, the government returned extensive tracts to the Passamaquoddy and Penobscot tribes. Facing financial difficulty, the tribes sold large tracts to developers, who in turn subdivided the land into 40-acre lots. Cottages appeared on Bottle Lake Stream and parts of Junior Lake in an area heretofore undeveloped.

Fortunately, Maine's strong regulations controlling development next to water require significant setbacks and stringent septic design. Conservation organizations are hard at work preserving several hundred thousand acres of land in this area. Just before you paddle into Bottle Lake proper, a channel to the right leads into Keg Lake, which we didn't explore. Bottle Lake's heavy development represents the kind of place we prefer to paddle through as quickly as possible.

You can use the north-end access, but to get to Sysladobsis, a small cove extending to the south provides much closer access. As mentioned above, low water levels may make access difficult. To find the portage, paddle around a small peninsula (almost an island) and behind a boathouse (gray when we visited). Though not marked or maintained, we are told this is an acceptable access for the 0.5-mile carry to or from Sysladobsis. From the boathouse, walk south on the dirt road a few hundred feet then bear right. In a few hundred yards, cross a larger gravel road and continue south for another few hundred yards until you see an access stream on the left. You can launch into this access stream or carry down the road next to the main lake.

Sysladobsis, or Dobsis (pronounced DOB-see), stretches about 9 miles northwest-southeast and is about 1.5 miles across at its widest. You will become well aware of its size with even a modest breeze from the north or south.

Some development has taken place along the shores but nothing like on Bottle Lake. Some summer residents pump their drinking water right out of the clear lake, and anglers regularly catch good-size salmon. You can explore the few coves and inlets along the lake if weather conditions permit leisurely paddling. We paddled a few hundred yards up Sysladobsis Creek, but rapids eventually blocked our way.

Few campsites exist along the lake; we failed to find the one near Cranberry Cove. Away from established campsites, finding a place to set up a tent among the rocks and hillocks is difficult.

Sysladobsis to Pocumcus Lake and Elsemore Landing. Near the south end of Dobsis, Big Island stretches almost 2 miles in length on a northwest-southeast axis. As you paddle southeast, keep to the left of the island unless you have time to explore it. Stick to the shoreline, and you will reach the lake outlet at Dobsis Dam and Dennison Portage, about 0.75 mile from the second point. There's a road-accessible campsite here that sees heavy use (fire permit required).

From the campsite, carry around the dam to Pocumcus. Launch into the stream on the dam's left (west) side for the 5-mile paddle back to Elsemore Landing. We loved paddling the marshy section through Pocumcus Narrows, with its cattails and stumps of long-dead trees.

48 | Scraggly Lake (Southern) and Pleasant Lake

Scraggly and Pleasant lakes provide a less-traveled wilderness experience amid marshy coves and varied shoreline, with a boreal forest backdrop. Look here for moose, loons, bald eagles, common terns, wood ducks, and more.

Location: Kossuth Township, Pukakon Township, T6 R1 NBPP
Maps: *Maine Atlas & Gazetteer*, Map 34: A2 and Map 45: E2, E3; USGS Scraggly Lake
Area: Scraggly Lake, 2,758 acres; Pleasant Lake, 1,574 acres
Time: All day or multiday trip
Habitat Type: Large, shallow lakes with marshy coves and long shoreline, much of it surrounded by northern boreal forest

Fish: Brook and lake trout, landlocked salmon, smallmouth bass, white perch, chain pickerel (see fish advisories, Appendix A)
Information: Maine Wilderness Camps, mainewildernesscamps.com; 370,000 acres, including most of Scraggly and Pleasant lakes as conservation easements, preserved by Down East Lakes Land Trust, downeastlakes.org
Take Note: Campfire permit required, 207-827-1800

GETTING THERE

Scraggly Lake. From I-95, Exit 227 northbound, turn right, go 3.9 miles southeast on Access Road/Route 116, and turn left on Route 2. Go 1.8 miles (cumulative: 5.7 miles) and turn right on Route 6. Go 35.1 miles (40.8 miles, and turn right on Amazon Road. Go 8.9 miles (49.7 miles) to the Hasty Cove access on the right. Access road may require high-clearance vehicle. You can also reach Scraggly Lake from Junior Lake (Trip 47). (45° 19.182′ N, 67° 56.778′ W)

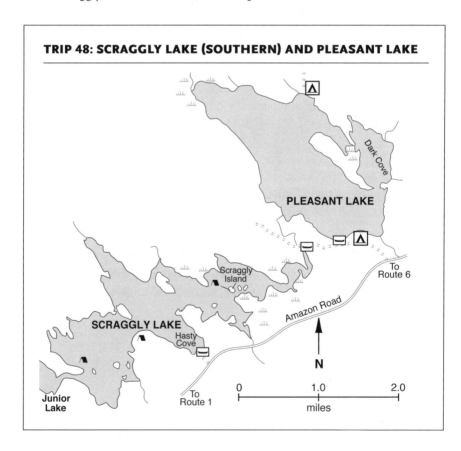

TRIP 48: SCRAGGLY LAKE (SOUTHERN) AND PLEASANT LAKE

Pleasant Lake. As above, except go 5.2 miles (46 miles) on Amazon Road and turn right. Go 0.6 mile (46.6 miles) to the access on the right. (45° 20.406′ N, 67° 54.486′ W)

WHAT YOU'LL SEE

We call this Scraggly Lake "southern" to distinguish it from another Scraggly Lake farther north (Trip 92). Although only 3.5 miles long, the lake's highly varied shoreline extends nearly 20 miles along marshy coves and undeveloped islands. Wild and remote, this is the paddler's ideal lake: too shallow for most motorboaters and with difficult access, so you have to do some work to get there.

We paddled into Scraggly as part of a loop trip starting at Elsemore Landing on Pocumcus Lake, extending through Junior and Sysladobsis lakes. Scraggly makes a wonderful 2- or 3-day detour. A more common one way trip starts at Maine Wilderness Camps on Pleasant Lake's northern shore, with a portage to the northeastern tip of Scraggly then on through to Junior Lake and either Pocumcus or West Grand Lake. Maine Wilderness Camps can shuttle you to a starting or ending point.

While paddling along Scraggly's northern shore in morning's first light, we surprised a magnificent bald eagle feeding at the water's edge. We saw a number of eagles here, along with wood ducks, loons, ring-necked ducks, deer, and a huge snapping turtle. During a morning paddle from Scraggly up into Pleasant Lake, we watched a playful family of otters in the glass-smooth water. We did not happen to see any moose, even though Scraggly sports superb moose habitat. You also may see common terns; we suspect they nest on large boulders visible from the Scraggly Island campsite.

A number of designated campsites dot Scraggly Island. The nicest requires a permit to camp but no permit for a fire; the other two require campfire permits. The island's camping areas include fire rings, picnic tables, outhouses, and lots of space for tents. During a visit at the end of June we found surprisingly few mosquitoes on Scraggly Island, although some surrounding marshy areas had many bugs. We enjoyed exploring the marshy area east and south of the island. At high water, you can find a passage around the large marsh.

A Side Trip to Pleasant Lake. To go from Scraggly Lake to Pleasant Lake, paddle to Scraggly's eastern tip and take your boat out at a steep ramp (too steep for trailers). Carry up to the road (about 50 feet), then right (east). You can carry all the way to the campground and launch onto Pleasant Lake (about 0.5 mile), or you can cut over to Pleasant Lake on a portage trail. When we paddled here, the trail seemed poorly marked and hard to follow due to recent logging activity.

We particularly enjoyed exploring Dark Cove. Hundreds of boulders sticking out of the water and hiding just beneath the surface near the mouth help minimize motorboat traffic. In the very clear water, you will see thousands of freshwater mussels poking out of the sand. Northern white cedar, the dominant tree here, grows alongside balsam fir, spruce, and white pine. Alder, bog laurel, sweetgale, and other northern species grow in profusion along the shore. We found a very pleasant campsite near the north end, nestled beneath a grove of red pines.

49 | Cold Stream

We paddle here to escape wind-driven waves on larger bodies of water and to hone our paddling skills in the endlessly meandering channel. You're likely to see ospreys, northern harriers, beavers, possibly moose, and typical bog vegetation.

Location: Passadumkeag
Maps: *Maine Atlas & Gazetteer*, Map 33: B5; USGS Passadumkeag
Length: 5 miles one way
Time: 4 hours; shorter trips possible
Habitat Type: Meandering stream through large, treeless marsh
Fish: Smallmouth bass (see fish advisories, Appendix A)
Take Note: No development; paddle here when wind makes lakes unsafe

GETTING THERE
From I-95, Exit 217 northbound, go 1.3 miles east on Routes 6 and 155, and turn right on Old County Road North. Go 0.9 mile (cumulative: 2.2 miles) and continue straight on Route 2. Go 3.4 miles (5.6 miles) and turn left on Pleasant Street. Go 1.9 miles (7.5 miles) and turn right on St. John/Goulds Ridge roads. Go 0.1 mile (7.6 miles) to the access on the left, just over the bridge. (45° 10.890′ N, 68° 34.662′ W)

TRIP 49: COLD STREAM

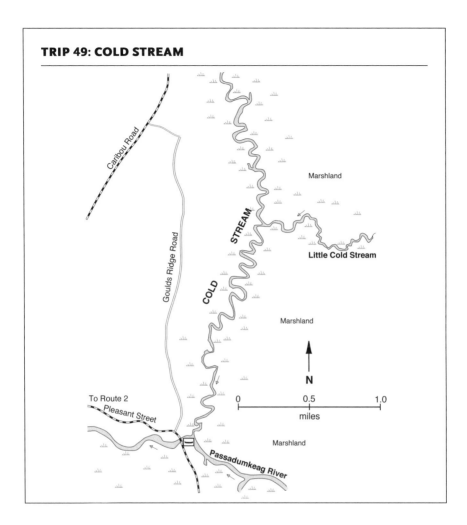

WHAT YOU'LL SEE

Cold Stream drains a huge bog in the towns of Passadumkeag and Lowell, about 20 miles north of Old Town. The stream itself, with all of its meanderings, only stretches about 5 miles. Together with its tributary, Little Cold Stream, Cold Stream flows into the Passadumkeag River, which immediately empties into the Penobscot River.

From the access on the Passadumkeag, paddle right (or upstream) for a very short way then take a left into the mouth of Cold Stream. At the rivers' confluence, you will find dwarf willow and alder. These give way to typical low-growing bog vegetation along the border of the 40-foot-wide channel. Sweetgale and several members of the heath family grow right to the water's edge.

At one point, the channel wanders nearer high ground, where you will find a thick grove of silver maples.

Wild country that sees few visitors except for the occasional angler, this is a great place to look for moose. Although we did not see any, we saw much evidence of their presence. We watched an osprey hover overhead, seemingly oblivious to us, waiting to dive on an unsuspecting fish in the clear water. We also watched a northern harrier glide over the marsh, skimming the tops of the vegetation, waiting to pounce on any rodents foolhardy enough to be out in the middle of the morning. Formerly called marsh hawk, the harrier's distinguishing characteristics include a white rump patch and its habit of buoyantly gliding over fields and marshes, tipping its upraised wings from side to side.

As we rounded one of the channel's never-ending bends, we surprised a beaver. In typical fashion, it dove, resurfaced, and slapped its tail on the water, splashing us as it dove again. Wherever you see patches of alder, look for beavers and beaver activity. We saw numerous cuttings, lodges, side channels dug out to provide access to more lush vegetation, and mudbanks where they had collected mud to plaster on their lodges and dams. If you paddle here in the evening, you should see several of these industrious little engineers.

You can also paddle quite a way up Little Cold Stream, at least during high water. We would paddle these two streams when wind turns nearby lakes and the Penobscot River to froth.

Beaver

50 | Folsom Pond, Crooked Pond, and Upper Pond

These three shallow ponds offer quiet paddling and suffer less from wind than larger lakes. We've seen many loons here, along with bald eagles and lots of waterfowl, all against a backdrop of wooded shores and rolling hills.

Location: Lincoln
Maps: *Maine Atlas & Gazetteer*, Map 34: A1, A2 and Map 44: E1; USGS Lincoln East
Area: Folsom Pond, 282 acres; Crooked Pond, 220 acres; Upper Pond, 506 acres
Time: 5 hours; shorter trips possible
Habitat Type: Shallow ponds
Fish: Upper Pond, brook trout, white perch; Folsom and Crooked ponds, smallmouth bass, white perch, chain pickerel (see fish advisories, Appendix A)
Take Note: Limited development; campfire permit required, 207-827-1800

GETTING THERE

Folsom Pond. From I-95, Exit 227 northbound, go 4.7 miles east on Access Road/Route 116 and turn left on Route 155, followed by an immediate right on Transalpine Road. Go 2.4 miles (cumulative: 7.1 miles) and turn left on Folsom Pond/Clay Road. To stay on Folsom Pond Road to the access, go 0.6 mile (7.7 miles) and turn left. Go 1 mile (8.7 miles) and turn right. Go 0.9 mile (9.6 miles) and turn right. Go 0.2 mile (9.8 miles) to the access on the left. (45° 20.454′ N, 68° 26.892′ W)

Upper Pond. From Folsom Pond access, go 0.4 mile southeast, and turn left on Pierce Webber Road. Go 0.9 mile (cumulative: 1.3 miles) to a junction; continue straight across to the access. (45° 20.064′ N, 68° 25.746′ W)

WHAT YOU'LL SEE

Folsom and Crooked Ponds. These ponds harbor very little development and lie in a gorgeous setting, with rolling hills in the background. Their three shallow sections, separated by narrow channels, grow thick with waterlilies and pickerelweed. A few small islands poke up here and there, and lush vegetation grows down to the water's edge. Great diversity of tree species characterizes this area, with white cedar, white pine, lots of hemlock, white birch, and red maple in evidence.

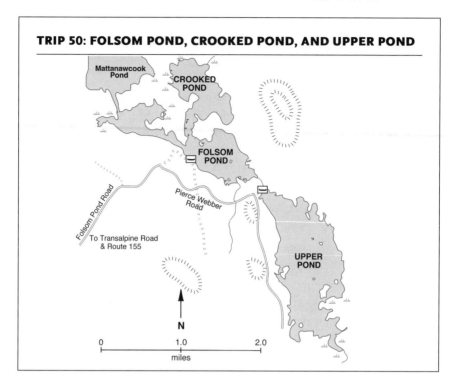

TRIP 50: FOLSOM POND, CROOKED POND, AND UPPER POND

Mattanawcook Pond

CROOKED POND

FOLSOM POND

Folsom Pond Road

Pierce Webber Road

To Transalpine Road & Route 155

UPPER POND

N

0   1.0   2.0

miles

We saw at least ten loons and many ducks feeding in the shallows. You also may see the resident bald eagle here. Explore the extensive marshy areas in the farther reaches of the undeveloped arms for wildlife, especially in early morning or evening.

Speaking of wildlife, they say that after about 500 mosquito bites in a season, you become immune, no longer swelling at the site of each attack. Anyone who paddles a lot in the spring in Maine should come to Folsom Pond in June. Spend about ten minutes out here, and you will not have to worry about mosquitoes for the rest of the season. Driving to the access, we had to go slowly due to hundreds of patrolling dragonflies. Clearly, they were not doing their job of controlling the mosquito population.

Upper Pond. A small stream separates Upper Pond from Folsom and Crooked ponds, and you have to drive to the Upper Pond access. Although much larger than the other two, it has only one marshy area, on the south shore, but aquatic vegetation appears regularly along the shoreline. The tree-species assembly resembles that of Folsom and Crooked ponds, and we saw just as many loons here—at least ten.

4 | WESTERN LAKES AND MOUNTAINS

Rugged mountains and abundant lakes populate this region, for which we include 17 trips. Flagstaff is the state's fourth largest lake, while the Rangeley Lakes—a system of 112 interconnected streams, lakes, and ponds—dominate the landscape and provide a paddler's paradise. The Western Lakes and Mountains Region borders New Hampshire and encompasses the eastern Maine portion of White Mountain National Forest. Featured trips include Lake Umbagog (Trip 61), with its abundant moose, loons, ospreys, and occasional bald eagles; huge Flagstaff Lake (Trip 63), where you may spot otters and rafts of migrating waterfowl; and Attean and Holeb Ponds and the Moose River Bow Loop (Trip 67), which provides a several-day trip on the Rangeley Lakes system, with beautiful mountains as a backdrop.

For the third edition, we added meandering Bog Stream (Trip 60) in the Mercer Bog Wildlife Management Area.

51 | Brownfield Bog

Depending on water levels, you can paddle with abandon or get bogged down, literally, among sphagnum hummocks. At any water level, this is a great place to look for ducks, geese, turtles, muskrat, deer, beavers, moose, and ospreys.

Location: Brownfield
Maps: *Maine Atlas & Gazetteer*, Map 4: B1, B2; USGS Brownfield
Area: 5,700 acres in wildlife management area
Time: 3 hours; shorter trips possible
Habitat Type: Shallow ponds filled with aquatic vegetation
Take Note: At low water levels, extremely slow paddling due to boggy islands and aquatic plants

GETTING THERE

From Fryeburg at the junction of Routes 5 and 113 and Route 302, go 7 miles southeast on Routes 5 and 113, and turn left on Route 160. Go 1.3 miles (cumulative: 8.3 miles) and turn left on Lord Hill Road. Go 0.1 mile (8.4 miles) and turn left on the access road. Go 0.7 mile (9.1 miles) to a small shed with a list of rules. Park here and put your boat in about 50 feet down the road. (43° 58.392′ N, 70° 53.508′ W)

Continue 1.5 miles (10.6 miles) to a more interesting place to paddle.

WHAT YOU'LL SEE

During the summer, when canoeists overrun the nearby Saco River, you can paddle undisturbed on Brownfield Bog. The Major Gregory Sanborn Wildlife Management Area contains hundreds of acres of marsh to explore. When we paddled here on a warm, sunny October day, bigtooth aspen leaves reflected golden light onto the water as we enjoyed a beautiful view of the snow-dusted White Mountains off in the distance.

The first access is on an old course of the Saco River; paddle north up the narrow, shallow channel. Depending on water levels, it may be difficult paddling here. The second access is at a more interesting small pond filled with floating sphagnum islands and aquatic vegetation. At times of high water, the area available for paddling expands dramatically. An extensive grassy area at road's end makes a scenic spot for a picnic.

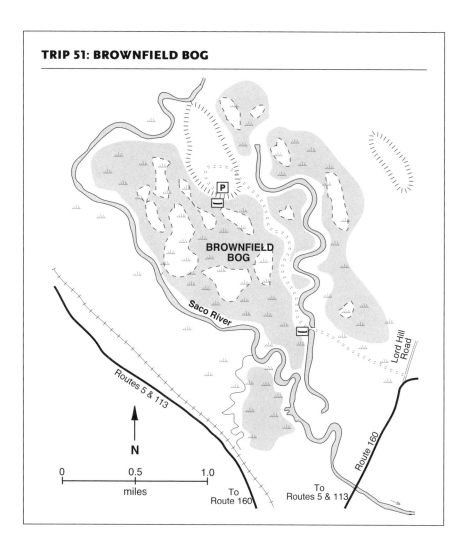

TRIP 51: BROWNFIELD BOG

BROWNFIELD BOG

Saco River

Routes 5 & 113

N

0   0.5   1.0

miles

To Route 160

To Routes 5 & 113

Lord Hill Road

Route 160

P

Brownfield Bog, very wild but relatively accessible, teems with wildlife. In addition to nesting waterfowl, you should see deer, beavers, muskrat, turtles, and—if you paddle here early in the morning or at dusk—an occasional moose. Just about every type of bog vegetation abounds, from pitcher plants and sundews to waterlilies, sweetgale, and rhodora.

Due to the huge amount of beaver activity and extensive bog vegetation, we progressed slowly through the hidden pathways. If you need more space, just push aside the small, floating islands dotting the marsh. Thanks to the large landmass within the marsh, you can paddle here unaffected by wind.

This area and south of here provides an ideal spot to look for oaks. White and red oaks cover the higher ground within and on the hillsides surrounding

Oak-covered hillsides form a backdrop for Brownfield Bog. Marshy islands keep these waters calm when wind-driven waves make more open water unsafe.

the marsh. Thought to have originated in Mexico and then radiated out to other areas, oaks comprise a genus with more than 500 species found throughout the warmer parts of the north temperate region. There are 58 native oak species in the United States, but as you would expect, the number of species present in a given area dwindles the farther you get from Mexico. For example, Texas has 29 species of oak, Illinois 20, Pennsylvania 18, New York 12, and Vermont 7. Maine has 8 species, with most of the rarer ones concentrated along the lower New Hampshire border and the coast.

With some searching at Brownfield Bog and along the southern New Hampshire border, expect to find swamp white oak, chestnut oak, bear oak, black oak, and scarlet oak, along with white oak and the ubiquitous northern red oak. Only bur oak, found in the Machias region, is absent from this area. We found a thick stand of bear oak along the shore of Black Pond in Porter, the next town south of Brownfield.

Brownfield Bog typifies the kind of wilderness experience that becomes increasingly difficult to find in Maine these days. It seems even the most remote ponds and lakes sprout cabins and camps overnight, and unfortunately more and more people adopt the sedentary TV-generation lifestyle by forsaking the traditional hand-powered Maine canoe for motorboats. Because the state owns the bog, it will not sprout cabins; and due to the bog's shallow and weedy character, those addicted to throbbing horsepower will have to get their thrills elsewhere. Gazing off through fall-colored, yellow-leaved birches and aspen at the layered hillsides and mountains, we are thankful Brownfield Bog remains wild and protected in such a heavily vacationed area.

52 | Pleasant Pond and Saco River

This trip affords a good way to get exercise because, after paddling down the Saco River to Pleasant Pond, you have to paddle back against the current. (At times of high water, you wouldn't be able to do so.) You will see wonderful views of the White Mountains, along with muskrat, deer, turtles, and more.

Location: Brownfield, Denmark, Fryeburg
Maps: *Maine Atlas & Gazetteer*, Map 4: A2; USGS Brownfield, Fryeburg
Area/Length: 239 acres; 2 miles one way
Time: 4 hours
Habitat Type: Shallow, marshy pond reached by Saco River
Fish: Largemouth bass, smallmouth bass, white perch, chain pickerel
(see fish advisories, Appendix A)
Take Note: Do not attempt this trip unless you can easily paddle upstream; novice paddlers should avoid this area during high water; wear PFD; campfire permit required, 207-624-3700

GETTING THERE
From Fryeburg at the junction of Routes 5 and 302, go 2.8 miles east on Route 302, cross the Saco River bridge, and park in the lot on the right. Lot fills on summer weekends, with cars spilling out onto adjacent road shoulders. (44° 1.806′ N, 70° 55.314′ W)

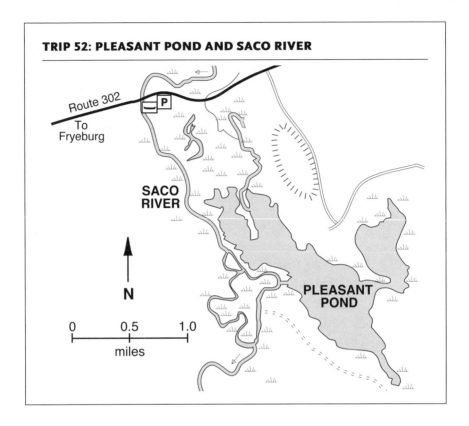

TRIP 52: PLEASANT POND AND SACO RIVER

Route 302

To Fryeburg

P

SACO RIVER

N

0   0.5   1.0
miles

PLEASANT POND

WHAT YOU'LL SEE

The Saco River, born among the highest peaks of the White Mountains in New Hampshire, gathers feeder streams and momentum as it roars down the steep valleys. By the time it reaches Fryeburg, though, it morphs into a tame, meandering, marshy meadow stream, popular with weekend canoeists. Thousands of people paddle this water on summer weekends. Very few of them, however, take the time to paddle out onto Pleasant Pond, accessible only from the Saco River. With layered hills and lofty peaks of the White Mountains as a backdrop, sitting out in the middle of the pond, gazing off at the multihued pastel layers retreating into the distance, we found it difficult to leave—even as the sun set over the mountains, meaning we would paddle back in semidarkness. A magical place, indeed.

The Saco's banks make it difficult to see out into the surrounding marsh. Although the current flows at a modest pace in the summer and fall, leave sufficient time to paddle back (at least 50 percent more time than it takes to paddle down to Pleasant Pond). Watch closely for the access stream to the left on a sharp, sweeping curve to the right. A black and orange No

Trespassing sign appears in front of you; high in a tree, a broken paddle reads, Pleasant.

Oaks line the Saco's banks, along with occasional groves of hemlock and scattered white pine. In addition, silver maple shows up in large numbers in some places. You can distinguish silver maple from the other swamp dweller—the red maple—by its deeply cleft, five-lobed leaves with silvery undersides. Red maple has shallow-cleft, three-lobed leaves. Silver maple has the largest-winged seeds of all native maples, reaching 3 inches in length and providing important food for squirrels, foxes, and mice, plus pine and evening grosbeaks. We spied a fat gray squirrel clambering among the silver maples, searching for seeds.

Pleasant Pond—shallow and marshy, especially along the north end, where the access stream enters—would take a few hours to explore fully. Look for beavers, muskrat, red-winged blackbirds, turtles, and deer lurking in the marshy inlets and coves. At quieter times, especially on the pond's north end, one might be lucky enough to see a moose browsing on the abundant vegetation.

Due to the extensive marshes, we found few areas where one could pitch a tent. It would be far easier to camp out under the oaks on unposted land along the Saco River. Please treat this private property with respect.

During spring high water, you would not be able to paddle the 2 miles back to the Route 302 bridge. You could take out at the Route 160 bridge, 5 or so miles downstream from Pleasant Pond. Given the summer crowds, we prefer to paddle here in the fall, when the hillsides have turned to golds, reds, and browns. We paddled here in October and saw not another soul; when we visited in June and August, cars jammed the parking areas, and canoes dotted the river.

53 | Kezar Pond

Although its round shape is atypical of the trips in this book, Kezar Pond deserves a mention for its important marshlands, Saco River Old Course, and views of the White Mountains. Expect to see loons, bald eagles, ospreys, great blue herons, and marshland species.

Location: Fryeburg
Maps: *Maine Atlas & Gazetteer*, Map 4: A2 and Map 10: E2; USGS Fryeburg, Pleasant Mountain

Area/Length: 1,447 acres; outlet stream, 1 mile each way
Time: 4 hours, longer if you paddle the Saco River's old course
Habitat Type: Large lake with extensive perimeter marshes
Fish: Largemouth bass, smallmouth bass, white perch, chain pickerel
(see fish advisories, Appendix A)
Take Note: Wind can make paddling here dangerous; under windy
conditions, stay on the old course of the Saco River

GETTING THERE

From Fryeburg at the junction of Routes 5 and 302, go 5.5 miles east on Route
302 and turn left on Hemlock Bridge Road. Go 3 miles (8.5 miles) to the Hemlock Covered Bridge. Park on the right before the bridge or on the left across
the bridge. If you launch before the bridge, paddle right. If you launch after
the bridge, paddle under the bridge and take the right channel. (44° 4.824′ N,
70° 54.342′ W)

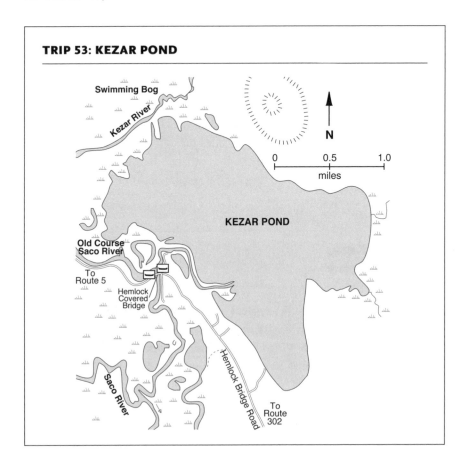

TRIP 53: KEZAR POND

You can also explore the old channel of the Saco River up to North Fryeburg or down to the Saco River and Pleasant Pond (Trip 52).

WHAT YOU'LL SEE

Kezar Pond, given its relatively round shape, might not seem like a great paddling spot, but we had a great time here despite a stiff southern breeze that made paddling difficult. From the beautiful covered bridge on the Saco River's old course, paddle north into the Kezar Pond outlet stream, which meanders gently on a barely perceptible current for about 1 mile, the sides lined with silver maple, gray birch, white pine, red maple, viburnum, and a few red oak. The creek traverses the 400-acre Kezar Pond Fen that contains Long's bulrush (*Scirpus longii*), a globally rare and federally threatened species.

The main pond affords an impressive and extensive view of the White Mountains to the west and of Smarts Hill, extending up from the pond's northeast side. Marshy coves to the right (south) of the outlet stream harbor stands of pickerelweed, bulrush, and waterlily, with great blue herons fishing the shallows. A few cottages on the southern lobe make up the bulk of the pond's modest development. After exploring the south end, we paddled across to avoid the developed areas then around the pond counterclockwise.

Two inlet streams on the east side provide great side explorations. The more southerly one—somewhat difficult to find—heads off near the northernmost house along the pond's east side. Silver maple, royal and sensitive ferns, and sweetgale line the deep, narrow, winding, sandy-bottomed channel. Near the creek outlet you also will find cranberry, whose large red berries in the fall dwarf the tiny oval leaves of this heath (related to blueberry and laurel).

In the pond's northeast lobe, you can explore some hidden coves and an inlet creek, also very easy to miss. We paddled 200 yards up this creek, our pace quickened by the mosquitoes in this wind-shielded area, until a beaver dam blocked our progress. Without the mosquitoes, we might have portaged over the dam and explored upstream, but we retreated back to the main pond and its protective wind. One learns to love and hate the wind!

We favor the north end, extending around to the western tip. This section adjoins an area known as Swimming Bog, a Maine priority wetland conservation area. Hillocks of grasses and pickerelweed dot the shallow shoreline here. When whitecaps fill the pond itself, the matrix of tiny islands damps the waves, keeping it fairly calm. We explored lazily through these hillocks and the acres of pondlilies. As we snaked our way west, we watched a bald eagle we had first spotted from the pond's east end (nearly 2 miles away) that had perched atop an old silver maple. (For more on the bald eagle, see "Bald Eagle: Our National Bird, Back from the Brink" on page 85.)

Hemlock Bridge, a historic wooden-truss structure built in 1857, spans the Old Course of the Saco River at the access to Kezar Pond.

54 | Five Kezar Ponds

This trip includes four of the Five Kezar Ponds. Although quite small, these ponds offer a lot: loons, pitcher plants, sundew, tamarack, black spruce, and the opportunity to see beavers in the evening; plus, you can enjoy paddling into the middle of a minerotrophic fen.

Location: Lovell, Stoneham, Waterford
Maps: *Maine Atlas & Gazetteer*, Map 10: D3; USGS North Waterford
Area: Middle Pond, 72 acres; Back Pond, 62 acres; Mud and Unnamed Pond, 45 acres
Time: 2 hours, longer if you study the plants
Habitat Type: Mud Pond, minerotrophic fen; wooded ponds
Fish: Brook trout, smallmouth bass, white perch, chain pickerel (see fish advisories, Appendix A)
Take Note: Some development; 10 HP limit

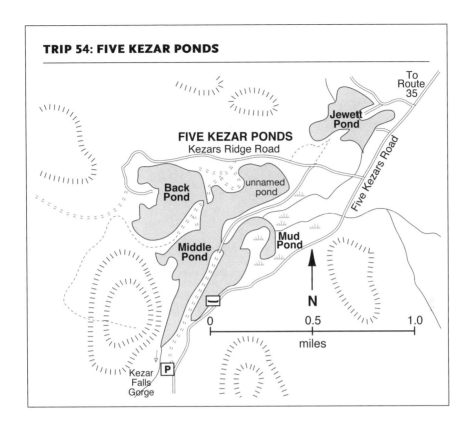

TRIP 54: FIVE KEZAR PONDS

FIVE KEZAR PONDS
Kezars Ridge Road

Jewett Pond

To Route 35

Five Kezars Road

Back Pond

unnamed pond

Mud Pond

Middle Pond

N

0   0.5   1.0
miles

Kezar Falls Gorge

P

GETTING THERE

From North Waterford at the junction of Routes 35 and 118, go 0.2 mile south on Route 35 and turn right on Five Kezars Road (right fork). Go 3 miles (cumulative: 3.2 miles) to a small turnout on the left. Carry across the road, down over the bank to the pond. (44° 12.216′ N, 70° 48.720′ W)

WHAT YOU'LL SEE

Of the Five Kezar Ponds, we cover Mud, Middle, Back, and one unnamed pond. Jewett Pond, not connected to the other four, has no public access. Although the ponds have pockets of development, we include this series of small, forested ponds because unusual natural features abound. With relatively little boat traffic, especially in the spring and fall, one can find hours of quiet paddling.

After paddling up the unnamed pond, before passing under the bridge on the left into Middle Pond, keep going northwest, curving around to the right into Mud Pond, a splendid example of a peatland minerotrophic fen. Scientists only recently started to distinguish between raised peatlands with no streams

Mud Pond's minerotrophic, or mineral-rich, fen offers quiet solitude.

flowing through, calling them bogs, and peatlands on slopes with water flowing through, calling them fens. Minerotrophic means "mineral nourished," from the flow-through of water. In contrast, in the classic domed bog with no flow-through—the huge 4,300-acre Great Heath, 20 miles due west of Machias—almost all nutrients come from rainfall and the air. In contrast to the dwarfed shrubs and trees of nutrient-poor bogs, the relatively large tamarack, red maple, and black spruce of the Mud Pond fen benefit from water flow-through that brings necessary minerals and carries away acids produced by sphagnum and plant degradation.

Beavers thrive in the shrubby environment of Mud Pond, opening watery paths to higher ground in order to drag succulent branches of alder, birch, and red maple back to their submerged winter food caches. Look for them by paddling quietly here in the evening. Pitcher plants and sundews, as well as many species of marshland shrubs, abound on the raised sphagnum clumps. It is so rare one can paddle back into such a beautiful, unspoiled peatland, this alone makes a trip to Five Kezar Ponds worthwhile.

But one more unusual natural feature draws us here: Kezar Falls Gorge. Paddle back out of Mud Pond and turn right under the bridge to Middle Pond. Turn left and paddle southwest to the five ponds' outlet. Where the pond narrows, pull your boat up on shore and hike the short distance to Kezar Falls Gorge. A surprising amount of water tumbles down through a steep-walled, beautifully sculpted canyon. To get a better view, climb up above on the left. You can also reach the gorge by continuing down the access road.

55 | Horseshoe Pond

Horseshoe Pond lies in a forested valley with views of the White Mountains all around. We saw fresh moose tracks on the road and enjoyed spotting common mergansers, great blue herons, and ospreys.

Location: Lovell, Stoneham
Maps: *Maine Atlas & Gazetteer*, Map 10: D1; USGS Center Lovell
Area: 132 acres
Time: 2 hours
Habitat Type: Narrow pond in wooded valley
Fish: Brown and brook trout, smallmouth bass, chain pickerel (see fish advisories, Appendix A)
Take Note: 6 HP limit

GETTING THERE

From Fryeburg at the junction of Routes 5 and 302, go 11.5 miles north on Route 5 and turn left on West Lovell Road. Go 2.7 miles (cumulative: 14.2 miles) and veer left on Foxboro Road. Go 2.1 miles (16.3 miles) and turn right on Horseshoe Pond Road. Go 0.9 mile (17.2 miles) to the access on the left. (44° 13.200′ N, 70° 56.712′ W)

WHAT YOU'LL SEE

Horseshoe Pond's magnificent setting, with steep hills hovering on all sides and two very different nearby hiking trails, prompted us to include it. Small and out of the way, it provides paddling solitude, especially when wind whips up whitecaps on Kezar Pond. A few small cabins stand on the pond's southern end, but the White Mountain National Forest protects the north end.

The tree-covered hillsides give way to dense shrubbery along the shore. Rhodora dominates the shoreline. Nearby Moose Pond more than makes up for the lack of marshy areas.

A moose left teeth marks on this red maple.

TRIP 55: HORSESHOE POND

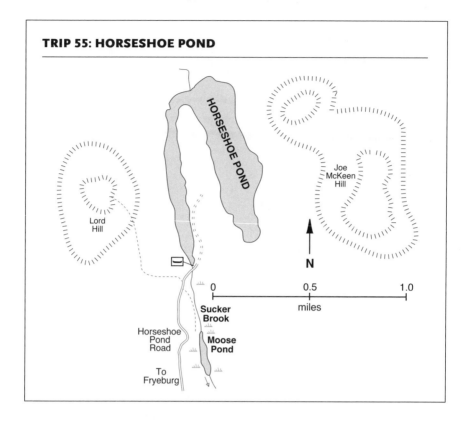

The presence along the shoreline of mostly shallow-rooted trees, such as spruce, red and white pines, hemlock, and white birch, indicates a shallow soil. In addition to stands of pines on the hillsides, you will find lots of oak and sugar maple. An osprey, great blue heron, and a flock of common mergansers—a colorful, fish-eating, diving duck with a narrow, serrated bill—greeted us as we paddled the narrow western arm.

While you're here, hike the short trail into Moose Pond. The Nature Conservancy maintains the Sucker Brook Nature Trail, which begins along the road on the left, just uphill from the access. When we hiked here in October, a moose had made fresh tracks on the road. After a short hike into Moose Pond, we found denuded red maple and alder trunks where a moose had recently browsed.

A trail immediately across the road leads up to Lord Hill, which towers 720 feet over Horseshoe Pond's west edge. Look for an abandoned mica mine at the top, and enjoy the beautiful view of the pond and the Sucker Brook valley.

56 | Virginia Lake

We include Virginia Lake for its out-of-the-way location and its mountain views. Look for loons, alder flycatchers, and moose here.

Location: Stoneham
Maps: *Maine Atlas & Gazetteer*, Map 10: C2; USGS East Stoneham
Area: 128 acres
Time: 2 hours
Habitat Type: Small, wooded pond
Fish: Brook trout, white perch, chain pickerel (see fish advisories, Appendix A)
Take Note: No personal watercraft

GETTING THERE

From Fryeburg at the junction of Routes 5 and 302, go 19.8 miles north on Route 5 and turn left on Birch Road. Go 0.4 mile (cumulative: 20.2 miles) and veer left on Virginia Lake Road. Go 0.6 mile (20.8 miles) and veer left. Go 0.3 mile (21.1 miles) to the access. (44° 16.206′ N, 70° 51.732′ W)

WHAT YOU'LL SEE

A part of the White Mountain National Forest since 1987, Virginia Lake sits just south of a string of peaks that stretches to 2,000 feet in elevation, some 1,200 feet above the lake. A real gem, Virginia Lake sees little boat traffic aside from a few fishermen. You can explore this scenic lake fully in a few hours. Loons nest here on floating platforms, and if you're lucky, you could see moose.

The forested shores on the west, south, and east—primarily oak—give way to marshy inlets on the north that drain the surrounding peaks. During spring high water, you should be able to paddle back into the swamp a little way. Besides the typical marsh vegetation, look for an alder swamp, the summer home of an uncommon warbler-sized bird, called, appropriately enough, the alder flycatcher. An inconspicuous little bird with an olive-brown back and pale yellow belly, with two white wing bars and a small white eye ring, this flycatcher—and the eight other similarly drab species found throughout the United States and Canada—sits upright on exposed branches, waiting to pounce on juicy insects that fly by. Listen for its song, a distinctive, falling, buzzy

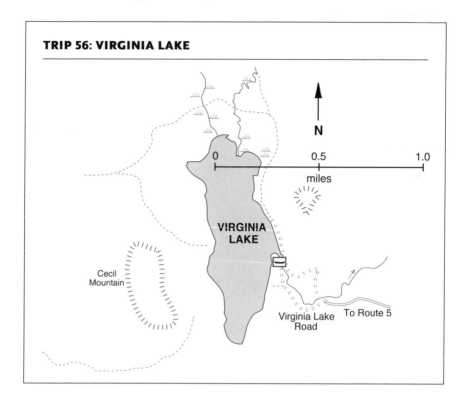

TRIP 56: VIRGINIA LAKE

VIRGINIA LAKE

Cecil Mountain

Virginia Lake Road

To Route 5

fee-bee-o anytime you are near alder stands in the spring and early summer.

When we paddled here in October, the alder flycatchers had long ago departed for warmer climes still abuzz with insects. Birches and maples along the northern shoreline had turned bright yellow and red, and hillside oaks, with their burnished reds, stood in contrast to the dark green of scattered conifer groves. Huge clumps of multicolored leaves clogged the surface of the lake's south end, driven there by breezes from the north, the same ones that carry ducks and geese southward. Reflections of the brightly colored hillsides shimmered on the lake's rippled surface. Although the paddling season sadly would end with leaf fall, we were reminded one can paddle in complete solitude almost anywhere in Maine after Labor Day, enjoying gloriously colored fall foliage and cool air, free of biting insects.

57 | North Pond

Spend anywhere from a few hours to most of a day paddling scenic North Pond. Going is slow as you wend your way through floating islands and aquatic vegetation. You should see a profusion of heath family members, bog orchids, loons, turtles, waterfowl in fall, ospreys, and possibly moose.

Location: Norway
Maps: *Maine Atlas & Gazetteer*, Map 10: C5 and Map 11: C1; USGS West Paris
Area: 147 acres
Time: 3 hours
Habitat Type: Shallow marsh slowly filling in
Fish: Chain pickerel (see fish advisories, Appendix A)
Take Note: Slow going due to floating islands and thick aquatic vegetation; deposits of at least 58 minerals found in Stoneham

GETTING THERE

From Norway at the junction of Paris and Main streets, go west on Routes 117/118 for 1.4 miles and turn right on Crockett Ridge Road. Go 2.5 miles (cumulative: 3.9 miles) and turn left on Round the Pond Road. Go 2.3 miles (6.2 miles) to the access on the right. (44° 16.176′ N, 70° 36.444′ W)

WHAT YOU'LL SEE

Wild and beautiful, particularly on the north and west ends, North Pond should be a sure bet for moose. The heavily forested hillsides of hemlock, birch, aspen, white pine, oak, maple, and many other tree species provide refuge during the day, while acres and acres of marsh vegetation provide food by night. That said, although we paddled here quietly at sunset, we did not see any moose.

We did not spend much time paddling the southeast arm, where several houses stand in stark contrast to the pond's pristine northern and western reaches. The north end's twisting channels meander their way in and out among islands and floating chunks of marsh vegetation. One could spend several hours paddling north along the east side then down the west side, exploring each of the extensive channels reaching back up into the surrounding hills.

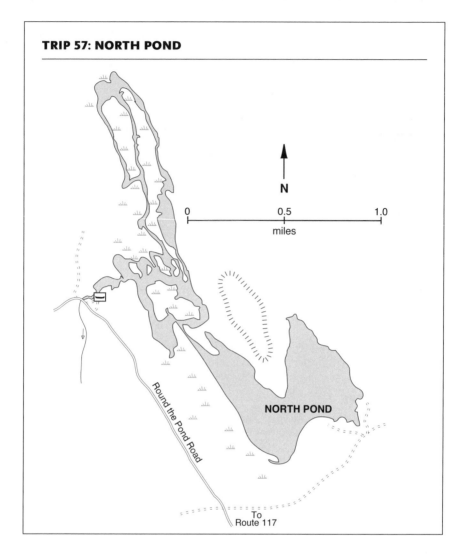

A fire tower rises on a hill in the north, and you can see a few farms off in the distance. From the access, paddle by an island covered with big white pines, almost to the eastern shore, and turn north, heading for the fire tower. You can paddle up this channel all the way back to the farms on those hills, exploring the many side channels along the way.

Although tamarack, black spruce, and white pine populate several low-lying islands, shrub vegetation predominates. Waterlilies float in shallow channels lined with cattails, and members of the heath family, many with evergreen leaves, dominate the swamps of North Pond. Some sport showy flowers, such as rhodora, with its beautiful rose-purple flowers that emerge before the leaves in

The low-growing American cranberry is in the same genus as the blueberry.

May; the summer-blooming swamp azalea, with its long, showy white flowers (near the northern limit of its range here); and the similar sheep laurel and bog laurel, with clusters of bright pink flowers. You can distinguish the latter two easily by the location of their flower whorls: Bog laurel (*Kalmia polifolia*) flowers at the ends of stems, whereas sheep laurel (*Kalmia angustifolia*) flowers below a terminal cluster of new leaves.

Other members of the swamp-loving heath family include Labrador tea, with its woolly brown leaf undersides; bog rosemary with its 2-inch-long, 0.25-inch-wide leaves with white undersides and its small, pink, urn-shaped flowers; and leatherleaf, with its aptly named leaves and long lines of upside-down, white, bell-shaped flowers. Perhaps the best known members of the heath family include highbush and lowbush blueberries, huckleberries, and cranberries. You can find some of these heaths in great numbers in and around North Pond.

People also travel here for the geology. Common minerals include pegmatite, a very large-crystal granite, and gem quality crystals of quartz, amethyst, and tourmaline. Unfortunately, Perham's, a 90-year-old institution in nearby West Paris, closed in 2009, with its collection—reputed to be the best in Maine at the time—now taking up residence at the new Maine Mineral and Gem Museum in Bethel.

58 | Bunganock Pond and Bunganock Brook

Although it doesn't take long to paddle here, it's worth the marshland experience. Expect to see great blue herons and other marsh birds, along with painted turtles and ubiquitous marsh vegetation.

Location: Hartford
Maps: *Maine Atlas & Gazetteer*, Map 11: B3; USGS Canton
Area/Length: 51 acres; 1 mile one way
Time: 2 hours
Habitat Type: Shallow, weedy pond and stream
Fish: Largemouth bass, chain pickerel (see fish advisories, Appendix A)
Take Note: No motors

GETTING THERE

From Auburn at the junction of Routes 4 and 202, go 14.3 miles north on Route 4 and turn left on Harlow Hill Road. Go 2.3 miles (cumulative: 16.6 miles) and turn left on Route 219. Go 4.8 miles (21.4 miles) and turn right on Route 140. Go 0.5 mile (21.9 miles) and turn right on a dirt road. Go 0.8 mile (22.7 miles) to the pond access on the left and stream access on the right. (44° 23.100′ N, 70° 20.460′ W)

WHAT YOU'LL SEE

The outlet stream, far more interesting to the quietwater paddler than Bunganock Pond itself, sees hardly any visitors. The undeveloped shore has only one visible cabin, but the pond's small, relatively round nature does not offer a lot of interesting features. We paddled the complete shoreline in less than an hour and then spent our remaining time paddling down and back on meandering Bunganock Stream.

Bunganock Pond. Many large white pines hug Bunganock Pond's shoreline, along with maple, birch, and other deciduous trees. Explore the marshy coves and enjoy the view of forested hills to the west. An abundance of vegetation, especially waterlilies, populates the pond's waters. Most floating-leaved pond vegetation, such as American white waterlily, yellow pondlily, watershield, and bladderwort, cannot grow in more than about 4 feet of water, although some less common aquatic plants tolerate deeper water.

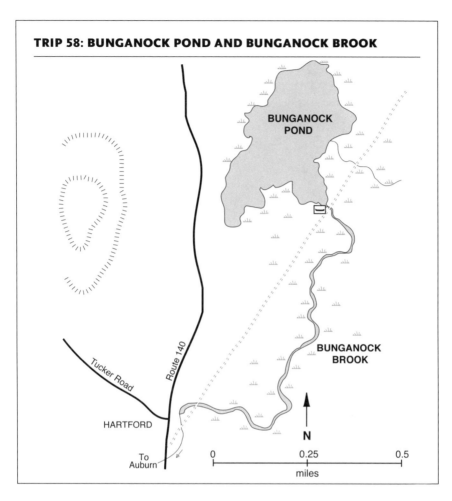

TRIP 58: BUNGANOCK POND AND BUNGANOCK BROOK

BUNGANOCK POND

BUNGANOCK BROOK

Tucker Road

Route 140

HARTFORD

To Auburn

N

0   0.25   0.5

miles

Bunganock Brook. Although we paddled here in July, we found relatively high water levels. We suspect that in late summer or during dry years, the outlet stream may be somewhat less navigable. Indeed, we had difficulty even getting into the pond's outlet stream, sliding the boat down the overgrown bank next to the bridge then following its path. We found the first 100 feet of the stream the most difficult, and we had to get out of the boat three times, portaging over beaver dams and through shallows before the channel widened out to an easy-to-paddle 30 feet. If your boat floats in this widened channel, you probably will find enough water to paddle to the end.

Wildlife, marsh vegetation, and solitude fill this place. We saw eastern kingbirds, great blue herons, song sparrows, and painted turtles that poked their heads up through floating vegetation and dived down through tea-colored water as we approached.

A great blue heron takes a break from fishing.

Abundant American white waterlilies and yellow pondlilies, along with pickerelweed and grasses, line the channel. Sweetgale and other shrubs crowd the shore in places, and water-tolerant trees, such as tamarack and red maple, encroach on the banks wherever the ground rises slightly above the marsh.

At bends in the stream, occasional large granite boulders stand like sentinels guarding the passageway. In those areas, beware of submerged boulders. We had little trouble if we stayed in the middle of the channel when near visible boulders.

The stream snakes around the large pine island in the middle of the marsh then seems to disappear at a dwarf tamarack and red maple forest. Instead, the stream abruptly turns right, continuing on for another few hundred yards before taking a sharp left turn down a narrow rocky channel. At this point you have reached the road at Hartford Center. Barely submerged rocks fill the narrow channel; time to turn around.

59 | Parker Pond

Under calm conditions, Parker Pond is a joy to paddle. Protruding flat rocks and islands provide spots for picnicking and swimming. Look for loons, bald eagles, ospreys, and kingfishers among granite boulders and pine-covered islands.

Location: Mount Vernon, Vienna
Maps: *Maine Atlas & Gazetteer, Map* 12: A2 and Map 20: E2; USGS Farmington Falls, Fayette
Area: 1,610 acres
Time: 5 hours
Habitat Type: Large, clear lake
Fish: Brook trout, landlocked salmon, largemouth bass, smallmouth bass, chain pickerel (see fish advisories, Appendix A)
Take Note: Modest development; motors limited by rocks; winds from the north or south can make paddling treacherous

GETTING THERE

From I-95, Exit 109 southbound, go 2.5 miles west on Routes 11, 17, 100, and 202 and turn right on Route 17. Go 9.7 miles (cumulative: 12.2 miles) and veer right on Route 41. Go 7.2 miles (19.4 miles) and turn sharply left on Seavey Corner Road. Go 1.5 miles (20.9 miles) to the access on the left; park on the right.

WHAT YOU'LL SEE

We include this large, scenic pond because there is so much to explore and because the numerous islands dotting the western shore screen much of the development. With all of the coves, bays, inlets, peninsulas, and islands, it would take all day to explore Parker Pond.

After leaving the access, head right. What appears to be a peninsula is really a series of islands. On their far side, a huge rock provides a great spot for swimming and picnicking. After exploring these islands, head around to the right, toward the northwest cove. A series of beautiful, pine-covered islands, many suitable for picnicking and swimming, extends down the pond's western side, standing sentinel over its many coves.

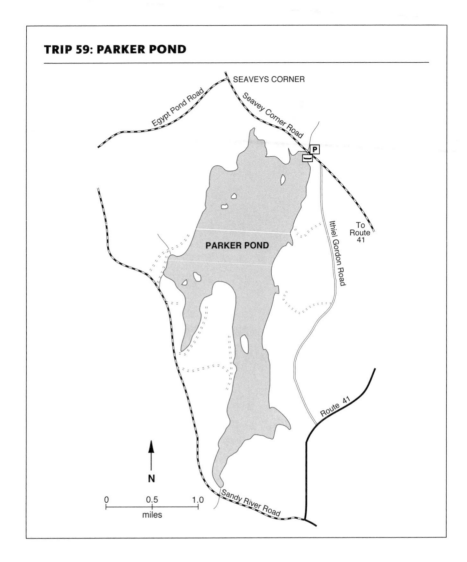

TRIP 59: PARKER POND

SEAVEYS CORNER

Egypt Pond Road

Seavey Corner Road

P

PARKER POND

Ithiel Gordon Road

To Route 41

Route 41

N

0   0.5   1.0
miles

Sandy River Road

Well out from shore, a series of large boulders extends up from the water's surface, creating more great places for swimming or picnicking, especially when biting insects seem to patrol every patch of vegetation. Quite clear water gives good views of the pond's rocky floor. We suspect that the large boulders gleaming up at us everywhere except the pond's center help keep motorboat traffic down.

We saw ospreys, loons, fifteen ring-billed gulls resting on a bare rock formation, kingfishers, and dozens of swallows. In Maine Audubon's 2014 loon survey, volunteers spotted 25 loon adults and 3 chicks. Besides the beautiful white pine covering the islands, balsam fir, hemlock, red and sugar maples, red oak, and gray birch line the western shore.

60 | Bog Stream

This out-of-the-way stream offers a few hours of quiet paddling through Mercer Bog Wildlife Management Area, which is filled with ducks, geese, and other birds typically found near pristine streams. In summer and fall, emergent vegetation can slow your paddling.

Location: Mercer
Maps: *Maine Atlas & Gazetteer*, Map 20: C3, D3; USGS Mercer
Length: 3 miles one way
Time: 3 hours
Habitat Type: Wide, shallow, heavily vegetated stream through wildlife management area
Fish: Smallmouth bass, chain pickerel (see fish advisories, Appendix A)
Take Note: Parking along highway with high traffic volume; floating vegetation can make launching difficult

GETTING THERE

From I-95, Exit 130 northbound, turn left (west) on Route 104, and go 2 miles to the junction with Route 139. Continue 10.6 miles (cumulative: 12.6 miles) on Route 139 and stay straight on Route 2 in Norridgewock. Go 8 miles (20.6 miles) west on Route 2 to the access on the left, just over the bridge. (44° 40.716′ N, 69° 56.382′ W)

WHAT YOU'LL SEE

Mercer Bog, a hidden treasure, offers a wonderful morning or afternoon of paddling and exploration. Technically, it isn't a bog but rather a widened section of Bog Stream formed by a dam in the town of Mercer.

When we paddled here in early September, we couldn't wait to escape the road noise from Route 2, which sees a lot of truck traffic. Around the bend, though, highway noise abates, and tranquility takes over.

What is initially a wide-open channel becomes thick, emergent, and floating vegetation as you paddle south, narrowing the waterway and impeding your progress. Watershield and pickerelweed dominate here, along with yellow pondlily, American white waterlily, bur-reed, and pondweed (*Potamogeton spp.*).

By midsummer, navigating the channel becomes fairly challenging. You have to weave a sinewy path, following the narrow band of open water. In places,

TRIP 60: BOG STREAM

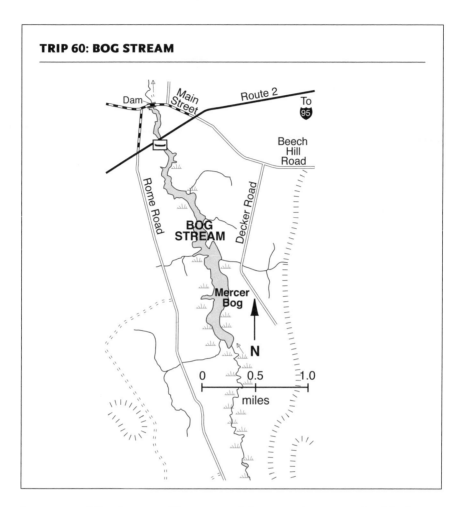

large mats of floating waterlily roots and decomposing vegetation block your progress. Expect to have to backtrack in places as you wend your way south.

We saw dozens of wood ducks, although they typically fly up well before you get close enough for a good look. We also saw great blue herons, kingfishers, a few cormorants, a flock of perhaps 100 Canada geese, several solitary sandpipers, and lots of painted turtles. And although we didn't see any on our visit, beaver sign abounds. Look for the animals themselves in the evenings.

A mix of deciduous and coniferous trees, including sugar and red maples; white, gray, and yellow birches; white pine; balsam fir; red spruce; red oak; beech; and a few quaking aspen populate the woodland away from the marsh.

We plan to come back here in the spring when one could likely paddle farther south. We made it about 2 miles down, but the bog extends another 0.5 mile. In spring, bird life would also be a lot richer.

You can also paddle under Route 2 and down about 0.5 mile to the dam that deepened Mercer Bog, a pleasant trip that passes just a few houses. We watched a deer grazing by the water's edge along here.

61 | Umbagog Lake

This huge, shallow lake straddles the Maine–New Hampshire border. Loons, ospreys, and bald eagles nest here, and the probability of seeing moose is high. Also look for beavers, otters, mink, black bears, and waterfowl.

Location: Magalloway PLT, Maine; Cambridge and Errol, New Hampshire
Maps: *Maine Atlas & Gazetteer*, Map 17: B5, C5 and Map 18: B1, C1; USGS Umbagog Lake North, Umbagog Lake South
Area: 7,850 acres
Time: Multiday
Habitat Type: Large, shallow, marshy lake with numerous coves and rivers
Fish: Brown trout, brook trout, landlocked salmon, chain pickerel (see fish advisories, Appendix A)
Information: Umbagog Lake Campground, nhstateparks.org, 603-482-7795; backcountry sites require reservations; towing to remote sites available for a fee; canoe rentals; Lake Umbagog National Wildlife Refuge, fws.gov/northeast/lakeumbagog
Take Note: Avoid open boats under windy conditions; always wear a PFD

GETTING THERE
Northern access. From Bethel, after crossing the Androscoggin River bridge on Routes 2 and 26, go 5.3 miles north on Routes 2 and 26, and turn left on Route 26. Go 22 miles (cumulative: 27.3 miles) to Errol, New Hampshire, and turn right on North Mountain Road, 0.1 mile before the Androscoggin River bridge. Go 1 mile (28.3 miles) to the access, veering left at the fork. (44° 47.236′ N, 71° 7.266′ W) The main lake is about 3 miles upriver.

 Southern access. From the Androscoggin River bridge in Errol, go 7 miles south on Route 26 to the access on the left. (44° 42.137′ N, 71° 3.316′ W) Backcountry campers may launch from Umbagog Lake State Park, 0.1 mile east.

TRIP 61: UMBAGOG LAKE

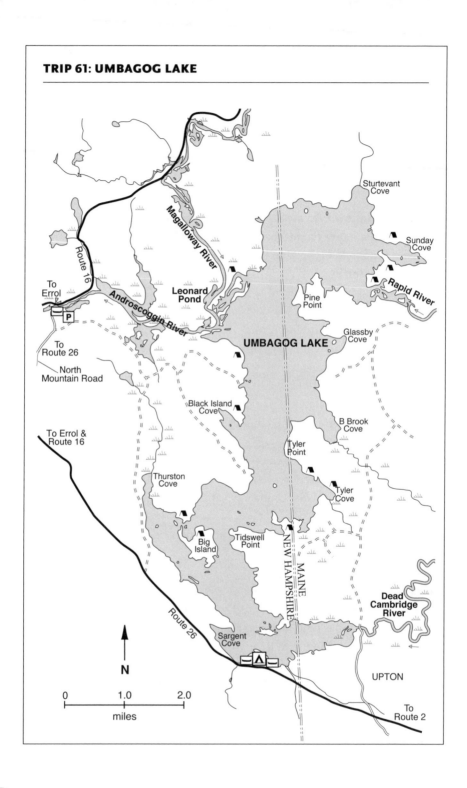

Sturtevant Cove

Sunday Cove

Rapid River

Magalloway River

Route 16

To Errol

P

Androscoggin River

Leonard Pond

Pine Point

Glassby Cove

UMBAGOG LAKE

To Route 26

North Mountain Road

Black Island Cove

B Brook Cove

To Errol & Route 16

Tyler Point

Thurston Cove

Tyler Cove

Big Island

Tidswell Point

MAINE

NEW HAMPSHIRE

Dead Cambridge River

Route 26

Sargent Cove

UPTON

N

0   1.0   2.0

miles

To Route 2

WHAT YOU'LL SEE

With the tremendous variety of wildlife and the number of ducks nesting here, we should not be surprised that Lake Umbagog has become one of the newest national wildlife refuges. Established in November 1992 with the purchase by the federal government of the first tracts of land, Lake Umbagog National Wildlife Refuge has grown to 32,000 acres already, but the U.S. Fish and Wildlife Service intends to obtain title or conservation easements that would increase the refuge to 70,000 acres.

Umbagog, pronounced "um-BAY-gog," straddles the Maine–New Hampshire border, covering more than 12 square miles. Oriented generally north-south, with a highly varied shoreline that extends more than 40 miles, plus dozens of islands, this magnificent lake exudes wildness. Readily accessible to the backcountry paddler, Lake Umbagog Campground manages 35 wilderness sites around the lake. A few private cottages and camps dot parts of the lake, and motorboat traffic has increased in recent years, but we expect very little future development. We should all encourage New Hampshire and Maine to restrict motorboat use for the protection of moose and nesting ducks, loons, and bald eagles.

A very shallow lake—Umbagog means "shallow water" in Abenaki—with average depths of only about 15 feet, the many marshy areas provide ideal nesting habitat for such species as ring-necked, black, mallard, and wood ducks, and hooded and common mergansers. Wood ducks and hooded mergansers, two common cavity nesters, use the approximately 100 nesting boxes around the lake.

Leonard Pond, the largest marshy area, near the northwestern corner of the lake, sports an extensive, grassy marsh that has supported nesting bald eagles since 1989—no eagle nested in New Hampshire from 1949 to 1988—right where the Magalloway River enters and the Androscoggin River exits the lake. The last nest left in 1949 was in the same tree as the new nest in 1989.

In 1989, the first chick died, but biologists placed in the nest a chick from a captive pair. The eagle adopted the foster chick and raised it successfully. In some years since, the pair nested successfully, in others years not. In the spring of 1994 during nesting, the male died from lead sinker ingestion. (On January 1, 2000, New Hampshire banned the use of lead sinkers weighing 1 ounce or less to protect loons and other waterfowl. Maine's ban came in 2013.) The female abandoned the lone egg but found a new mate. In the summer of 1997, nesting failed, but in 1998 they raised two young successfully. In 1999, they successfully raised another pair. In 2000, although the Umbagog hatchlings died, probably

Paddlers enjoy the early morning mist on Umbagog Lake. Photo: Jerelyn Wilson.

due to cold, wet weather, the year marked a new first, with a pair attempting nesting at nearby Pontook Reservoir.

By 2001, neither the original female nor male were still alive. Other eagle pairs inhabited the nest with limited success for a few years, but in 2006 three young fledged from the Leonard Pond site.

This mirrors what has happened nationally in the lower 48 states: From a low of 417 pairs in 1963, the population rebounded to 791 pairs in 1974; 1,188 pairs in 1981; 3,035 in 1990; 4,712 in 1995; and more than 6,000 in 2000. Due to the remarkable recovery of the population following the ban of DDT, which caused disastrous eggshell thinning, then-President Clinton announced in 1995 that the bald eagle's status would change from endangered to threatened. In 2007, with more than 10,000 nesting pairs—a number that has remained relatively constant since—U.S. Fish & Wildlife removed the bald eagle from the endangered and threatened species list, capping an amazing comeback story.

Ospreys, meanwhile, have had an even better time of it. In 1994, approximately 25 pairs nested in the vicinity of Umbagog, and they successfully reared 35 chicks. They continue to be common on Umbagog. Loons have had mixed success. A lot of loons summer on the lake: Of 22 territorial pairs, 13 pairs actually nested, fledging a total of 11 chicks in 1994. In late July 1997, however, when we paddled here, biologists told us that few chicks had survived the late, cold spring. In what may be a portent of things to come, in 2016 a loon with avian malaria, a tropical disease not previously seen in loons, was found dead in Umbagog. During May, June, and July, be particularly careful about nesting loons. Even a quiet paddler inadvertently getting too close to a nest can result in the adults abandoning it, and loons always nest very close to the water.

Our favorite places on Umbagog include Leonard Pond, coves along the inlet of Rapid River on the northeast, and small coves and islands east of Tidswell Point. Big Island, purchased by the Society for the Protection of New Hampshire Forests in the 1980s, is also wonderful and includes six campsites. For camping with kids, sites on the north shore of Tyler Cove (numbers 21, 22, and 23) stand out for the protected, sandy swimming beach at the cove's end.

We also enjoy paddling the slow-flowing, meandering Androscoggin and Magalloway Rivers. Paddling toward Umbagog on either river, a number of marshy ponds both to the right and left await your exploration. Keep an eye out for moose, otters, and mink.

Moose abound. Look for them standing belly-deep in the Magalloway River, in ponds on either side of the Androscoggin, or in any of the lake's numerous coves. In early morning light, in a cove just east of Tidswell Point, we watched three moose browsing by the water's edge. At the far southeastern end, the most developed part of the lake, we got our closest look at a moose not 200 yards from a cottage near the mouth of the Dead Cambridge River. We also have watched them swim across open water in early morning, moving along at a brisk pace.

The varied vegetation around Umbagog includes conifers that predominate in most areas: balsam fir, spruce, northern white cedar, hemlock, and white pine. In other areas, deciduous trees, including yellow and paper birches, red maple, and an occasional red oak, predominate. We also saw a few relatively rare jack pine.

Potentially dangerous winds and waves can come up very quickly on this large lake, making open-boat paddling hazardous. Paddling around the lake during a 2-day period in August, we got into heavy winds both afternoons, even though the water was like glass on each of those mornings. Wind blowing from the north or northwest across several miles of shallow water can build up sizable waves!

Many fish inhabit the lake, as evidenced by the large osprey population. In mid-August we caught yellow perch, smallmouth bass, and lots of lake chub (a whitefish with large scales and a deeply forked tail) up to a few pounds each. With the right bait, lures, or flies, one should not have too much trouble pulling a few tasty meals out of the lake.

62 | Upper Richardson Lake and Lower Richardson Lake

Really just one lake joined at The Narrows, long, narrow Richardson can give you a real workout, which is best over a multiday trip. Look here for loons, bald eagles, ospreys, moose, and otters.

Location: Magalloway PLT, Richardsontown Township, Township C
Maps: *Maine Atlas & Gazetteer*, Map 18: A1, A2, B1, B2, C2; USGS Andover, Metallak Mountain, Middle Dam, Richardson Pond, Oquossoc
Area: Upper Richardson, 4,200 acres; Lower Richardson, 2,900 acres
Time: Multiday
Habitat Type: Deep, clear lakes; scenic hillsides
Fish: Brown trout, brook trout, lake trout, landlocked salmon (see fish advisories, Appendix A)
Information: The Pingree family and New England Forestry Foundation developed a 762,000-acre conservation easement, including the west shore of Upper Richardson (the state owns the east shore) and the north shore of Lower Richardson, newenglandforestry.org
Take Note: Treacherous paddling under windy conditions; no personal watercraft; campfire permits required, 207-827-1800

GETTING THERE
South End. From Andover, at the junction of Routes 5 and 120, go 0.6 mile and turn left on South Arm Road in North Oxford. Go 2.5 miles (cumulative: 3.1 miles) and turn left on South Arm Road. Go 9.1 miles (12.2 miles) to the access on the left, 0.4 mile past the campground entrance. (44° 45.132´ N, 70° 50.562´ W)

    North End. From Rangeley, at the junction of Routes 4 and 16, go 6.5 miles west on Routes 4 and 16, and turn right on Route 16. Go 14 miles (cumulative: 20.5 miles), turn left on Mill Brook Road, and go 1 mile (21.5 miles) to the access. (44° 54.426´ N, 70° 54.438´ W)

WHAT YOU'LL SEE
Upper and Lower Richardson, once distinct lakes, merged at The Narrows with the construction of 22-foot Middle Dam on Lower Richardson in the early 1900s. The combined lake covers more than 11 square miles and extends

TRIP 62: UPPER RICHARDSON LAKE AND LOWER RICHARDSON LAKE

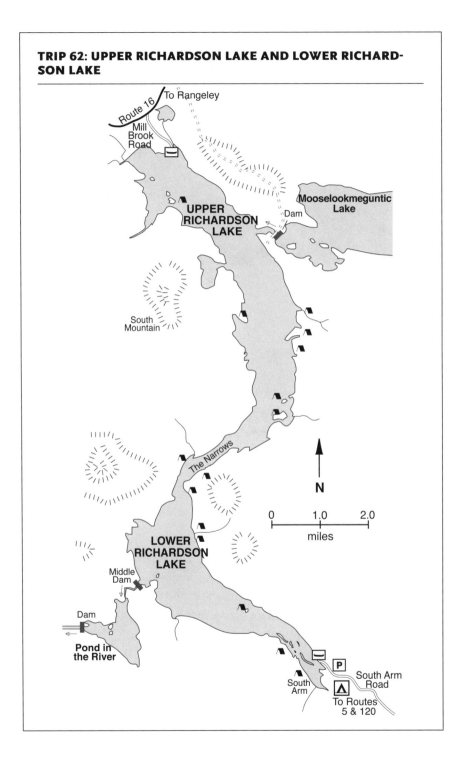

A telephoto lens gives a close-up view of a common loon, *Gavia immer*. Maine's loon population has been increasing.

roughly 15 miles in an S-curving, north-south direction. The lake ranges in width from a few hundred yards at The Narrows to about 1.5 miles at the widest section of Lower Richardson.

The lake's size and orientation make it quite dangerous in bad weather, when wind-driven waves can build up over more than 5 miles of open water. In bad conditions, wear PFDs, use extreme caution, and stay close to shore.

The rocky shoreline gives way to a generally sandy bottom, and the deep, clear water supports an excellent coldwater trout and salmon fishery. Spruce, fir, cedar, and white pine predominate in this young forest, extensively cut prior to state acquisition.

Nearly all of Upper Richardson's eastern shore consists of public reserve land. The state acquired 80 percent of this 22,800-acre tract in 1984 from the Pingree heirs (Seven Islands Land Company) and James River Corporation, and the other 20 percent in 1978 from the Brown Company. The state manages the Richardson Unit for recreation, wildlife habitat, and timber. Within sight of the lake, the first two uses generally take precedence over the last. The Appalachian Trail passes a few miles east.

Thirty-eight primitive campsites, managed by South Arm Campground, dot the shores of Richardson Lake and its islands. Some of the nicer campsites you pass paddling north from the campground include Spirit Island; Sand Banks, which has a great sandy beach area; Portland Point at the Narrows, with a protected sandy cove; Pine Island and Metallak Island, in Upper Richardson (Pine Island used to have a bald eagle nest); Half Moon Cove, on the west shore with two campsites; and Big Beaver Island.

If you paddle in Upper Richardson's north end, also check out Cranberry Cove, the most remote and protected part of either section. At low-water levels, you have to pick your way carefully among the rocks. The shoreline of Cranberry Cove harbors a typical northern fen ecosystem, with tamarack, leatherleaf, bog rosemary, pitcher plant, and sphagnum.

63 | Flagstaff Lake

Massive Flagstaff Lake, Maine's fourth largest, offers many paddling opportunities and multiday trips. Although it's large, you can often find quiet places to paddle when the wind blows. You will see loons, ducks, ospreys, ravens, and possibly moose and otters.

Location: Bigelow Township, Carrying Place Town Township, Dead River Township, Eustis, Flagstaff Township, T3 R4 BKP WKR
Maps: *Maine Atlas & Gazetteer*, Map 29: B2, B3, B4, B5, C2, C5 and Map 30: B1; USGS Little Bigelow Mountain, Stratton, the Horns
Area: 20,300 acres
Time: Multiday; shorter trips possible
Habitat Type: Large, shallow lake with numerous coves and islands
Fish: Brook trout, landlocked salmon, chain pickerel (see fish advisories, Appendix A)
Take Note: No personal watercraft; wind can make paddling hazardous; campfire permits required, 207-827-1800

GETTING THERE
From Rangeley at the junction of Routes 4 and 16, go 0.2 mile north on Route 16 and turn right, staying on Route 16. Go 18.4 miles (cumulative: 18.6 miles) and turn left on Route 27. Go 4.1 miles (22.7 miles) and turn right on Flagstaff Road. Go 2.5 miles (25.2 miles) to the access. (45° 11.328′ N, 70° 24.888′ W) This northern access avoids development on the southwest arm.

WHAT YOU'LL SEE
The beautiful Bigelow Mountains just to the south carry the Appalachian Trail to 4,000 feet—some 3,000 feet above the lake's surface. To the north, Flagstaff

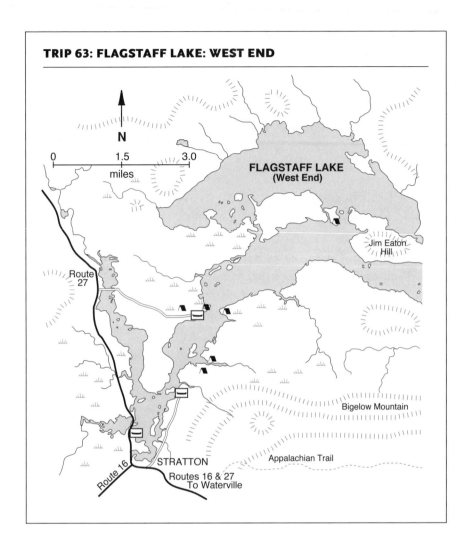

TRIP 63: FLAGSTAFF LAKE: WEST END

FLAGSTAFF LAKE
(West End)

N

0   1.5   3.0
miles

Jim Eaton Hill

Route 27

Bigelow Mountain

STRATTON

Route 16

Appalachian Trail

Routes 16 & 27
To Waterville

Mountain stretches to 2,500 feet, while layered hillsides recede into the distance at other compass points. The beautiful setting amid the northern boreal forest, with its pointed spires of fir, spruce, and tamarack, provides reason enough to travel to this remote area in the Rangeley Lakes region.

You could spend a week exploring the islands, coves, and shoreline of huge Flagstaff Lake, Maine's fourth largest, as it courses west to east for more than 18 miles through the dammed-up Dead River valley. Although wind could present hazardous conditions, you should be able to find relatively calm water from one or more of the ten access points. (See the Maine Atlas.) When we paddled here

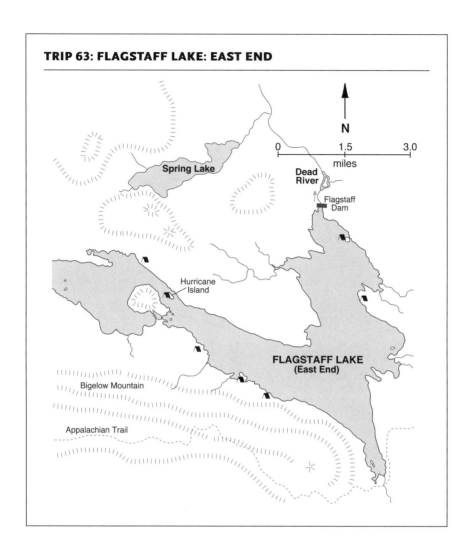

on a day with south winds, we snuck behind islands and into protected coves. In one of those coves, we watched an otter fish the waters as a pair of ravens called overhead. In other coves, we found fish carcasses on rocks, leftovers from otter feasts. With west winds, we would explore the North Branch of the Dead River, which you can paddle up for several miles.

Much of the land surrounding Flagstaff Lake, particularly the southern shore, lies within Maine Public Reserve Lands, which protects nearly 20 miles of shoreline and contains the entire Bigelow Range within its 35,000 acres. In this wild country, expect to see moose, otters, beavers, bears, mink, loons, ospreys, and lots of other wildlife.

RIVER OTTER: PLAYFUL MEMBER OF THE WEASEL FAMILY

The river otter, *Lutra canadensis*, inhabits New England's remote lakes and rivers. We have seen dozens throughout Maine, mostly in the less-populated North Country, but also on more southern waterways, sometimes surprisingly close to urban areas. Look for them in early morning and late afternoon.

The otter once inhabited virtually every U.S. watercourse, from sun-warmed southwestern rivers to icy far-northern lakes and streams. Today, thanks to 250 years of trapping, water pollution, and encroaching development, the otter has retreated to the far corners of its former range. Because it eats at the top of the food chain, the otter also suffers from pollution and toxic chemicals in the environment, such as heavy metals, DDT derivatives, dioxin, and PCBs.

With its long, thin body and relatively thick, sharply tapered tail, it can reach 4 feet in length and weigh up to 25 pounds. Long prized by trappers, its dense dark-brown fur above gives way to lighter colors on the belly and throat.

The otter has adapted well to its aquatic environment. Its nose and ears close when underwater, and webbed toes aid in swimming. Although it swims fast enough to catch trout, it usually preys on slower-moving suckers, minnows, crayfish, tadpoles, and salamanders. It often thrusts its head up above the surface, looking around and exhaling loudly.

While adapted for water, the otter does well on land, with its typical weasel-family undulating gait. Clocked at up to 18 MPH on land, it can travel 100 miles overland in search of new territory. It generally chooses dens—abandoned beaver lodges or natural cavities under tree roots—at the water's edge, with an underwater entrance.

The otter consumes smaller fish and crayfish in the water and larger prey on shore or on protruding rocks. An ingenious hunter, it sometimes herds fish into shallows or punches a hole in a beaver dam, allowing water to escape before wading in and feasting on flopping fish. Because it hunts so successfully, it has plenty of time to play—a famous trait.

Animal behaviorists believe that play among young mammals provides practice for future hunting, territorial interactions, and courtship. But the adult otter continues to play, chasing one another, and repeatedly climbing snow- and mudbanks then sliding down into the water.

The otter mates in late winter; birth follows almost a year later. As with many weasel-family members, the otter delays embryo implantation, stopping development until the subsequent winter, followed by the birth of two to four cubs anytime between November and April. Cubs emerge fully furred, but with eyes closed and no teeth. They venture outside the den after about three months. Although the mother provides the initial care, the father may rejoin the family to help with rearing after the cubs reach about six months.

Although the otter is curious and relatively bold, keep your distance. Interference from humans may cause it to move away and search for a more remote location.

64 | Gilman Pond

Gilman Pond, along with its inlet and outlet streams, provides a good place to paddle, especially for birdwatchers, plant enthusiasts, and fishermen. Other fish eaters seen here include loons, ospreys, and kingfishers. You could also see sandhill cranes in migration.

Location: Lexington Township, New Portland
Maps: *Maine Atlas & Gazetteer*, Map 30: E2; USGS New Portland
Area/Length: 242 acres; 2.5 miles one way
Time: 4 hours
Habitat Type: Shallow pond with inlet and outlet streams

Fish: Brown trout, largemouth bass, chain pickerel (see fish advisories, Appendix A)

Take Note: Private access, fee charged

GETTING THERE

From Norridgewock at the junction of Routes 2 and 201A, go 12.6 miles north on Route 201A and turn left on Route 16. Go 9.5 miles (cumulative: 22.1 miles), turning sharply left in New North Portland, and turn right on Gilman Pond Road. Go 1.9 miles (24 miles) to the private access on the right (fee). (44° 56.982′ N, 70° 3.360′ W)

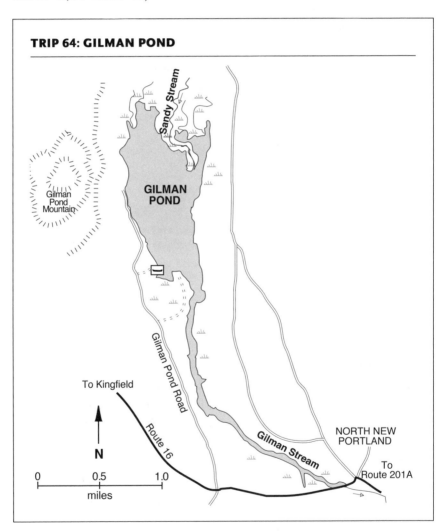

TRIP 64: GILMAN POND

Puffy, white, ball-like flowers of buttonbush, *Cephalanthus occidentalis*, a shrub that can withstand root immersion for periods of time, bloom in summer.

WHAT YOU'LL SEE

Gilman Pond, a delightful little out-of-the way pond in the Rangeley Lakes region, nestles into a valley surrounded by forested hills. This picturesque pond offers the opportunity for several hours of quiet paddling, especially if you paddle down to Route 16, a round-trip distance of about 5 miles. Paddle here when the wind blows on nearby Richardson and Flagstaff lakes.

Although we found the outlet stream the most interesting, we also enjoyed paddling the pond's north end, choked with sedges, equisetum, buttonbush, and other aquatic vegetation. Note Sandy Stream flowing down through scattered silver maples along the northern peninsula. Although it has good flow, impenetrable sedges choke the waterway, indicating boats do not ply these waters in great numbers. The cove on the peninsula's northeast side is quieter and marshier than the one on the other side.

The shoreline sports a wide variety of tree species, including cedar, birch, spruce, hemlock, and balsam fir on the north end. As you travel down the eastern shore (a small amount of development clusters along the western shore) to the outlet, note the large number of tall red oaks. White and yellow birches, aspen, and maple show up in good numbers, as well.

Birdwatchers trek here from all over the Northeast for the bird diversity, including the possibility of seeing sandhill cranes in migration. When we paddled here, loons called from the pond, kingfishers darted down the shore in front of us, and an osprey fished near the outlet. The presence of these three fish-eating birds together indicates a healthy fish population. Local anglers told us fishing is pretty good for chain pickerel and an occasional lunker brown trout. Recently, largemouth bass were introduced, which has kicked up fishing pressure.

Paddling down the outlet, note the very tall tamaracks on the right-hand shore. An extensive marshy area covers the left-hand side. After passing it, you can turn left and paddle into it. In mid-July when we visited, still-high water covered the roots of many shoreline trees, especially red maples. Their leaves had started to wilt, obviously not due to lack of water. Instead, standing water impeded gas exchange between the air and their roots.

Many beautiful wild swamp roses bloomed up and down the outlet, and extensive dogwood and viburnum blooms abounded. Islands of buttonbush, with its terminal Osage orangelike green balls that later turn into large, round, puffy white flowers, occurred in large clumps out in the water. Rushes filled the side channels. Sweetgale, with aromatic leaves that give off a wonderful scent when crushed, dotted the shoreline in marshy areas. With the diversity of plants and the opportunity to see many flowers in bloom, this is a great spot for plant lovers.

65 | Pierce Pond and Upper Pierce Pond

Out-of-the-way Pierce ponds offer deep, clear water that supports a productive coldwater fishery, scenic hillsides, and relative solitude. You could spend one or several days here. Expect to see several loons. In the spring, the woods fill with songbirds and wildflowers.

Location: Pierce Pond Township
Maps: *Maine Atlas & Gazetteer*, Map 30: A1, A2, B1, B2;
USGS East Carry Pond, Pierce Pond
Area: 1,650 acres
Time: 5 hours or multiday
Habitat Type: Deep, clear ponds

Fish: Brook trout, landlocked salmon, chain pickerel (see fish advisories, Appendix A)

Information: Harrison's Pierce Pond Camps, 207-672-3625; Cobb's Pierce Pond Camps, 207-628-2819

Take Note: Conservation easements protect the shoreline from further development; no personal watercraft; camping at established sites only; no fires

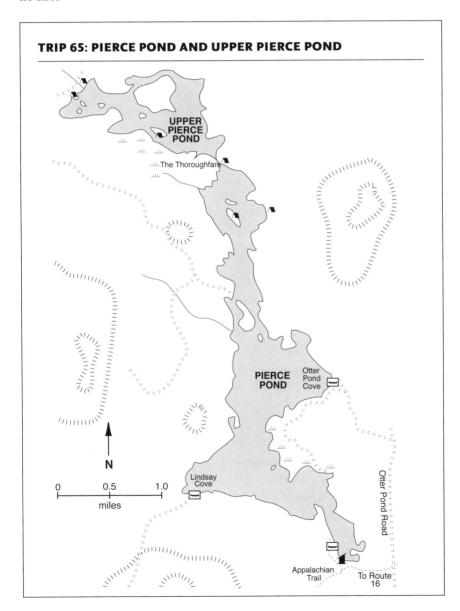

TRIP 65: PIERCE POND AND UPPER PIERCE POND

GETTING THERE

Otter Pond Cove. Pickup trucks only due to rocks in road. If you get stuck, there is at times a caretaker at Otter Pond Cove. From Bingham at the junction of Routes 16 and 201, cross the Kennebec River on Route 16 and turn immediately right on Ridge Road/Pleasant Ridge Road. Go 4.1 miles and turn right on Carry Pond Road. Go 8.6 miles (cumulative: 12.7 miles) and veer right on Otter Pond Road. Go 3.5 miles (16.2 miles) and turn right followed by a quick left on Otter Pond Road. Go 4 miles (20.2 miles), passing Harrison's Pierce Pond Sporting Camps on the left and the Appalachian Trail, and turn left on the access road. Go 1.7 miles (21.9 miles) to the access. (45° 15.762′ N, 70° 3.576′ W)

Harrison's Access. If you are staying at the camp, you can launch your boat there. (45° 14.250′ N, 70° 3.002′ W)

Cobb's Camps, Lindsay Cove. Fee to launch here. As above to Otter Pond Road (12.7 miles). From the junction of Otter Pond Road and Cary Pond Road, go 2.4 miles (cumulative: 15.1 miles) north on Otter Pond Road and turn left on Scott Road/Carrying Place Road. Go 6.3 miles (21.4 miles), turn right on Cobb's Camp Road, and follow it to the end. (45° 14.814′ N, 70° 5.322′ W)

WHAT YOU'LL SEE

Pierce Pond's deep, cold, well-oxygenated substratum makes it an excellent coldwater fishery and brings a fair number of anglers to its shores. Thanks to difficult access and more than 2.5 square miles of surface area, you can paddle in relative solitude here.

Beautiful forested hillsides surround both ponds, with conifers dominating the eastern shore, and mixed conifers and deciduous trees sharing the western shore. Heavily forested islands lend a scenic quality, especially to the northern section. The islands break up the view of open water, making the ponds seem deceptively small. Lots of beautiful boulders poke up everywhere, especially guarding channels going up the right side of the middle and northern sections of Pierce Pond and in Upper Pierce Pond. The huge number of these rocks, some barely submerged, belie the depths under open water.

There seems to be a camping spot on the Thoroughfare that connects the two ponds, as well as sites in the upper bay of Pierce Pond, one on the eastern shore and one on the western side of the two islands out in the middle. If you camp here, you will have to share the shore with a monster beaver lodge and its inhabitants. Upper Pierce Pond has a couple of camping spots, one on the south end of an island to the left. When we paddled here, passing between the ponds required a portage over some slippery boards, dodging the beaver cuttings. The depth here is deceptive due to very clear water.

Lots of loons plied the waters of the ponds as we paddled this wild place nearly alone on a beautiful late-July weekend. Purple damselflies, with their backswept wings, landed on our paddles and arms. Northern white cedar, white birch, white pine, and red pine covered the islands and hillsides. One could easily spend several days exploring this wonderful spot.

66 | Spencer Lake and Fish Pond

The backdrop for Fish Pond and Spencer Lake is incredibly scenic, with mountain views all around. The privately owned lakeshore remains open as long as we treat it well. You will see loons, ospreys, ravens, and Canada geese, along with spectacular views.

Location: Hobbstown Township, T3 R5 BKP WKR
Maps: *Maine Atlas & Gazetteer*, Map 39: D4, E4; USGS King and Bartlett Lake, Spencer Lake
Area: 1,819 acres
Time: 5 hours
Habitat Type: Deep, clear lake
Fish: Brook trout, lake trout, landlocked salmon (see fish advisories, Appendix A)
Information: Take Note: No personal watercraft; campfire permits required, 207-827-1800; camping permits required, 207-243-3020

GETTING THERE
From The Forks at the junction of Route 201 and Lake Moxie Road, go 13.9 miles north on Route 201 and turn left on Hardscrabble/Spencer roads. Go 12.8 miles (cumulative: 26.7 miles) and turn left on Fish Pond Road. Go 0.3 mile (27 miles), turn right, and go slowly down a potholed road lined with balsam fir and red and striped maples to the access. (45° 26.610′ N, 70° 18.108′ W)

WHAT YOU'LL SEE
Breathtaking views of surrounding mountains—Number 5, Three Slide, Hardwood, and Hardscrabble—await you as you drive to these bodies of water. At the access, we were greeted by the view of several Canada goose families grazing on flat grasslands across the pond. As we watched the low afternoon sun turn the

TRIP 66: SPENCER LAKE AND FISH POND

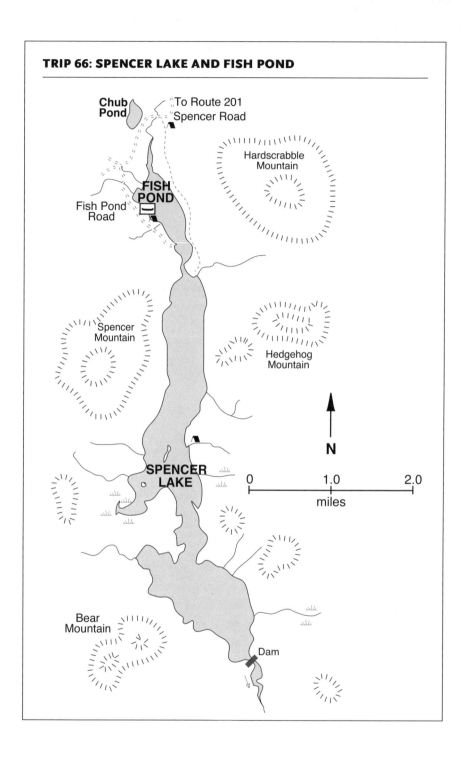

clouds billowing over Spencer Mountain to shades of gold and red, we knew we had come to a wild place. Other than the few people who fish for trout and salmon, you should paddle here pretty much alone, although the campsites at the access fill up on weekends.

Nestled between two parallel ridges and ringed with peaks rising 1,300 feet above the water level, Spencer Lake fills a deep gorge, giving it depth not found in other lakes in this area. This depth keeps the lower layers—down to 135 feet—quite cold, much to the liking of the lake trout, brook trout, and salmon populations.

When we paddled here, ravens croaked out their hoarse cries, and loons filled the air with haunting songs, adding to the already incredible feeling of wilderness. Ospreys, great blue herons, and kingfishers fished the surface waters. Spotted sandpipers bobbed their tails along the shore, and warblers hunted for insects in the trees hanging over the water.

As we paddled through the access stream between Fish Pond and Spencer Lake, we encountered submerged stumps, a sand beach, and shallow water, which could be a problem at low water levels. The expected conifers—white and red pine, spruce, balsam fir, and northern white cedar—dominate the shoreline, intermingling with white birch, red maple, and alder. Conifers and hardwoods share the western hillsides about equally, but deciduous trees dominate the eastern hillsides. Past logging practices may have altered the species composition in this area of the northern spruce, pine, and fir forest.

As you paddle south into Spencer Lake, a fair amount of marshland surrounds the large peninsula, while a rocky shoreline contains the rest of the lake. Several campsites exist on Fish Pond and Spencer Lake.

A lodge with several cabins appears on the left, and farther down the lake, after passing a series of islands, another cluster of cabins appears, also on the left. Continued access and shoreline use lie in the hands of the cable TV billionaire John Malone, who has said access will remain open as long as the land is not abused.

In July 2000, Malone purchased the remaining shoreline of Spencer Lake as a 7,500-acre parcel from Plum Creek for $1,330 per acre. He previously had purchased a 7,400-acre parcel surrounding the lake from International Paper for $470 per acre. Malone has now purchased more than 1 million acres in Maine and, as of 2011, was the largest U.S. private landowner, with more than 2 million acres nationwide. The good news is he's a past national board member of The Nature Conservancy and has expressed strong interest in land conservation.

67 | Attean Pond, Holeb Pond, and Moose River Bow Loop

Attean and Holeb ponds, with their many islands and coves, make wonderful places to paddle, but most people travel here for the Moose River Bow loop, which begins and ends on Attean Pond. This wild area teems with wildlife: loons, bald eagles, ospreys, moose, beavers, muskrat, and otters.

Location: Attean Township, Bradstreet Township, Holeb Township, T5 R7 BKP WKR
Maps: *Maine Atlas & Gazetteer*, Map 39: C3, D3; USGS Attean Pond, Catheart Mountain, Holeb
Area/Length: Attean Pond, 2,745 acres; Holeb Pond, 1,055 acres; 34-mile loop
Time: 3 to 5 days
Habitat Type: Large, shallow lakes; Attean Pond dotted with islands; marshy stream
Fish: Brook trout, lake trout, landlocked salmon (see fish advisories, Appendix A)
Take Note: Wind from the west can make paddling these large ponds treacherous; no personal watercraft on Attean Pond; all sites require campfire permits, 207-827-1800

GETTING THERE

From Jackman at the railroad crossing on Route 201, go 0.6 mile south and turn right on Attean Road. Go 2.4 miles (cumulative: 3 miles) to the access. (45° 35.358′ N, 70° 15.660′ W)

WHAT YOU'LL SEE

We cover Attean and Holeb ponds together because they form part of the popular Moose River Bow trip. We paddled this scenic 34-mile loop in August over a three-day weekend. To maximize wildlife viewing and allow thorough exploration of the two ponds and some side channels on the river, 4 days would be better. To avoid crowded campsites on the river, try to start your trip on a Thursday or earlier in the week.

Maine's Bureau of Parks and Lands' Public Reserved Lands system protects Attean and Holeb ponds and the neighboring part of Moose River. Bogs, fens,

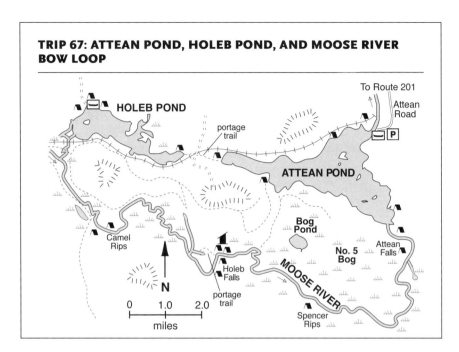

TRIP 67: ATTEAN POND, HOLEB POND, AND MOOSE RIVER BOW LOOP

To Route 201

Attean Road

HOLEB POND

portage trail

ATTEAN POND

P

Bog Pond

Camel Rips

No. 5 Bog

Attean Falls

Holeb Falls

N

MOOSE RIVER

0   1.0   2.0   portage trail

miles

Spencer Rips

and marshes cover the landscape, supporting a large moose population. We saw two moose on our trip, and friends who made the same trip a year earlier saw five. In the evening, beavers swam in front of us, eventually slapping the water with their tails before diving out of sight as we ventured too near.

The Moose River Bow loop totally encloses Number 5 Bog, a National Natural Landmark. Inaccessible except by foot down an old logging road that takes off north from Spencer Rips, this unique, pristine fen of more than 1,500 acres may be the most remote of the Northeast's large peatlands. Formed 10,000 years ago as glaciers retreated and now protected from logging and other development, Number 5 Bog sports large stands of jack pine, tamarack, and white cedar. Its sphagnum-covered open areas provide habitat for many plant species, including several rare orchids. The area, wetter than most other peatlands in Maine, such as the Great Heath just northeast of Cherryfield, even boasts a substantial 90-acre pond, Bog Pond.

Other natural wonders abound in this area, starting with Attean Pond. Extraordinarily scenic, the pond's nearly 60 islands scatter across 4 square miles, with forested mountains all around. As you approach Jackman on Route 201, stop at the turnout overlooking the pond for a bird's-eye view of this often-photographed wonder.

The loop trip starts at the Attean Pond access. After paddling to the right (west) 4 miles across Attean Pond, portage 1.2 miles into Holeb Pond on a well-

Clouds roll above a kayaker on Attean Pond. Photo: Jerry and Marcy Monkman/ Ecophotography

marked trail with boardwalks across swampy areas. When you get to the wide logging road after 1 mile, turn right, cross the railroad track, watch for a small sign, and take an immediate left for the last little segment down to Holeb Pond. Paddle across Holeb Pond to its outlet, Holeb Stream, which joins the Moose River, which, in turn, flows back into Attean Pond.

Smaller than Attean and with many fewer islands, Holeb Pond also sits among beautiful surroundings, with mountains off in the distance. Large granite boulders at the put-in enhance the scenic quality. Holeb Pond generally sees less traffic due to more difficult access, much to the liking of the mature bald eagle we watched as it perched in a large white pine. If you have time, explore the coves and islands on the right, midway down the pond.

Note the tall, steeplelike spires of the many large balsam firs along the Moose River. Some very large tamaracks mix in among the firs, while alders cover the shoreline for miles and miles. Occasional marshy openings intrude on the alders, and these locations, along with entering streams and side channels, provide moose viewing opportunities.

In most places, the Moose River moves along slowly, but because the water drops 73 feet between Holeb and Attean ponds, you must portage around a few falls; some you can run during high water. By August in most years, you must portage Camel Rips and Spencer Rips, along with Holeb Falls and Attean Falls. Mercifully, these relatively short portages—some just a few feet—do not compare with the long portage into Holeb Pond. Campsites lie adjacent to these portages. Finding the portage at Holeb Falls can present quite a challenge.

As shown on the map, paddle to the left into the side channel then take an immediate right, looking for moose to the left. Go over two short drops on this, the Moose River's left channel. Then, after about 0.5 mile, take a sharp left down an easy-to-miss, very narrow side channel, and go about 150 feet to the take-out.

Holeb Falls, just past the trip's midpoint, is back out on the main river. To see it, after the portage, cross the river to the campsite at the base of the riffle. From there a trail takes you up to the falls.

Between Holeb and Attean falls, the river can seem a little monotonous. You eventually will hope never to see alders again, and you wholeheartedly will root for the beaver in its attempt to gorge on alder bark. To break the monotony, take the time to explore the streams, side channels, and marshy areas along the banks. The marshiest area on the loop—and the best area to look for moose— lies between the falls. We saw a great horned owl along here. Just as the river turns north toward Attean Pond, Catheart and other tall peaks appear off to the east and should help take your mind off the endless alders.

Two short, marked portages confront you at Attean Falls, the first on the left, the second on the right. You paddle a few hundred feet between them.

Upon returning to Attean Pond, it will look as though the pond had shrunk. Most islands cluster between Moose River inlet and the take-out point, blocking the rest of the lake from view. These islands effectively damp wind-driven swells that might be a problem on more open water. Navigating through them can be somewhat of a challenge, especially if you don't use your compass. A hint: Three narrow valleys, with no hills, lead down to the water. You have just left one, the Moose River. The one to the left leads to Holeb Pond. Head for the one to the right to get to the access by paddling north-northwest about 2 miles and then northeast.

Tamarack

This region spans hundreds of miles of forests, lakes, rivers, and mountains in central and northwestern Maine; we include 14 destinations here. Moosehead Lake, at 117 square miles, is the largest lake contained within a single state east of the Mississippi. Just to the east of it lies the 100-Mile Wilderness, running from Monson to Baxter State Park and Mount Katahdin. Within this region, AMC's Maine Woods land contains Long Pond (Trip 73), with its spectacular views of surrounding mountains and AMC's Gorman Chairback Lodge & Cabins at its eastern end, as well as many other ponds, some of which boast increasingly rare populations of native brook trout. In 2004, AMC began to operate Little Lyford Lodge & Cabins, a traditional Maine sporting camp dating back to 1874, which serves as an excellent base for exploring the area. Since then, AMC has acquired more land, including around First, Second, and Third Branch ponds (Trip 75), which we added for the 3rd edition, and the Roach ponds (Trip 74), where we added Second Roach to Third and Fourth Roach ponds. At the time of this writing, AMC's rebuilt Medawisla Lodge & Cabins is slated to open in 2017 at Second Roach Pond's western end. For more information, see "Maine Woods: Great Northern Forest Resource," on page 256.

Other featured trips include Bald Mountain Pond (Trip 69), nestled along the Appalachian Trail, where you should see moose; Debsconeag lakes (Trip 78), protected in a 41,000-acre wilderness, where you paddle with Mount Katahdin as a backdrop; and spectacular Lobster Lake (Trip 80), with its unique geology and stands of old-growth red pine.

68 | Branns Mill Pond

Branns Mill Pond takes relatively little time to explore compared with larger lakes, but the mile or so you can paddle up the inlet brook into a wildlife management area greatly increases your chance of spotting animals and interesting plants. Expect to see loons, ospreys, possibly otters and white-tailed deer, and high aquatic plant diversity.

Location: Dover-Foxcroft
Maps: *Maine Atlas & Gazetteer*, Map 32: C2, C3; USGS Garland
Area: 271 acres
Time: 4 hours
Habitat Type: Shallow, marshy pond and stream
Fish: Brook trout, white perch, chain pickerel (see fish advisories, Appendix A)
Take Note: Some development

GETTING THERE
From Dexter at the junction of Routes 7 and 23/Grove Street, go 6.9 miles north on Route 7 and turn right on Merrills Mills Road. Go 1.5 miles (cumulative: 8.4 miles) and turn right on Notch Road. Go 0.9 mile (9.3 miles) to the access on the left. (45° 6.294′ N, 69° 9.990′ W).

WHAT YOU'LL SEE
Branns Mill Pond, a real gem, brims with wildlife and provides a wonderful place to explore, especially in early morning or late afternoon. On a windy day when the area's other lakes bristle with whitecaps, this pond remains much quieter and more suitable for paddling.

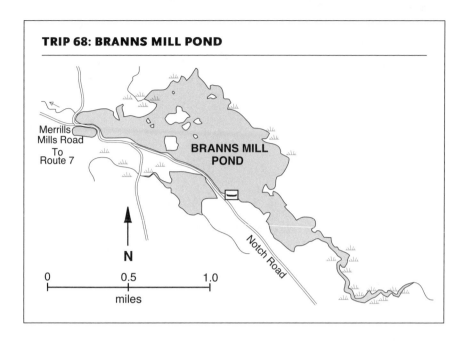

TRIP 68: BRANNS MILL POND

Merrills
Mills Road
To
Route 7

BRANNS MILL
POND

N

Notch Road

0   0.5   1.0

miles

From the access, paddle southeast through the pond's narrow section into the inlet brook. This lazy channel winds about 1 mile through biologically rich and highly diverse marsh habitat. Floating aquatic plants, especially yellow pondlily, crowd the channel by early summer. Dense stands of cattail occur in places, but elsewhere sedges, rushes, alders, sphagnum, and heaths dominate the marsh. Part of the creek lies within the Bud Leavitt Wildlife Management Area.

As we paddled quietly along here, we suddenly heard a distinct munching sound. Muskrat? Beaver? Then, 15 feet away, the bushes rustled, and out swam an otter. From the sound, one can only conclude they enjoy eating as much as they seem to enjoy everything else. As dusk approached, we also saw a muskrat swimming along the creek and several beavers that loudly announced our passage with slapping tails.

As you paddle up the creek, the channel narrows gradually and the current picks up. After poling over the remains of an old beaver dam, the sound of running water meant we were nearing the end of our upstream explorations. At the channel's end, we came to a large stone wall and the ruins of a structure—probably Branns Mill, but we have not been able to learn anything of the history.

Notice that trees growing on the banks get progressively shorter closer to the stream, evidence of a narrowing channel. Aquatic plants and sphagnum gradually expand out over the water's surface. Then shrubs, such as leatherleaf and alder, take hold. As a root mat builds up, tamarack and cedar become established. You can see this succession clearly as you look from water's edge to the forest on higher ground.

An interesting geology underlies this area. Unlike the granite covering most of central and northern Maine, sedimentary rock lies here. In places, the layered rock tilted up before the stream channel eroded it so you'll pass jagged rocks extending out of the water like tombstones. Use caution paddling here; unlike rounded granite boulders, this jagged shale could puncture your boat.

While we would choose the inlet channel first for exploration, we enjoyed the rest of the pond, as well. The narrow section between the access and the inlet creek, as well as the far western tip by the dam, suffer from development, but most of the pond remains fairly natural. Marshy areas, rich with wildlife, extend along the northern shore. We saw at least one loon pair and suspect they nest on one of the many islands, relatively safe from predators. Open areas on a few of these islands would make nice picnic spots, but we do not suggest overnight camping.

69 | Bald Mountain Pond

Scenic vistas await you at Bald Mountain Pond, with the Appalachian Trail skirting the north shore. This popular lake is best paddled midweek or early or late in the season. It's a great place to see loons, moose, and other wildlife.

Location: Bald Mountain Township
Maps: *Maine Atlas & Gazetteer*, Map 31: A1, B1; USGS Bald Mountain Pond
Area: 1,152 acres
Time: All day
Habitat Type: Deep, clear pond; forested hillsides
Fish: Brook trout, blueback trout (see fish advisories, Appendix A)
Take Note: No personal watercraft; campfire permits required, 207-827-1800

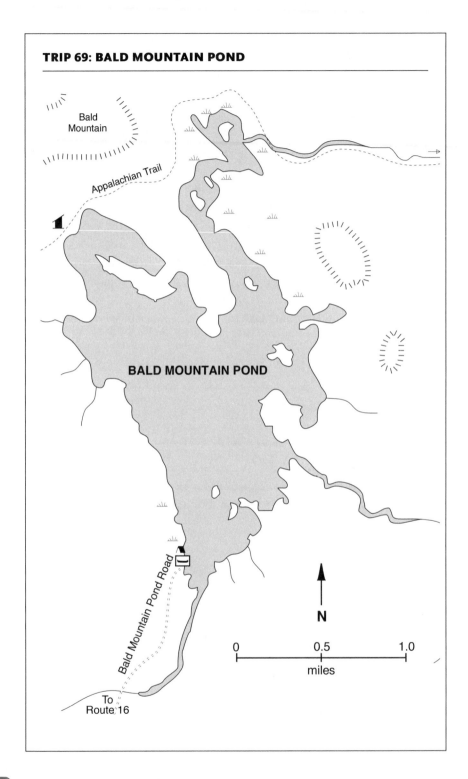

GETTING THERE

From Bingham, at the junction of Routes 16 and 201, go 5.4 miles east on Route 16 and turn left on Townline Road. Go 2.8 miles (cumulative: 8.2 miles) and turn right on Deadwater Road. Go 0.1 mile (8.3 miles) and veer left. Go 2.1 miles (10.4 miles) and veer right. Go 1.8 miles (12.2 miles) and turn diagonally right onto Bald Mountain Pond Road. Go 4.6 miles (16.8 miles) and stay left. Go 3 miles (19.8 miles) straight to the access. (45° 14.598′ N, 69° 44.004′ W)

WHAT YOU'LL SEE

The Appalachian Trail skirts Bald Mountain Pond's northern shore, part of the Maine Public Reserve Land system. A wild place in a beautiful setting, aptly named Bald Mountain dominates the western skyline. The pond draws large crowds on summer weekends, although fewer people camp here than at nearby Austin Pond. A visit here would be more satisfying during the week or after Labor Day.

When we paddled out on the last Sunday in July at 6:30 A.M., the resident loons were the only other bodies making ripples on the placid surface for the first hour and a half after sunrise, while the weekend partiers slept in. The only noise, other than an occasional loon call, came from the large population of white-throated sparrows, with their *Old Sam Peabody, Peabody, Peabody* call. We saw lots of wildlife, including a cow moose in the northeast cove, submerged to her nostrils in an attempt to escape a huge cloud of biting flies. Several of these tenacious flies broke off from the pack and annoyed us for half an hour after our encounter with the moose.

Heavily forested islands enhance the picturesque nature of Bald Mountain Pond. Hundreds of granite boulders dimple the surface in places; unfortunately for boat hulls, many of these rocks hide out barely submerged. Go cautiously when paddling near shore and when exploring the many inlets. The boulder-strewn northern inlet is one of the most scenic areas, making paddling up there well worthwhile.

White and red pine, cedar, balsam fir, and spruce grow right down to the water, and a fair number of yellow birch, maple, and white birch appear in and among the conifers. American white waterlilies abound in the coves and shallower parts. Bird species include ring-billed gulls, red-breasted mergansers, loons, black ducks, belted kingfishers, and double-crested cormorants.

Thanks to the many coves and inlets dotting the 14-mile-long shoreline, it takes several hours to explore fully this wonderful place. Paddle out early to maximize wildlife viewing, and come during the week to avoid the weekend camping parties.

70 | West Shirley Bog

West Shirley Bog, one of the best places in the Moosehead Lake region to see moose, provides hours of quietwater paddling. Look for beavers, moose, deer, and bog vegetation, including sundew, pitcher plants, bog laurel, and dragon's mouth orchid.

Location: Moose Junction Township, Shirley
Maps: *Maine Atlas & Gazetteer*, Map 41: E1, E2; USGS Bald Mountain Pond, Big Squaw Pond
Area: 275 acres
Time: 4 hours
Habitat Type: Shallow, marshy pond
Fish: Brook trout (see fish advisories, Appendix A)
Take Note: Limited parking along road

GETTING THERE
From Monson, at the junction of Routes 6 and 15 with Water Street, go 6.8 miles northwest on Routes 6 and 15, and turn left on Lower Shirley Corner Road. Go 1.8 miles (cumulative: 8.6 miles) and bear left on West/CCC roads. Go 3.4 miles (12 miles) to the access on the right, just before the bridge. (45° 21.360′ N, 69° 41.220′ W)

WHAT YOU'LL SEE
West Shirley Bog, a quiet, secluded marshy section of the West Branch Piscataquis River near its headwaters, grows thick with northern bog vegetation. During an early-July paddle, hundreds of northern pitcher plant (*Sarracenia purpurea*) flowers peaked above the surrounding vegetation, along with bog laurel (*Kalmia polifolia*) and dragon's mouth orchid (*Arethusa bulbosa*). Sweetgale dominates here, interspersed with leatherleaf, bog rosemary, cranberry, and a wide variety of grasses, sedges, and rushes. Having explored so much of New England in more southern areas, we were struck by the total absence of invasive plants here.

An arm of the bog extends to the northwest shortly after you head out from the hand-carry access by the bridge. This arm gets progressively narrower as you paddle away from the main channel, eventually ending in some inlet creeks with passage blocked by alders. Tall, conical spires of balsam fir stand farther from the water.

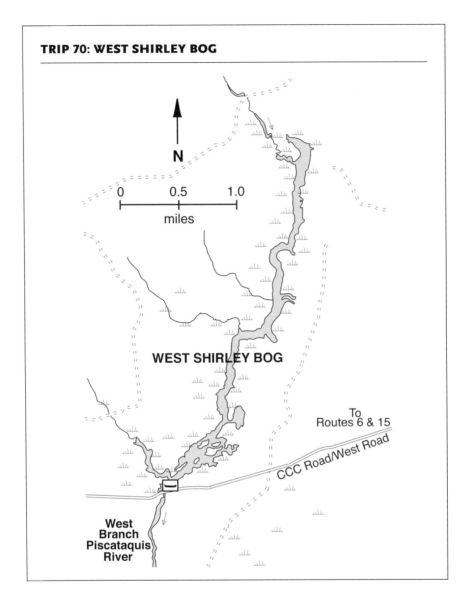

The main channel continues northeast then north for several miles of wonderful paddling. The farther north, the wilder it seems, with feathery tamarack trees giving the place a very northern feel. Along with the deep pinks from bog laurel, sizeable patches of bright-yellow horned bladderwort (*Utricularia cornuta*) grace the water's edge, providing lots of visual diversity. You may also see blue flag iris (*Iris versicolor*), which grows sparsely here.

On the right side after leaving the access, you can explore some deep,

We saw a black bear near this spot, the access to West Shirley Bog.

protected coves and connected ponds. Look for an island here with a stand of trees in its center. We didn't think we would be able to navigate around it with the summer growth of vegetation, but we managed to sneak through—after running into a few dead ends and almost giving up. By late summer, this may not be possible, especially in a dry year, but in spring you should have no problem making your way around.

Surprisingly, about halfway up the waterway a rock outcropping on the western side juts out into the water, making a wonderful spot for a picnic lunch or a rest. If nothing else, it provides an easy place to pull up and get out of your boat to stretch. At the northern end, you can explore the inlet brooks a short way, but your passage soon will be blocked.

We saw ample sign of beavers and moose, both often spotted here. We heard lots of songbirds, and we also saw a bear along the road, near the access.

71 | Indian Pond

Indian Pond provides one or more days of paddling in the heart of moose country. The long, relatively narrow lake can suffer from south winds, but much of the shore is usually protected. Besides moose, expect to see loons, bald eagles, ospreys, beavers, and more.

Location: Big Moose Township, Chase Stream Township, Indian Stream Township, Sapling Township
Maps: *Maine Atlas & Gazetteer*, Map 40: C4, C5, D4, D5; USGS Indian Pond North, Indian Pond South
Area: 3,746 acres
Time: All day or multiday trip
Habitat Type: Long, large, deep lake
Fish: Brook trout, lake trout, landlocked salmon (see fish advisories, Appendix A)
Information: Indian Pond Campground, 800-371-7774
Take Note: Wind from the south can cause treacherous conditions; campfire permits required, 207-827-1800

GETTING THERE
There are three access points; easiest is the southern access.

Southern Access. From The Forks, at the junction of Route 201 and Lake Moxie Road, go 5.2 miles on Lake Moxie Road and turn left on Indian Pond Road. Go 7.3 miles (cumulative: 12.5 miles), veer left, and go 0.6 mile (13.1 miles) to Indian Pond Campground and the access on the right. (45° 27.390′ N, 69° 51.726′ W)

Northeast Access. High-clearance vehicle necessary. From Rockwood, at the junction of Routes 6 and 15 with Village Road south, go 10.2 miles south on Routes 6/15 and turn right. Go 4.3 miles (cumulative: 14.5 miles), staying straight at junctions, to the access. (45° 32.880′ N, 69° 46.446′ W)

West Outlet. High-clearance vehicle necessary. From Rockwood, at the junction of Routes 6 and 15 with Village Road south, go 1.3 miles south on Routes 6/15 and turn right on Somerset Road. Go 4.8 miles (cumulative: 6.1 miles), veer left, and go 2.8 miles (8.9 miles) to the access. (45° 33.810′ N, 69° 47.616′ W)

TRIP 71: INDIAN POND

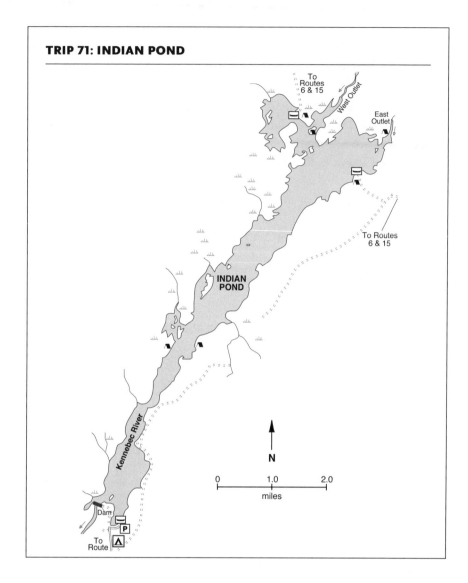

WHAT YOU'LL SEE

Indian Pond, large and very scenic, truly is the country of the pointed firs. Little development intrudes on the shoreline, and the few boats plying the water have 35 miles of shoreline and nearly 6 square miles of surface to share. This wild-life paradise sports healthy populations of deer, moose, bears, coyotes, foxes, beavers, ospreys, eagles, loons, and fish. One must be wary of winds, but it still represents a great opportunity for a two- to four-day family trip.

In preparation for your trip here, you can camp overnight at Indian Pond Campground (reservations advised). A tremendous amount of congestion

A kayaker fishes on Indian Pond. Photo: Jerry and Marcy Monkman/EcoPhotography

occurs on the roads and at the pond's southern end, most of it from rafters and kayakers testing their ability to float after getting dumped on the Class IV and V rapids of the Kennebec River Gorge below Indian Pond. When we paddled here, as we gazed out from the access over the picturesque southern end of Indian Pond, we could see only one other boat.

Make sure you paddle the more scenic north end. It sees far fewer people and motorboats. Most of the marshy areas and islands occur from the midpoint up to the north end, the heart of moose country. We saw five moose along the road while driving from Greenville to Rockwood late one evening, and every time we've come here, we've seen moose. The shallow, marshy northern end provides the best chance. Be sure to explore the two large, marshy coves about halfway up the left side. Both contain plenty of moose habitat.

White and red pines, balsam fir, tamarack, cedar, and spruce blanket the shores and islands on the lake's north end. Occasional red maple and white birch occur here and there, and a well-developed understory lines the shore. Lots of drowned stumps populate the northwest arm, a legacy of the 50-year-old Harris Dam at the south end.

We saw many species of birds here in addition to ospreys and loons, including song sparrows, spotted sandpipers, hermit thrushes, ring-billed gulls, and cedar waxwings.

72 | Prong Pond

Prong Pond's long arms provide lots of shoreline to paddle and also offer wind protection. Besides the bog vegetation and surrounding boreal forest, this is one of the best places to look for moose in the early morning or evening. You should also see loons here.

Location: Beaver Cove, Greenville
Maps: *Maine Atlas & Gazetteer*, Map 41: C3; USGS Lily Bay
Area: 427 acres
Time: 4 hours
Habitat Type: Shallow pond with many marshy areas
Fish: Brook trout, smallmouth bass (see fish advisories, Appendix A)
Take Note: Campfire permits required, 207-827-1800

GETTING THERE

From Greenville, where Routes 6 and 15 turn left, go 6.8 miles north on Main Street/Lily Bay Road, turn right on Prong Pond Road, and immediately turn right again. Go 0.2 mile (cumulative: 7 miles) to the access. (45° 32.784′ N, 69° 32.484′ W)

WHAT YOU'LL SEE

Prong Pond, a little-noticed pond on the southeast side of giant Moosehead Lake, can provide a pleasant day of paddling, especially when wind has whipped Moosehead and other large lakes in the region to a froth. Although it looks small, the pond offers 9 miles of perimeter to explore, extending in several long, narrow arms, or prongs. Cedar, white pine, spruce, paper birch, and hemlock line the pond's rocky shoreline. Along some sections, stately red pine groves rise from shore; a nice campsite lies under some of these pines on a point of land along the pond's eastern shore.

Narrow arms extending east and west provide a great opportunity to observe northern bog flora, including pitcher plant, with its nodding flowers extending above the grasses; sedges; sweetgale; leatherleaf; swamp rose; cranberry; and other low vegetation. At ground level, amid the sphagnum, look for the diminutive red leaves of sundew. Both pitcher plants and sundews obtain some of their nourishment from insects; see "Carnivorous Plants: The Table is Turned," on page 108.

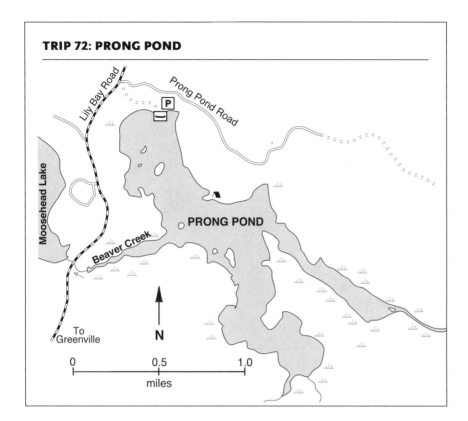

TRIP 72: PRONG POND

(Map labels:) Lily Bay Road · Prong Pond Road · P · Moosehead Lake · PRONG POND · Beaver Creek · To Greenville · N · 0   0.5   1.0 · miles

Though by no means as common as pitcher plants and sundews, keep an eye out for two of Maine's most beautiful orchids: rose pogonia and *Calopogon*, or grass pink. We saw several good-size patches of rose pogonia (*Pogonia ophioglossoides*), which has one or two flowers on the stem and a small lanceolate leaf. We saw only two *Calopogon* orchids (*Calopogon pulchellus*), which has three or more flowers and long, grasslike leaves. We watched a fascinating and beautiful crab spider on the *Calopogon* flower, waiting for an insect to come along. The spider, all white except for a pink band on either side of its globelike body and well camouflaged against the flower backdrop, sat motionless with eight long legs outstretched in four pairs and fangs no doubt ready to impart a fatal dose of venom to a visiting pollinator. This spider has the ability to adapt its coloration to that of different plants.

Prong's long, shallow east arm has an extremely mucky bottom. Even if your paddle does not sink into muck, agitation will stir up sediment and release bubbles of swamp gas, mostly methane. In some places, the water seemed to boil behind us as we paddled along. At the arm's far eastern tip, you will reach a beaver dam and lodge.

A paddler passes a sunny day on Prong Pond. Photo: Jerry and Marcy Monkman/EcoPhotography

Beaver Creek, the boglike arm extending to the west, has the same plants as the east arm. We noticed more tamarack, the larger ones farther back from the water marking the encroachment of land into the quiet stream. The many dead trees along here—sun-whitened snags and stumps—provide nesting habitat for tree swallows. We watched a sharp-shinned hawk dart between these snags as it tried to elude some blackbirds. Along with the possibility of camping on the pond, Lily Bay State Park offers camping a few miles away. Located on one of the prettiest areas of mammoth Moosehead Lake, dozens of islands protect the bay from wind.

73 | Long Pond

AMC's Long Pond sits among scenic, forested peaks: White Cap, Chairback, Barren, and Baker mountains. You should see loons, white-tailed deer, moose, otters, and beavers.

Location: Bowdoin College Grant East and West, Elliotsville Township, T7 R9 NWP

Maps: *Maine Atlas & Gazetteer*, Map 41: D5 and Map 42: D1; USGS Barren Mountain West

Area: 643 acres

Time: 4 hours

Habitat Type: Narrow pond elongated on an east-west axis

Fish: Brook trout, lake trout, landlocked salmon (see fish advisories, Appendix A)

Information: Lodging at AMC's Gorman Chairback Lodge & Cabins (on Long Pond) and AMC's Little Lyford Lodge & Cabins (nearby), outdoors.org/lodging, 603-466-2727; for hiking opportunities, see *Maine Mountain Guide*, by Carey Michael Kish (AMC Books, outdoors.org/amcstore)

Take Note: Campfire permit required, 207-827-1800; Ki-Jo Mary Multiple Use Forest camping and entrance fees required, northmainewoods.org; 4WD with good clearance recommended

GETTING THERE

From Greenville, where Routes 6 and 15 turn left, go north on Main Street/Lily Bay Road for 100 yards and turn right on Pleasant Street/East Road. Go straight 12.4 miles to the Hedgehog Checkpoint (fee). Continue 1.8 miles (cumulative: 14.2 miles) and turn right on Greenville–KI Road. Go 1.1 miles (15.3 miles) and turn right on Long Pond Road. Go 2.2 miles (17.5 miles) to the bridge over Trout Brook then go another 100 yards, turn left, and go 0.2 mile (17.7 miles) to the campsite. (45° 27.840′ N, 69° 22.824′ W)

WHAT YOU'LL SEE

Long Pond, which lies within a 70,000-acre parcel now owned and managed by the Appalachian Mountain Club, provides a wonderful place to paddle, especially when winds from the north or south turn the region's larger lakes into

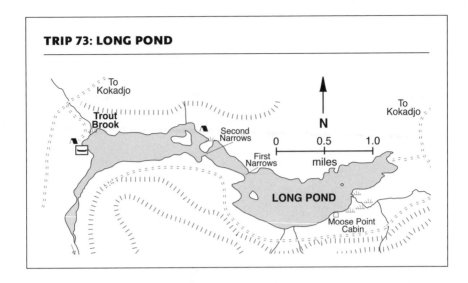

TRIP 73: LONG POND

a foaming froth. Long Pond's east-west axis, islands, and narrow width provide not only wind protection but also a lengthy shoreline to explore. For a map of the greater area, see page 257.

Deciduous trees have repopulated logged areas on the hillsides. Look for large stands of conifers on steeper slopes and on the spectacular, distant mountains you can see from many vantage points around the pond. Portage around the right side of an old dam at the outlet to explore a small flowage of about 75 acres. Look here for deer and moose that often frequent this area. You also may see beavers and otters. Besides the area at the outlet, two more small, marshy areas are located on the pond's east side.

The few camps along the shore—including rustic log cabins that date to the 1800s—do not mar the wild feel of Long Pond. The pond is also known for its great spring fishing.

While in this area, you may wish to visit two popular hiking destinations, The Hermitage and Gulf Hagas, both accessible from the Appalachian Trail where it crosses Greenville–KI Road, about 0.5 mile east of the turnoff onto Long Pond Road. The Hermitage, a National Natural Landmark, consists of a 35-acre stand of old-growth pine on a bluff overlooking the West Branch of the Pleasant River, about 0.5 mile from the road. Gulf Hagas—the 4-mile chasm known as "the Grand Canyon of Maine," with five major and many smaller waterfalls, also a National Natural Landmark—lies along Gulf Hagas Rim Trail. This strenuous loop hike takes off from the Appalachian Trail about 1.5 miles from the road and requires fording the West Branch of Pleasant River, which

Gulf Hagas, a spectacular gorge cut through the lush 100-Mile Wilderness by the West Branch of the Pleasant River, lies not far from Long Pond. Photo: Sarah Jane Shangraw

may be decidedly unpleasant at times of high water. That said, it is worth the effort to view the falls and sheer slate walls rising 400 feet above the streambed. Viewing fall foliage in the gorge makes the trip even more spectacular; watch your footing on the rim trail, particularly when covered by wet leaves or at any time when wet.

74 | Second, Third, and Fourth Roach Ponds

The scenic Roach ponds, now part of AMC's Maine Woods land, no longer suffer from extensive clear-cutting. These remote ponds offer an outstanding opportunity to see wildlife. We've spotted loons, bald eagles, ospreys, moose, otters, beavers, and black bears here.

Location: Shawtown Township, T1 R12 WELS
Maps: *Maine Atlas & Gazetteer*, Map 42: A1, B1, B2; USGS Farrar Mountain, Wadleigh Mountain

Area: Second Roach Pond, 970 acres; Third Roach Pond, 570 acres; Fourth Roach Pond, 266 acres
Time: Multiday; shorter trips possible
Habitat Type: Wilderness ponds, rich with wildlife
Fish: Brook trout, landlocked salmon, white perch (see fish advisories, Appendix A)
Information: Lodging at AMC's Medawisla Lodge & Cabins, outdoors.org/lodging, 207-358-5187 (scheduled to open in 2017)
Take Note: No personal watercraft; campfire permits required, 207-827-1800

GETTING THERE

Second Roach Pond. From Greenville, go north about 18 miles on Main Street/Lily Bay Road to Kokadjo. After crossing the bridge in Kokadjo, go 0.4 mile on North Shore Road and turn left on Sias Hill Road. Go 1.5 miles (cumulative: 1.9 miles) and turn right on Smithtown Road. Stay on the main road for 5.9 miles (7.8 miles) and turn left to AMC's Medawisla Lodge and Second Roach Pond. (45° 40.560′ N, 69° 19.584′ W)

   Fourth Roach Pond. From the Medawisla access road, continue 4.3 miles (cumulative: 12.1 miles) on Smithtown Road, park next to a green gate, and carry your boat 0.5 mile to the pond. A boat dolly may be available. (45° 38.256′N, 69° 15.810′ W)

   Third Roach Pond Southeast Arm. From the Medawisla access road, continue 6.8 miles (cumulative: 14.6 miles) on Smithtown Road to a small parking area on the left. Carry your boat 250 yards downhill to the pond. (45° 37.986′ N, 69° 13.140′ W)

   Third Roach Pond Northeast Arm. From the Medawisla access road, continue 8.7 miles (cumulative: 16.5 miles) on Smithtown Road, staying on main road, then turn left at the T. Go 1 mile (17.5 miles) to the access on the left: the third of three unimproved roads in quick succession. Carry your boat 200 yards down to the pond. (45° 39.642′ N, 69° 13.740′W)

WHAT YOU'LL SEE

The abundant wildlife that awaits you makes the trip into remote Second, Third, and Fourth Roach ponds well worth the effort. If you camp at the primitive campsites, you would likely have the whole place to yourself—along with the moose, deer, otters, eagles, and other wildlife that abounds.

   During two days on Third and Fourth Roach ponds in late July, we saw four moose, including a very large bull; a deer with two fawns; two otters; loons,

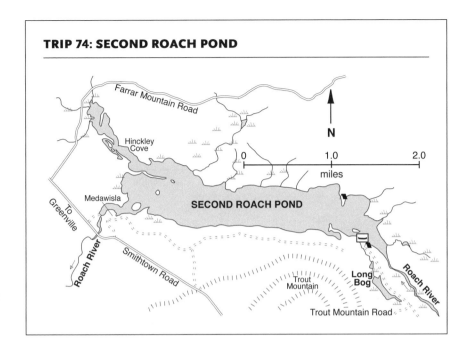

TRIP 74: SECOND ROACH POND

including one pair with two chicks; a large family of common mergansers; and a bald eagles. During a more recent visit, camping at one of the new campsites on Second Road Pond, we were treated to spectacular skies and several industrious beaver. In the amount and variety of wildlife we have seen, these ponds rank near the top.

A typical northern Maine woodland of spruce, balsam fir, white pine, cedar, and paper birch extends away from the rocky shoreline. On the long point of land reaching south from Third into Fourth Roach Pond, however, you will see a very different red pine forest. You can get out and walk, picnic, or camp under the open red pine canopy very easily, unlike most other forest types in this area.

Marshy areas occur at the ends of the various fingers. At the northeast end of Third Roach, the water becomes very shallow, with yellow pondlilies and other floating vegetation, while grasses and sedges grow along the perimeter. Right at the tip, we watched a bull moose neck-deep in the ooze, grazing on this vegetation while protecting itself from biting flies. It is remarkable how moose can extract themselves after wallowing in the underlying muck.

Third and Fourth Roach ponds connect via a small, rocky stream. In spring, you can probably paddle between these ponds, but by midsummer, you need to wade through the couple hundred feet of this stream, pulling your boat.

From these ponds, one used to get a clear view of extensive clear-cutting that

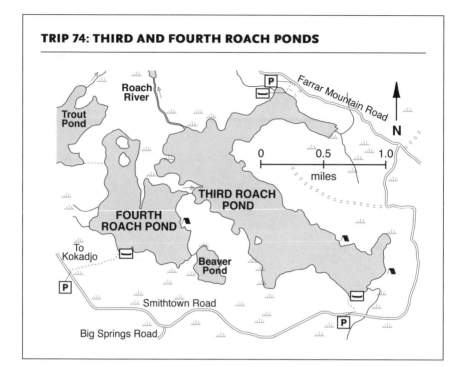

TRIP 74: THIRD AND FOURTH ROACH PONDS

Roach River

Trout Pond

Roach River

Farrar Mountain Road

N

0   0.5   1.0
miles

THIRD ROACH POND

FOURTH ROACH POND

To Kokadjo

Beaver Pond

Smithtown Road

Big Springs Road

A bull moose makes for tree cover at the northeastern cove on Third Roach Pond.

long took place on the surrounding hills, separated only by a paper-thin "beauty strip"—that ribbon of un-cut woods left along the perimeter of most ponds. But since AMC acquired the Roach Ponds Tract, the logging scars are healing, although some limited clear-cutting will continue, including the gradual removal of plantation trees planted by Plum Creek Timber Company.

The wonderful campsite at Third Roach Pond's southeast end backs up against a hill rising 700 feet from the pond and offers a protected sandy beach for a relaxing swim after a day of exploration.

Second Roach Pond is now the most accessible of these three ponds, with paddling access near the rebuilt Medawisla Lodge & Cabins, replacing the old buildings that were torn down (scheduled to open in 2017). Medawisla is an American Indian name for loon, and the 1981 movie *On Golden Pond* featured loon recordings made here.

75 | First, Second, and Third West Branch Ponds

These small ponds, surrounded by deep woodlands and scenic peaks, are great places to look for wildlife, including loons, bald eagles, moose, otters, and more.

Location: Shawtown Township
Maps: *Maine Atlas & Gazetteer*, Map 42: B1, B2, C1; USGS Hay Mountain
Area: First West Branch Pond, 119 acres; Second and Third West Branch ponds, 214 acres
Time: 4 hours
Habitat Type: Shallow ponds with wooded and marshy shorelines
Fish: Brook trout (see fish advisories, Appendix A)
Take Note: Requires driving for 10 miles on a gravel road; last few miles fairly rough; campfire permit required, 207-827-1800

GETTING THERE
First West Branch Pond. From Greenville, where Routes 6 and 15 turn left, go 17.5 miles north on Main Street/Lily Bay Road and turn right on Frenchtown Road. Go 10.6 miles (cumulative: 28.1 miles) to the access on the right. (45° 35.370′ N, 69° 17.058′ W)

   Second and Third West Branch ponds. As above, then continue 0.5 mile (cumulative: 28.6 miles) on Frenchtown Road, staying right at the fork, to the access on the left. Carry about 100 yards to the water. (45° 35.304′ N, 69° 16.542′ W)

WHAT YOU'LL SEE
When we arrived at Second West Branch Pond on an early evening in early July, a cow moose grazed belly-deep on wetland vegetation perhaps 100 feet from the access—seemingly unperturbed by our activities. A loon pair watched from about the same distance.

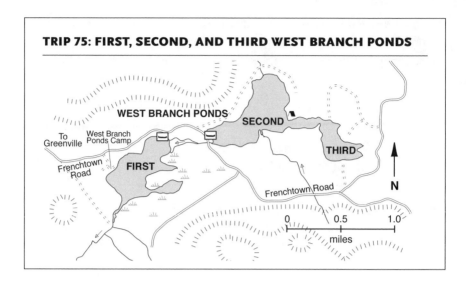

TRIP 75: FIRST, SECOND, AND THIRD WEST BRANCH PONDS

Most of Second West Branch Pond is now owned by the Appalachian Mountain Club and is part of the 29,500-acre Roach Pond Tract AMC acquired from Plum Creek Timber Company in 2009. This tract is part of AMC's 70,000 acres of land that contributes to a protected, 60-mile corridor from Moosehead Lake to Baxter State Park in an area known as the 100-Mile Wilderness.

One can see why AMC acquired this land, in the heart of the North Maine Woods. The spectacular West Branch ponds nestle beneath White Cap Mountain, Hay Mountain, and West Peak to the south, which carry the Appalachian Trail. Smaller Hedgehog Mountain and Black Pinnacle lie to the west and north.

Second West Branch Pond has a remote feel to it, surrounded by deep, diverse woodlands consisting of northern white cedar, balsam fir, red spruce, red pine, white pine (not many), white birch, and sugar maple. Marshy shoreline areas grow thick with sweetgale, some leatherleaf, bog laurel (in bloom in early July), alder, and other wetland shrubs. In the marshy shallows, a variety of grasses, rushes, and sedges grow. Where pond depth allows, you will find floating vegetation as well.

Along with the moose near the access, we saw a deer in one of the pond's coves, and we watched a beaver hard at work building up its winter store of branches.

Of the three, Second West Branch Pond is our favorite. At the access you will see more than a dozen canoes, rowboats, and kayaks stored there, but we don't get the sense that many of these boats are widely used.

In 2016 AMC built a nice campsite on the western shore, just north of the narrow extension into Third West Branch Pond, including several nice tenting sites and a new outhouse.

Boats are available for paddling or rowing on scenic First West Branch Pond.

From Second West Branch Pond you can—barely—thread your way through to the smaller Third West Branch Pond via a shallow, boulder-strewn connector. Expect to get a few scratches on your boat if you paddle through here; you might want to avoid bringing a treasured cedar-strip canoe. Paddling back into Second, one of us got out and waded in the shallow water between the many boulders, guiding the canoe along. There are a few cabins and camps on Third West Branch Pond, but we didn't see any people.

After leaving Second West Branch Pond, we drove to the access to First West Branch Pond. Much like Second, First West Branch Pond is also mostly within the AMC Roach Pond Tract. Not too far from the access, you will come to West Branch Ponds Camp, which is a wonderful, family-owned (since around 1870) sporting camp. This is the only non-AMC land on First West Branch Pond. There are a half-dozen cabins, and guests are served three meals a day. Cabin rentals come with a canoe, so you don't have to bring your own—as long as you're content to limit your paddling to First West Branch Pond.

76 | Seboeis Lake

Seboeis Lake affords spectacular views of Katahdin off in the distance. The lake sees quite a few fishermen, but its 19 miles of shoreline provide plenty of opportunity for solitude. Expect to see loons, bald eagles, ospreys, common terns, moose, otters, and more.

Location: Lake View PLT, T4 R9 NWP
Maps: *Maine Atlas & Gazetteer*, Map 42: D5 and Map 43: C1, D1, E1; USGS Endless Lake, Ragged Mountain, Seboeis Lake
Area: 4,201 acres
Time: All day or multiday; shorter trips possible
Habitat Type: Large, deep lake
Fish: Brook trout (streams only), splake, landlocked salmon, smallmouth bass, white perch, chain pickerel (see fish advisories, Appendix A)
Information: Seboeis Lake guide, maine.gov/dacf/
Take Note: Winds from the north or south can make paddling here treacherous; no fire permits needed for designated sites; other sites, no fires allowed

GETTING THERE

Northern Access. From Millinocket, at the T-junction of Routes 11 and 157 with Katahdin Avenue, turn left on Route 11/Katahdin Avenue, go 0.3 mile, and turn right on Route 11. Go 12.5 miles (cumulative: 12.8 miles) and turn left on West Seboeis Road. Go 0.6 mile (13.4 miles) and turn left, staying on West Seboeis Road. Go 0.5 mile (13.9 miles) and stay straight. Continue 1.9 miles (15.8 miles) to the access. (45° 30.036′ N, 68° 53.382′ W)

Outlet. As above, up to where you stay straight (13.9 miles). Instead, turn left at the junction, go 5.7 miles (19.6 miles), crossing the outlet stream bridge, and turn right. Do not block access to the cottage or dam. (45° 27.240′ N, 68° 51.204′ W)

WHAT YOU'LL SEE

We paddled Seboeis Lake in July and August, entering from the northern access and from the east arm. Public Reserve Lands surround the lake.

Seboeis sees relatively heavy traffic from anglers in small boats. At times, upward of a dozen boat trailers park at the northern access. Fortunately, this

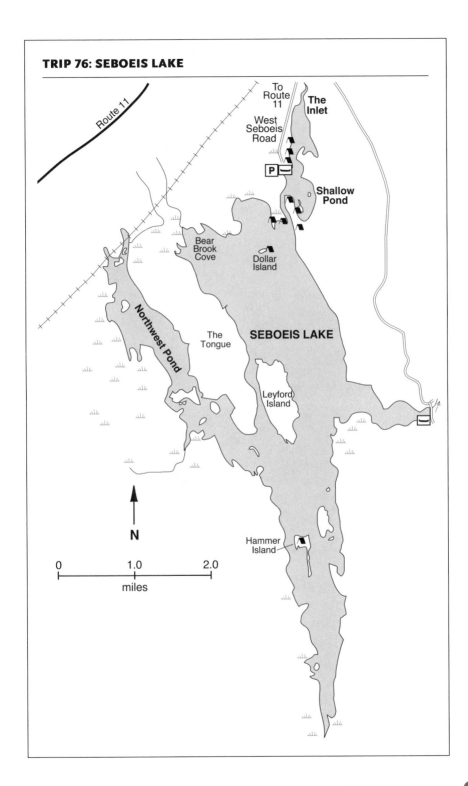

TRIP 76: SEBOEIS LAKE

Route 11

To Route 11

The Inlet

West Seboeis Road

P

Shallow Pond

Bear Brook Cove

Dollar Island

Northwest Pond

The Tongue

SEBOEIS LAKE

Leyford Island

N

Hammer Island

0   1.0   2.0
miles

Fall arrives on Seboeis Lake. Photo: Jerry and Marcy Monkman/Ecophotography

large lake provides plenty of room on its 6.5-square-mile surface. One August morning, we paddled alone until another boat appeared at 8:30 A.M.

There are 16 primitive campsites, including a few right at the access. Seven are accessible only by water. Look for one on Hammer Island's north end and one on Burn Island. By evening on a July weekend, each of these campsites probably will have an occupant. On our trips here, however, we saw at least one open campsite at the access. Sites at the access do not require fire permits.

We use the word "spectacular" to describe Seboeis Lake. You can see Mount Katahdin in Baxter State Park to the north. Beautiful, tree-covered islands are numerous, including at the entrance to Bear Brook Cove, at Northwest Pond, down in the southern arm, and up in the inlet. Large boulders line much of the shore, and if you paddle back into the outlet on the eastern shore halfway down the lake, you will see an extraordinary number of boulders both sticking up out of the water and submerged. A number of fairly large northern white cedars appear along the shore in this cove, along with cattails and other marsh vegetation.

We enjoyed exploring Shallow Pond and the inlet, particularly the marshy islands of Shallow Pond. Be wary of barely submerged stumps when you paddle in this area. Going down the channel that separates the inlet from the main lake, you will see large white and red pines lining the eastern shore. Indeed, pines and other conifers dominate the shoreline most everywhere.

Leyford Island, at 237 acres the largest island in the Bureau of Public Lands eastern holdings, is a special protection resource, with only camping and hiking allowed. Moose and deer frequent the marshy coves, particularly those along the northwest shore and in Northwest Pond.

Expect to see bald eagles, ospreys, belted kingfishers, dozens of loons, and a colony of common terns, all using different methods to catch fish in these fertile waters. Anglers come here to fish for landlocked salmon, brook trout, splake, smallmouth bass, and chain pickerel.

MOOSE: NORTH WOODS GIANT

Coming across a moose is often the high point of trips into the North Woods. We see most moose during the early morning and early evening hours, although one can see them at any time.

In nearly 25 years of doing research for three editions of this book, we've often had to drive Maine's back roads at night, and we've seen way too many moose in the middle of the road. Hard to see—both because their spindly, nearly invisible legs usually are all that show up in headlights and because their dark brown bodies blend in so well with the dark forest background—the moose presents a real road hazard. We make it a practice to drive below the speed limit on North Country back roads.

The moose, *Alces alces*, is the world's largest member of the deer family. Bull moose can stand 7 feet tall at the shoulders and range in weight from 900 to 1,800 pounds, with cow moose typically three-quarters as large. The average cow in Maine weighs about 850 pounds and the average bull about 1,100 pounds. Among North American land mammals, only bison and

Alaskan brown bears (a grizzly bear subspecies) commonly exceed the moose in weight; none approaches it in height.

The typical moose ranges over a small territory, usually just a few square miles. Well adapted to the marsh environment, moose often forage for aquatic plants in ponds and streams, sometimes standing neck-deep in water to escape hordes of biting flies. Long legs allow moose to reach tree branches and wade into bogs and snow. Thick, dense fur, sometimes 6 inches long around the neck and shoulders, helps protect the animals from biting flies. Moose have a keen sense of hearing and smell, but poor vision. When frightened, they run at speeds up to 35 MPH for short distances. Long legs help them run through bogs. They swim slowly but have been known to swim as far as 12 miles.

Moose derive most of their nourishment by browsing on trees and aquatic vegetation, but they also graze on grasses, mosses, lichens, and low herbaceous plants. Due to their long legs and short necks, they often need to bend or spread their front legs, or even drop to their knees, to feed. They may rear up to feed on tree branches, and they sometimes "ride down" saplings by straddling them and walking forward to bring upper branches into reach.

Rutting season extends from September through October but may range into November and even early December. After an eight-month gestation period, cows bear one or two calves in May or June. Younger cows generally produce just one offspring. As one might expect, a direct correlation exists between the incidence of twins and the availability of forage.

The Northeastern moose population fluctuated considerably in the last two centuries. For Colonial settlers, moose provided an important food source. Because moose were so easily killed, populations plummeted. By the mid-1800s, moose had been extirpated in New York, and fewer than 15 lived in New Hampshire, with even fewer in Vermont. Because some northernmost Maine counties remained fairly inaccessible, they continued to harbor moose. In 1930, one estimate put the population at about 2,000.

With protection from hunting in 1936 and with the proliferation of low-growing browse after extensive clearcutting, moose populations rebounded dramatically, to the point where about 300 moose die each year in collisions with cars in New Hampshire and Vermont, and nearly 400 in Maine. Moose populations in New Hampshire and Vermont reached more than 10,000, and about 75,000 in Maine, in 2012. Moose have just started to repopulate New York.

A limited, 700-permit, annual moose-hunting season was insti-
tuted in Maine in 1980. Over time, permits allowed by the legislature increased to 3,000, but in 2000, the legislature turned permit decisions
over to Maine's Department of Inland Fisheries & Wildlife. Recently, the
number of permits has been reduced, from a high of more than 4,000 to
fewer than 3,000, due to severe winter mortality from tick infestations.

Brainworm infestations, fatal to moose, keep populations from building
in southern areas due to the presence of large numbers of deer. Although unaffected by these parasites, deer carry them and deposit them in their feces,
which passes them to land snails. If moose browse on plants hosting snails,
a likely occurrence at lower elevations in southern Maine, they contract the
disease and die.

Winter tick infestations, caused by warm fall and winter weather, have
very recently begun to devastate moose populations. New Hampshire and
Vermont populations have fallen almost by half, and Maine's population is
probably well below 60,000 and heading downward. Moose, like other wildlife,
always have suffered from ticks. But whereas wood and deer ticks engorge
with blood then drop off, winter ticks, which in the colder years of the past
would be killed by snow and freezing rain, have now proliferated. They grab
on to moose and remain attached through the winter, causing widespread
fatal anemia in calves and even killing adult moose. Adults, trying to rid
themselves of the tick burden, rub off their fur on trees. We've included a

A young bull moose in spring shows massive hair loss from winter tick infestation.

photo of a nearly hairless young male moose we saw in northern Maine in late May 2016.

Many wonderful paddling destinations exist in Maine, where you have a good chance of seeing moose. We never tire of that exhilarating feeling we get from paddling into a marshy cove and coming suddenly upon an enormous bull moose or a cow with calf. We have seen hundreds of these majestic mammals, and we hope you see as many on your travels. But continued global warming, which is driving increases in winter tick populations, will reduce moose numbers, especially in the southern part of its range. Let's hope populations stabilize at some point. Perhaps biologists can find a way to lessen mortality. Time will tell.

77 | Cooper Brook Deadwater, Lower Jo-Mary Lake, Middle Jo-Mary Lake, and Turkey Tail Lake

These scenic lakes, with Katahdin as a backdrop, are filled with interesting nooks and crannies, along with loads of wildlife. You will see loons, bald eagles, ospreys, moose, and possibly otters.

Location: T4 Indian Purchase Township, TA R10 WELS, T1 R9 WELS, T1 R10 WELS
Maps: *Maine Atlas & Gazetteer*, Map 42: A4, A5, B5 and Map 43: B1; USGS Nahmakanta Stream, Pemadumcook Lake, Ragged Mountain
Area: Lower Jo-Mary Lake, 1,912 acres; Middle Jo-Mary and Turkey Tail lakes, 1,152 acres
Time: Multiday; shorter trips possible

Habitat Type: Shallow, marshy lakes and streams

Fish: Brook trout, lake trout, landlocked salmon, white perch, chain pickerel (see fish advisories, Appendix A)

Take Note: No personal watercraft on Lower Jo-Mary; campfire permits required, 207-827-1800

GETTING THERE

From Millinocket, at the T-junction of Routes 11 and 157 with Katahdin Avenue, turn left on Route 11/Katahdin Avenue, go 0.3 mile, and turn right on Route 11. Go 9.6 miles (cumulative: 9.9 miles) and turn right on Lincolnridge Road. Go 4 miles (13.9 miles) and merge onto Turkey Trail Road. Go 0.9 mile (14.8 miles) and veer left on Fire Road 3. Go 0.7 mile (15.5 miles) and veer right. Go 1.1 miles (16.6 miles) to Jo-Mary Stream and Turkey Tail access on the right. (45° 37.458′ N, 68° 56.172′ W)

WHAT YOU'LL SEE

We treasure this rarely explored string of connected lakes: Turkey Tail, Middle Jo-Mary, and Lower Jo-Mary. A few summer homes intrude on Turkey Tail and the south end of Middle Jo-Mary, but you quickly leave those behind as you paddle north toward Lower Jo-Mary.

Cooper Brook Deadwater

These lakes include about 25 miles of highly varied shoreline, but we find the winding channel of Cooper Brook, between Middle and Lower Jo-Mary lakes, the most interesting. This slow-moving creek and the Cooper Brook Deadwater it becomes provide superb, marshy wildlife habitat. We saw two moose here, lots of beaver activity, ring-necked ducks, wood ducks, great blue herons, American bittern, and songbirds galore.

If you paddle from Middle Jo-Mary to Lower Jo-Mary via this creek, you travel upstream initially, then downstream, though on hardly perceptible current. Cooper Brook and Mud Brook enter from the west, and the current divides, with half flowing north into Lower Jo-Mary and half south into Middle Jo-Mary. By midsummer in a dry year, you might not be able to paddle through easily. We paddled here in mid-May, before black flies and mosquitoes, with plenty of water.

You might have difficulty finding the brook from the Cooper Brook Deadwater, especially later in summer with taller vegetation restricting your view. You simply have to explore the area, winding among the grassy islands and floating peat mats that form the shoreline. Once you find the brook, you

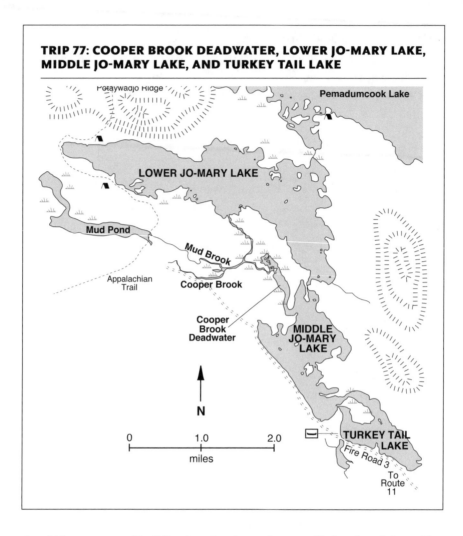

TRIP 77: COOPER BROOK DEADWATER, LOWER JO-MARY LAKE, MIDDLE JO-MARY LAKE, AND TURKEY TAIL LAKE

Potaywadjo Ridge

Pemadumcook Lake

LOWER JO-MARY LAKE

Mud Pond

Mud Brook

Appalachian Trail

Cooper Brook

Cooper Brook Deadwater

MIDDLE JO-MARY LAKE

N

0   1.0   2.0

miles

TURKEY TAIL LAKE

Fire Road 3

To Route 11

should have no trouble following the channel, generally lined with low alder and various heath: blueberry, leatherleaf, bog rosemary, and sheep laurel. About 0.5 mile from the Deadwater, you will reach a fork in the creek—really, a brook coming in from the left that divides. To get to Lower Jo-Mary, bear to the right (northeast). If you have some time and there's enough water, first explore to the left, paddling upstream on both Cooper and Mud brooks. The Appalachian Trail traverses these brooks.

As you continue downstream toward Lower Jo-Mary, you pass a rocky area that could be a problem at low water levels. You may have to cross beaver dams, as well. As you paddle out onto Lower Jo-Mary, take a careful look at the several tall white pines so you can find the creek access if you return by the same route.

Jo-Mary Lakes. Rounded granite boulders extend above—and lurk just below—the water surface along the rocky south shore. In a cove hidden by an island about 0.5 mile west of Cooper Brook, we watched a moose browse on low cedar branches. We saw a number of loon pairs and watched two bald eagle soaring. Northern white cedar dominates the south shoreline. Thick, generally impenetrable shrubs line the banks.

Traversing the south shore, you get great views of Mount Katahdin across the lake. About 1 mile from the lake's western tip, the Maine Appalachian Trail Club maintains a wonderful campsite, nestled beneath a stand of tall red pine.

Lower Jo-Mary's north shore—especially the west half, with its sandy banks—differs from the south shore. With full southern exposure, the drier woods support more deciduous trees, such as maple, beech, ash, and oak, along with paper birch and aspen. Once the lake widens out farther east, though, and you leave the steep Potaywadjo Ridge, the shoreline returns to the wet, swampy, cedar-dominated vegetation you will see on the south shore and around most of this region's other lakes.

We had hoped to find a portage path into Pemadumcook Lake from the northeastern tip of Lower Jo-Mary, but we could not. New logging roads, however, could provide a route. Skilled paddlers could negotiate the 50 yards of whitewater under and below the bridge at the outlet; in mid-May we found this water fairly rough. Returning upstream, though, would be a real chore through almost impenetrable woods, as the connecting stream would be too deep and too fast to wade.

While we did not fish when we visited here, we saw many large trout or salmon in the stream connecting Lower Jo-Mary and Pemadumcook lakes. The several ospreys we saw here provided further evidence of the superb fishing.

Several attractive islands dot the northeast corner of Lower Jo-Mary, but none had campsites we could find. (The western end of Lower Jo-Mary contains the best campsite on these lakes.) Paddling south from these islands into the southeast tip, you will find another access, larger than the Cooper Brook access, into Middle Jo-Mary. You can make a nice, one-day loop trip by paddling into Lower Jo-Mary on Cooper Brook then returning via this more southern connecting channel.

On Middle Jo-Mary, just below the connecting creek, sits a classic old private fishing and hunting camp: Buckhorn Camps, dating to the late 1800s, accessible by boat or floatplane. The small, rustic cabins are of a different age.

78 | First, Second, and Third Debsconeag Lakes and Debsconeag Deadwater

Protected by The Nature Conservancy and among the most pristine lakes in the Northeast, Debsconeag lakes provide a fabulous paddling resource. A high-clearance vehicle is necessary for the access road. Expect to see loons, bald eagles, common terns, beavers, moose, and views of Katahdin. This is also a great place to see bog plants.

Location: T1 R9 WELS, T1 R10 WELS, T2 R9 WELS, T2 R10 WELS
Maps: *Maine Atlas & Gazetteer*, Map 42: A3, A4 and Map 50: E3, E4, E5; USGS Abol Pond, Nahmakanta Stream, Rainbow Lake East
Area: First Debsconeag Lake, 320 acres; Second Debsconeag Lake, 189 acres; Third Debsconeag Lake, 1,011 acres
Time: Multiday; shorter trips possible
Habitat Type: Deep lakes with scenic mountains; marshy areas on Second Debsconeag and Debsconeag Deadwater
Fish: Brook trout, lake trout, landlocked salmon, white perch (see fish advisories, Appendix A)
Take Note: High-clearance vehicle required; camping in designated sites only; campfire permits required, 207-827-1800

GETTING THERE

From Millinocket, at the T-junction of Routes 11 and 157 with Katahdin Avenue, turn right on Katahdin Avenue, go 0.2 mile, and turn left on Bates Street/Millinocket Lake Road/Baxter Park Road. Go 9.2 miles (cumulative: 9.4 miles) and turn left on Sawdust Pile Road, followed by an immediate right on Golden Road. Go 3.5 miles (12.9 miles), and veer diagonally left on Debsconeag Road. Go 3.5 miles (16.4 miles) to the Omaha Beach access on Debsconeag Deadwater. High-clearance vehicle required. (45° 46.086′ N, 68° 56.448′ W)

WHAT YOU'LL SEE

Wild, remote, pristine, and magical, the Debsconeag lakes represent the essence of the Maine Woods. Fortunately, through the foresight of Great Northern Paper, which kept this area unharvested and nonmotorized for more than 70 years, and with the aid of The Nature Conservancy, the 41,000-acre Debsconeag Wilderness now protects all of this area from development. Paddling here on

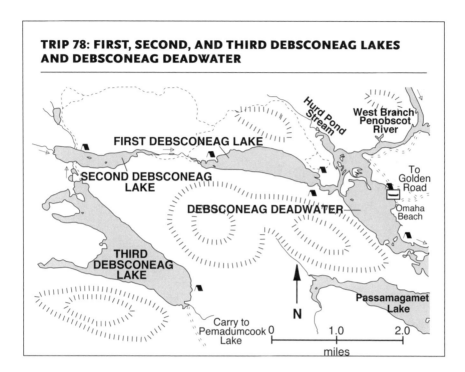

TRIP 78: FIRST, SECOND, AND THIRD DEBSCONEAG LAKES AND DEBSCONEAG DEADWATER

FIRST DEBSCONEAG LAKE

Hurd Pond Stream

West Branch Penobscot River

SECOND DEBSCONEAG LAKE

To Golden Road

Omaha Beach

DEBSCONEAG DEADWATER

THIRD DEBSCONEAG LAKE

Passamagamet Lake

Carry to Pemadumcook Lake

N

0   1.0   2.0
miles

a quiet morning or listening to the wail of ever-present loons from one of the rustic campsites, you can imagine what much of this country once must have been like.

Rushing brooks and portage paths connect several lakes; depending on your energy level and time, you can stay on one lake or carry through to the others. The more adventuresome can arrange a dropoff and paddle an extended one way trip through these lakes then on to Pemadumcook and either Ambajejus or the Jo-Mary lakes.

Debsconeag Deadwater. The access delivers you to Omaha Beach on Debsconeag Deadwater. Loons may greet your arrival, as does Mount Katahdin to the north, which stands sentinel over many lakes in this region. Along the shore, you will see northern white cedar, jack pine, red maple, paper birch, balsam fir, red spruce, and a few hemlock. The unusual swampy island area at the northern end provides nesting habitat for wood ducks and keeps the many resident beavers happy.

The north end of Debsconeag Deadwater narrows to a swampy channel where Hurd Pond Stream enters. We saw a bald eagle searching for its next meal here. There are several campsites on Deadwater: Omaha Beach, with its

Katahdin, snow covered in late May, rises over Omaha Beach at Debsconeag Deadwater.

wonderful, white-sand swimming beach; on the northeastern end, where the Penobscot flows in; and at the inlet from First Debsconeag.

First Debsconeag Lake. Debsconeag Deadwater and First Debsconeag Lake connect through an open, readily paddleable channel. The fair current in the spring subsides later in the season. Stronger current flows along the narrows between the island and the southwest shore—where water from the Penobscot River circles around the island. You will find great campsites on both sides of the channel here.

Paddling along the southern shore of First Debsconeag, you will get a spectacular view of Mount Katahdin—when not enshrouded in clouds. Because of the view, one could easily miss the granite boulders waiting to scrape boat bottoms and the freshwater mussels that populate the clean, sandy bottom. From the north shore, marked by a small sign, a trail leads to some ice caves.

Oddly, our favorite thing about Debsconeag lakes is not the water at all but the surrounding banks and woodland, with their carpets of mosses, club mosses, lichens, ferns, and wildflowers. Trailing arbutus, wintergreen, and creeping snowberry (all diminutive members of the heath family) grow thickly in some areas. Dense cushions of moss and polypody fern drape over many of the boulders here.

Second Debsconeag Lake. For a great way to see the woods, portage into Second Debsconeag. Even if you don't want to carry your boat, walk the easy 0.75-mile trail anyway. The first part runs parallel to the connecting creek, where you can dangle your feet over the edge and watch the rushing cataract. Despite the 30-foot elevation rise, the portage remains generally flat and remarkably dry—even when some pockets of snow remain, as we found in mid-May. We got a good view of ruffed grouse on the walk. With gear, the portage should take about 25 minutes.

Paddling close to shore on Second Lake—much rockier than First, especially on the west end—you will almost certainly scrape bottom once or twice, but the rounded granite boulders should not do much damage. A couple of islands and a nice campsite sit along the west shore, roughly opposite the inlet brook. In boggy areas, look for the reddish leaves of pitcher plants. Because you can get into Second Lake only by portaging or by floatplane, you should not see any motorboats here.

Third Debsconeag Lake. You can portage from Second into Third Lake via a trail that starts about 100 yards east of the inlet brook on the south shore. This trail, both harder to find and steeper in places than the trail connecting First and Second lakes, runs for only half the length. A side trail leads down to one of two small ponds between the lakes. The portage should take 15 minutes one way.

Third Debsconeag Lake seems just as wild as Second but much larger. Keep an eye out for common terns. We believe they nest on large granite boulders protruding from the water near the north end. In Minister Cove, we saw lots of beaver activity, as well as seemingly ever-present loons and common mergansers.

MAINE WOODS: GREAT NORTHERN FOREST RESOURCE

For many, the Maine Woods—or North Woods—conjures up thoughts of huge tracts of relatively undeveloped forestland in western and northern Maine. Who can resist the allure of its mountain chains, clear blue ponds and lakes, thousands of miles of streams and rivers, and abundant wildlife? The Appalachian Trail runs through it; the Allagash, St. John, Kennebec, and Penobscot drain it; and Maine preserves some of its finest treasures, such as Katahdin and Baxter State Park, within its borders.

On a broader regional scale, the Maine Woods forms the largest component of the Northern Forest, which spans the northern tier of New York,

Vermont, New Hampshire, and Maine, encompassing more than 26 million acres. This largest expanse of forestland in the eastern United States includes deep woods and provides a home to a rich variety of wildlife. It boasts an abundance of moose, deer, black bears, otters, loons, ospreys, and bald eagles. Less common but also present are bobcats, fishers, martins, and even the Canada lynx—the only stable population of this threatened species in the eastern United States. More than 230 species of birds nest here or migrate through the area. And it provides some of the best paddling east of Minnesota.

In the late 1980s, paper and timber investment companies started selling land throughout the region, some to development companies. Conservation organizations and individuals took note, identifying the region as the "Northern Forest" and beginning efforts to protect it. In Maine, in particular, timberland has changed hands at an alarming rate, and the marketing of these parcels of land usually touts development potential. Between 1998 and 2013, 9 million acres of Maine timberland, or 40 percent of the state's land area, changed hands.

Even so, cooperation among environmentalists and recreationists, politicians from opposite poles, and diverse organizations with widely differing priorities has been remarkable. The Appalachian Mountain Club, The Nature Conservancy, a host of other conservation organizations, individuals, the state of Maine, outdoor clubs, and local communities have worked to protect key swaths of land.

In December 2003, AMC embarked on the largest conservation effort in its 127-year history: the Maine Woods Initiative. The initiative seeks to address the ecological and economic needs of the Maine Woods region by supporting local forest-products jobs and traditional recreation, creating new multiday backcountry experiences for visitors, and attracting new nature-based tourism to the region. The region identified for this project is the 100-Mile Wilderness, a roadless corridor stretching from Monson to Katahdin that contains a segment of the Appalachian Trail, as well as Gulf Hagas, a magnificent gorge known as the "Grand Canyon of Maine" and a National Natural Landmark. AMC's investment will make paddling, hiking, skiing, and snowshoeing available to visitors while reducing overuse on some portions of the Appalachian Trail.

In the initiative's first phase, AMC purchased 37,000-acres from International Paper known as the Katahdin Iron Works Tract. In 2009, the orga nization acquired an adjoining 29,500 acres. AMC has drawn on its long history in Maine and New Hampshire in developing new trails, campsites, and wilderness lodges that are scaled appropriately for the area's natural resources. AMC purchases ensure that tens of thousands of acres—rich with opportunities for paddling, hiking, cross-country skiing, and snowshoeing—will be protected and remain open to the public for recreational use. For more information about the Maine Woods Initiative, see outdoors.org/mwi.

Meanwhile, the entrepreneur and conservationist Roxanne Quimby, who made her fortune through Burt's Bees, the company she cofounded with Burt Shavitz, acquired 120,000 acres in northern Maine, directly east of Baxter State Park. In August 2016, she donated 87,500 acres of this land to the federal government to become Katahdin Woods and Waters National Monument. President Obama announced the land's national monument designation on the 100th anniversary of the National Park Service's formation.

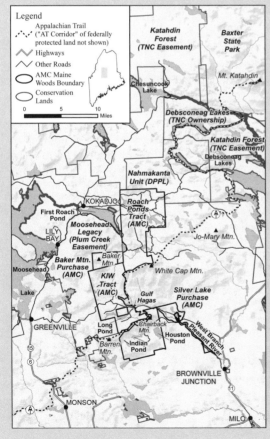

The 100-Mile Wilderness, AMC's Maine Woods Initiative project area. Map: Catherine J. Poppenwimer, AMC

79 | Upper Togue Pond, Lower Togue Pond, and Abol Pond

These small ponds are worth paddling, simply for the spectacular views of Katahdin reaching 4,700 feet above the water. You should see loons, beavers, and myriad bog plants.

Location: T2 R9 WELS
Maps: *Maine Atlas & Gazetteer,* Map 50: E5 and Map 51: E1; USGS Abol Pond, Trout Mountain
Area: Upper Togue Pond, 294 acres; Lower Togue Pond, 384 acres; Abol Pond, 70 acres
Time: 5 hours
Habitat Type: Small ponds with spectacular views; some marshy areas
Fish: Brook trout, landlocked salmon, white perch, chain pickerel (see fish advisories, Appendix A)
Information: Baxter State Park, baxterstateparkauthority.com, 207-723-5140; camping reservations required
Take Note: 10 HP limit; some development, including scout camps on Lower Togue and Abol ponds

GETTING THERE
Togue Ponds. From Millinocket, at the T-junction of Routes 11 and 157 with Katahdin Avenue, turn right on Katahdin Avenue, go 0.2 mile, and turn left on Bates Street/Millinocket Lake Road/Baxter Park Road. Go 15 miles (cumulative: 15.2 miles) and turn right. Go 1.5 miles (16.7 miles) to the access on the left. (45° 49.464′ N, 68° 53.172′ W)

   Abol Pond. Continue past Togue ponds to the Togue Pond Gate (fee required). Go 2.9 miles northwest on Park Tote Road, turn left, and go 0.4 mile (cumulative: 3.3 miles) to the Abol Beach Picnic Area and access. (45° 50.430′ N, 68° 56.328′ W)

WHAT YOU'LL SEE
It just does not get much more beautiful than the view of Mount Katahdin from Togue ponds. Located just 6 miles to the north, Baxter Peak rises 4,670 feet above pond level. In the spring (ice-out typically in early May), the dramatic snow-capped peak dominates the landscape, just as the Rockies do in the West.

TRIP 79: UPPER TOGUE POND AND LOWER TOGUE POND

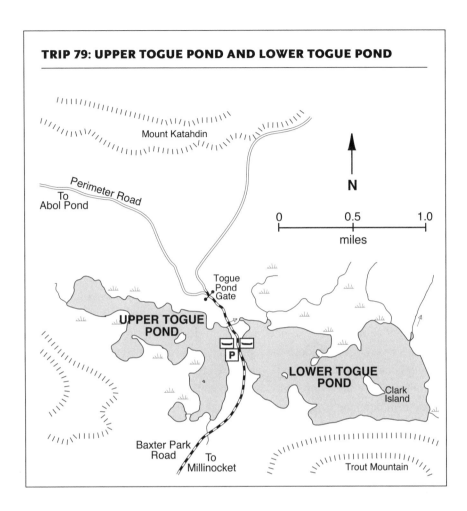

Of the two ponds, Upper Togue (west side of the road), a little more remote, also sports a more varied shoreline. Red pine dominates here—notice the reddish bark, long needles in bundles of two, and small cones—but you will also find white pine (five needles per bundle), jack pine (very short needles with two per bundle), some northern white cedar along the shore, a few red spruce and balsam fir, red maple, and paper birch. Various low, bushy shrubs of the heath family—blueberry, sheep laurel, leatherleaf, bog rosemary, and Labrador tea—grow thickly along the shoreline, mixed in with bracken fern, alder, and a wide range of mosses and lichens. In coves and along Lower Togue's northern shore, look for pitcher plants growing on sphagnum hummocks.

Natural tannins color the water reddish brown. The sandy bottom harbors freshwater mussels, which stick partway out of the sand, filtering out microscopic

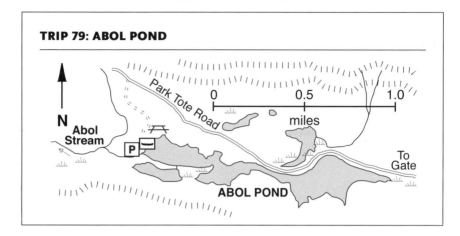

TRIP 79: ABOL POND

algae and other prey. We saw several loon pairs here, a broad-winged hawk, and lots of warblers (including yellow-rumped warblers and yellowthroats) and other songbirds at the far western inlet on Upper Togue. We also saw a half-dozen painted turtles at the inlet.

Beavers abound, as evidenced by several lodges and lots of stumps. The residents of a very active lodge in Upper Togue's cove that extends farthest south had cut over a hillside, with aspen and birch trees strewn as if part of a logging operation. In the boggy inlet into Lower Togue, we watched a mink scurry along the shore looking for its next meal. If you catch a glimpse of one, wait around and chances are pretty good it will come out of hiding to take another peek at you.

Lower Togue Pond provides spectacular views of Katahdin throughout the paddling season.

Abol Pond

While in the area, you might also want to paddle Abol Pond, a narrow pond that runs along Park Tote Road, just in from the Togue Pond gate. Abol Pond has a nice sand beach and picnic area and offers a pleasant few hours of paddling. The shallow pond grows thick with vegetation: waterlilies, bur-reed, and lots of submerged plants. In a few boggy areas, you can find pitcher plants, cranberry, sphagnum, tamarack, and other northern fen species. We saw a deer and a loon pair with chick while paddling here on an August afternoon.

80 | Lobster Lake

Lobster Lake represents one of the finest paddling and camping lakes in Maine. We have seen many moose here. Look for loons, common terns, ducks, and possibly otters.

Location: Lobster Township, Northeast Carry Township
Maps: *Maine Atlas & Gazetteer*, Map 49: D3, D4, E3, E4;
USGS Big Spencer Mountain, Lobster Mountain, Penobscot Farm
Area: 3,475 acres
Time: All day or multiday trip
Habitat Type: Deep lake with marshy coves and sand beaches
Fish: Brook trout, lake trout, landlocked salmon, white perch (see fish advisories, Appendix A)
Take Note: Fill up with gas in Millinocket or Greenville; no personal watercraft; North Maine Woods camping and entrance fees required, northmainewoods.org; camping only in designated sites, first-come basis; no fire permits required

GETTING THERE

From Millinocket. At the T-junction of Routes 11 and 157 with Katahdin Avenue, turn right on Katahdin Avenue, go 0.2 mile, and turn left on Bates Street/Millinocket Lake Road/Baxter Park Road. Go 9.2 miles (cumulative: 9.4 miles) and turn left on Sawdust Pile Road, followed by an immediate right on Golden Road. Go 43.2 miles (52.6 miles), passing through Caribou Checkpoint (pay fees), and turn left on a connector road. Go 0.8 mile (53.4 miles) and veer right

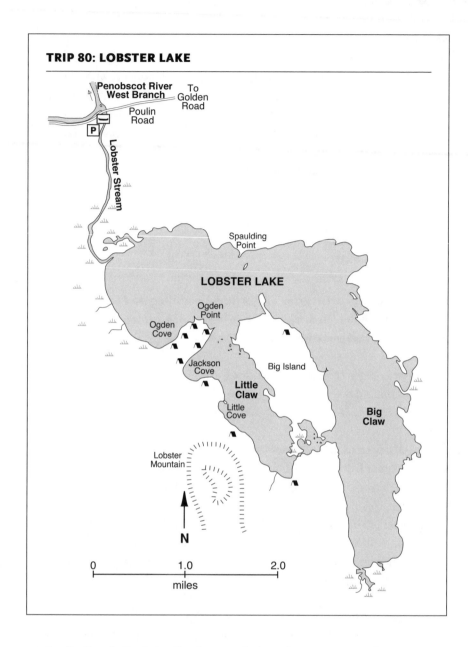

TRIP 80: LOBSTER LAKE

Penobscot River West Branch

To Golden Road

Poulin Road

P

Lobster Stream

Spaulding Point

LOBSTER LAKE

Ogden Point

Ogden Cove

Jackson Cove

Big Island

Little Claw

Little Cove

Big Claw

Lobster Mountain

N

0   1.0   2.0

miles

on Poulin Road. Go 2.7 miles (56.1 miles) to the access on Lobster Stream. (45° 53.532′ N, 69° 33.888′ W)

From Greenville. Where Routes 6 and 15 turn left, go 18.8 miles north on Main Street/Lily Bay Road and turn left on Sias Hill/Greenville Road. Go 14.3 miles (cumulative: 33.1 miles) and turn left on Golden Road. Go 15.3 miles, passing through Caribou Checkpoint (pay fees), and continue as above.

WHAT YOU'LL SEE

Lobster Lake, shaped like the two parts of a lobster claw, certainly represents one of the finest paddling and camping lakes in Maine. To reach the lake, paddle up Lobster Stream from the confluence of Lobster Stream and the Penobscot River West Branch. The 2-mile paddle traverses a wide, deep stream with a barely perceptible current. In fact, the stream actually changes direction depending on the volume of water coming down the West Branch. At high flow in spring, Lobster Stream can reverse direction and serve as an inlet into Lobster Lake. The marshy shoreline, dense with alder, sweetgale, and other water-tolerant plants, provides a home for beavers and moose.

After paddling up Lobster Stream and entering the lake, head left (north) where several coves extend into the marsh. We came upon a moose here, along with a family of common goldeneye.

Several well-maintained campsites—complete with picnic tables, fire rings, sites for at least half a dozen tents, and superb sandy beaches for swimming—lie across the way in Ogden Cove. Because shallow water extends quite a way out, young children love this spot. Three separate campsites occupy Ogden Point (Ogden North, Ogden Point, and Ogden South), each with room for multiple tents. All sites have sandy swimming beaches and great views over the lake and across to Big Island. Three other fine campsites lie farther south along Little Claw's western shore: Jackson Cove, Little Cove, and Little Claw.

Around Ogden Point from Ogden Cove, you enter Little Claw. In windy conditions, this section feels more protected. Rounding Ogden Point and looking down into Little Claw almost takes your breath away. Gulls and terns nest on the small, protruding, rocky islands, and jagged cliffs extend down into the clear blue water, interspersed here and there with sandy coves. Wind-sculpted cedars and pines perch precariously on the high overlooks, and mosses and ferns festoon the rocks, all nestled beneath picturesque mountains. In our paddling throughout Maine, we have not seen a more scenic spot.

Particularly attractive Big Island separates Big Claw and Little Claw. The 2,000-acre island includes tall cliffs, sandy beaches, and protected marshy coves. Quoting from the Maine Geological Survey: "Along the shores of this beautiful lake . . . is some of the most spectacular geology found anywhere in the state. In outcrop after outcrop, the shore of the lake reveals a complex geological story that begins with deep-sea sediments, is punctuated by several periods of igneous activity and folding, and ends with shallow marine sediment that is profusely fossiliferous."

Thick groves of protected old-growth red pine (only 1 percent of which remains in Maine) and some huge hemlocks grow on the island's higher sections.

A cow moose browses aquatic plants at the south end of Lobster Lake's Big Claw.

Northern white cedar, white pine, and the atypical jack pine grow along the shore. A rare tree in Maine, jack pine grows in profusion here, including some unusually large specimens. The very short needles (0.34 to 1.5 inches) twist at the base and grow in bundles of two. The cones take two years to grow and, until mature, remain oddly twisted. After maturing, they may stay on the tree for more than a dozen years. Fires help open the cones and disperse seeds.

At Big Island's south end, you can paddle through a narrow channel into Big Claw. Lined with sedges and thinly sprinkled with yellow pondlily, American white waterlily, and bur-reed, the marshy channel provides rich habitat for moose and numerous bird species. Paddling here in late July, sounds of songbirds filled the air, and we saw several wood ducks in the vegetation along the shore.

The Big Claw portion of Lobster Lake has much less variation than Little Claw. At 3.5 miles in length and as much as 1 mile across, Big Claw can also get pretty rough in windy conditions. At the lake's southern tip, a wonderful marshy area begs to be explored. Rounding a point of land into this marshy cove during an evening paddle, three moose greeted us: a cow with calf and a yearling cow. Grasses, sedges, bulrushes, and the aromatic sweet flag (*Acorus americanus*) grow in profusion here.

In 1981, the state acquired from Great Northern Paper a permanent conservation easement to the shoreline of Lobster Lake, extending back 500 feet from the high-water line. The easement protects the shoreline from development and timber harvesting.

81 | Canada Falls Lake

Canada Falls Lake, formed by a dam on the South Branch of the Penobscot River, is surrounded by scenic views of the northern boreal forest. The campground at the dam can get crowded, but the lake, with all of its many coves, provides plenty of solitude. Look for loons, ospreys, white-tailed deer, and moose.

Location: Alder Brook Township, Pittston Academy Grant, Soldiertown Township
Maps: *Maine Atlas & Gazetteer*, Map 48: D1, D2, D3, E2; USGS Canada Falls Lake, Tomhegan Pond
Area: 2,627 acres
Time: All day or multiday
Habitat Type: Large, shallow lake
Fish: Brook trout (see fish advisories, Appendix A)
Take Note: Camping and entrance fees required; campfire permits required, 207-827-1800

GETTING THERE
From Rockwood on Routes 6 and 15, cross the Moose River on Northern Road, veering immediately right, then left, and go 20 miles on Northern/20 Mile roads, following signs to Seboomook Wilderness Campground. Turn left and go 0.7 mile (cumulative: 20.7 miles) on 20 Mile/Seboomook roads, stopping at the 20 Mile Checkpoint to pay fees, and turn left on Canada Falls Road. Go 2.2 miles (22.9 miles) to the access at the dam. (45° 52.326′ N, 70° 0.024′ W)

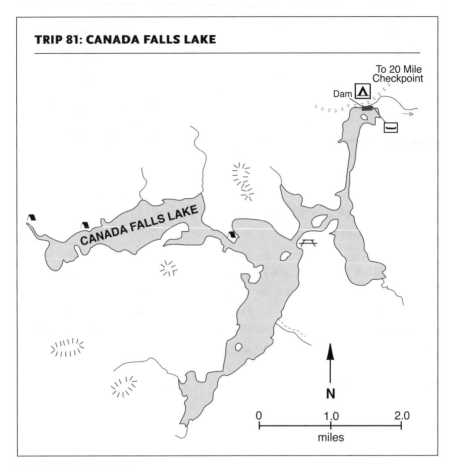

TRIP 81: CANADA FALLS LAKE

To 20 Mile Checkpoint

Dam

CANADA FALLS LAKE

N

0   1.0   2.0

miles

WHAT YOU'LL SEE

Don't be shocked when you arrive at the Canada Falls Lake access. The relatively large campground fills with campers, dogs, children, beer cans, and noise in the middle of the season. We could not wait to get out onto the much more peaceful lake. When we paddled here on a weekend at the end of July, with only light breezes rippling the surface, we saw one other boat up close on the water, trolling at idle speed down the long outlet channel. Fishermen seem to like Canada Falls Lake for the same reason that signs warn away the high-speed boating crowd. A gazillion submerged and not-so-submerged stumps provide plenty of hiding space for fish and make speedboating dangerous.

A jumble of roots, stumps, and downed timber covers the shore in many places, which detracts a bit from the dark-hued rows of pointed fir and spruce receding back into the many-layered hillsides. Entering the main lake, one is immediately taken with the beauty of three saw-toothed peaks in the distance.

Osprey

Hearing enchanting loon calls from a remote campsite as the sun sets over distant peaks is far preferable to barking dogs at the campground.

We watched in solitude as an osprey wheeled about, doing aerial acrobatics in search of a meal. It seemed as if some invisible hook held one wingtip fixed as it pivoted in the sky for a better look, eventually flying off to a quieter cove with improved visibility into the water below. Ring-billed gulls, white-throated sparrows, cormorants, black ducks, loons, great blue herons, and many other birds announced their presence. A female merganser with a raft of young in tow fled before us, ducking under the safety of some downed timber.

The northern coniferous forest dominates the shoreline and hillsides surrounding Canada Falls Lake, but spruce, pine, and fir have not totally squeezed out the deciduous species, as we saw many small red maple and paper birch, along with some quite large yellow birch. In places, beavers had stripped some of the deciduous trees of their bark. As we came around through the marshy area behind the big island, at the end of the outlet channel, we surprised a deer that had come down for a drink.

Although we found few marshy areas to explore, we very much enjoyed our paddle on Canada Falls Lake, with its long arms and lots of nooks and crannies to explore, including the inlet channel of the South Branch Penobscot River on the west end. We recommend spending more than one day to fully explore the extensive shoreline of this wonderful place.

6 | NORTHERN MAINE

This remote region offers solitude and wildness to the intrepid paddler.
The Northern Region encompasses 200,000-acre Baxter State Park, home to
Mount Katahdin, Maine's tallest peak at 5,267 feet. Aroostook County, so large
and remote it is known simply as "The County," composes most of the North-
ern Region. The largest county east of the Mississippi, it covers more land than
Connecticut and Rhode Island combined. The County contains 2,000 lakes,
rivers, and streams, including the spectacular Allagash Wilderness Waterway,
a 92-mile-long corridor of state-protected waterways winding through the
North Maine Woods. Featured trips include Penobscot River West Branch and
Chesuncook Lake (Trip 85), where Thoreau made a historic journey; remote
Allagash Lake (Trip 88), devilishly difficult to reach but loaded with wildlife;
Sawtelle Deadwater (Trip 91), just north of Baxter State Park, where we have
seen moose on every trip; and Deboullie, Pushineer, Gardner, and Togue ponds
(Trip 93), exuding wilderness and our farthest north trip.

New for the third edition are Baskahegan Lake (Trip 82), with its many coves
and islands, and Pine Stream Flowage, filled with waterfowl and moose, which
we've added to the existing Trip 85.

82 | Baskahegan Lake

Large, scenic Baskahegan Lake is a joy to paddle, at least with mild winds. It takes more than a day to circumnavigate its complete shoreline. Surrounded primarily by diverse boreal forest with pointed spires, the lake's deep coves and inlet streams wait to be explored. Bald eagles and loons nest here, and expect to see common terns, great blue herons, common mergansers, ducks, geese, and possibly moose.

Location: Brookton Township, Topsfield
Maps: *Maine Atlas & Gazetteer,* Map 45: C3, C4, D3, D4; USGS Brookton, Dill Hill, Farrow Mountain, Stetson Mountain
Area: 6,944 acres
Time: All day or multiday trip
Habitat Type: Large, shallow lake with marshy coves and several islands
Fish: Brook trout (streams only), smallmouth bass, white perch, chain pickerel (see fish advisories, Appendix A)
Information: Baskahegan Company, baskahegan.com; Canoe the Wild, canoethewild.com; Baskahegan Lodge, northernmaineguide.com
Take Note: Wind can make paddling hazardous; campfire permit required, 207-827-1800.

GETTING THERE
From Topsfield, at the junction of Routes 1 and 6, go 8.3 miles north on Route 1 and turn left on Baskahegan Lake Road. Go 1 mile (cumulative: 9.3 miles) to the access. (45° 31.620´ N, 67° 47.058´ W)

WHAT YOU'LL SEE
Baskahegan, a large lake with many coves, provides a great paddling resource under calm wind conditions. Wind blowing over 3 or 4 miles of shallow, open water can produce large waves. We've visited when dangerous whitecaps filled the lake's surface, and we've visited when the surface barely rippled. If you're caught out when the wind starts blowing, Baskahegan's several protected coves can provide a respite. Indeed, those coves amplify the lake's shoreline to an amazing 41 miles. Note the windpower machines lining the hillside across the lake from the access.

The lake's shallow waters also hide many granite boulders just under the surface, which keeps high-speed boating at bay. Most people who enjoy this scenic lake come to fish for smallmouth bass and white perch. Even during prime fishing season in May and June, you can still find plenty of solitude on the lake.

The Baskahegan Company, founded in 1920, owns the land surrounding the lake and also most of the land surrounding Crooked Brook Flowage (Trip 83) and Baskahegan Stream, which connects the two, and allows free public access. A study from 2010 showed serious damage at most campsites. As a result of this study, in succeeding summers groups of student and parent volunteers led by Dave Conley of Canoe the Wild hauled away boatloads of trash and upgraded campsites with new picnic tables, signs, outboxes (for toilet paper and human waste), and improved fire pits. Grants from several agencies funded this work. Self-policing campsites require us to keep them clean for the next user. Camp-

We often see common mergansers while paddling Maine's ponds and streams.

ing not your cup of tea? You could stay at Baskahegan Lodge, a hunting and fishing camp dating to 1926.

Roger Milliken, manager of his family's timber company, spent three years from 2008 to 2011 as board chairman of The Nature Conservancy, which helps explain the Baskahegan Company's firm commitment to sustainability and its forest operations certified by the Forest Stewardship Council. This explains, in large measure, the forest diversity surrounding the lake, which also promotes wildlife diversity. Respect for this property will keep it open for all to enjoy.

The surrounding boreal forest, with its pointed spires of several conifer species, draws bird watchers from across the Northeast to see boreal forest specialties, such as the red crossbill, white-winged crossbill, gray jay, olive-sided flycatcher, black-backed woodpecker, spruce grouse, and boreal chickadee. Out on the water and in the inlet streams, you'll see bald eagles that nest on an island here, as well as loons, common terns, great blue herons, common mergansers, ducks, and geese.

83 | Crooked Brook Flowage

Shallow Crooked Brook Flowage and the surrounding marsh represent nearly a quarter of the high quality marshland in Washington County, producing lots of ducks. It also supports a sizable beaver population; look for them in the evening. You could see moose here.

Location: Danforth
Maps: *Maine Atlas & Gazetteer*, Map 45: B3, B4; USGS Brookton, Danforth, Stetson Mountain
Area: 1,645 acres
Time: 5 hours
Habitat Type: Shallow, marshy lake
Fish: Smallmouth bass, white perch, chain pickerel (see fish advisories, Appendix A)
Take Note: Wind from the north or south can cause treacherous conditions; campfire permit required, 207-827-1800

GETTING THERE
From Danforth at the junction of Routes 1 and 169, go 0.4 mile and turn left to the Danforth Public Landing. (45° 39.366′ N, 67° 52.206′ W)

WHAT YOU'LL SEE
Paddling out from the access maintained by the town of Danforth, you will see numerous exposed stumps and rocks on the upper part of Crooked Brook Flowage. This long and narrow section also funnels wind. When the wind blows strongly out of the north or south, deep swells and whitecaps can develop.

Several unobtrusive houses perch along the bluff above the western shore, near the lake's north end. They soon disappear from view, and evidence of human presence abates until you get to the far end of the southeast arm. Deciduous trees predominate here, with occasional hemlocks and pines thrown in. Aspen, paper birch, red maple, and alder grow throughout.

The two southern arms provide lots of coves to explore, many with inlet streams. The shallow coves grow thick with cattails and other marsh vegetation. Islands dot the surface of the southeast arm. We saw dozens of feeding ducks

TRIP 83: CROOKED BROOK FLOWAGE

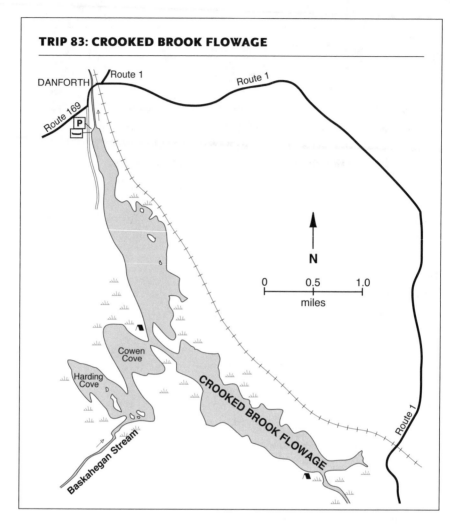

behind the large alder-covered island in Harding Cove's huge marsh. You can paddle back up Baskahegan Stream about 100 yards, until you run into a series of riffles cascading down into the flowage. The clear-cut alders make us wonder if the resident beavers are in training for paper company careers.

Most of the flowage away from the access is owned by the conservation-minded Baskahegan Company (see Trip 82). Crooked Brook and its surrounding marshlands represent nearly a quarter of Washington County's high-quality wetlands, which explains the large waterfowl presence.

84 | Mattawamkeag Lake

Theodore Roosevelt spent several weeks here in the 1870s, and it's easy to see why. Scenic vistas await you. You should see loons, bald eagles, ospreys, beavers, and possibly otters and moose.

Location: Island Falls, T4 R3 WELS
Maps: *Maine Atlas & Gazetteer,* Map 52: C4, C5; USGS Mattawamkeag Lake, Oakfield
Area/Length: 3,330 acres; 4 miles one way to Mattawamkeag Lake
Time: All day or multiday trips
Habitat Type: Winding river and large, shallow, scenic lake with islands
Fish: Brook trout, landlocked salmon, smallmouth bass, white perch, chain pickerel (see fish advisories, Appendix A)
Take Note: Development on Upper Mattawamkeag Lake; campfire permit required, 207-435-7963

GETTING THERE

Mattawamkeag River From I-95, Exit 276 northbound, go 0.6 mile east on Route 159 and turn right on Route 2. Go 0.6 mile (cumulative: 1.2 miles) and turn left on Michaud Road. Go 0.1 mile (1.3 miles) and turn left on Merriman Road. Go 0.9 mile (2.2 miles) or 1.5 miles (2.8 miles) to either of the accesses on the left. (45° 59.922′ N, 68° 15.180′ W).

Upper Mattawamkeag Lake. From I-95, Exit 276 northbound, go 0.6 mile east on Route 159 and turn left on Route 2. Go 1.8 miles (cumulative: 2.4 miles) and turn right on Brooks Road. Go 0.2 mile (2.6 miles) to the access. (46° 1.350′ N, 68° 14.316′ W)

WHAT YOU'LL SEE

In addition to paddling Mattawamkeag Lake, one can also paddle the very scenic, fairly wide West Branch Mattawamkeag River. Except for a few anglers, the river sees little boat traffic and is an excellent choice when the wind blows. Due to the river's meandering path, the wind has few lengthy and straight sections to build up waves. When we paddled here one August afternoon and evening, 3-foot swells greeted us out on the lake, while the river could only dish up a few ripples. In the lazy, late-summer current, the slightest breeze blew us back upstream.

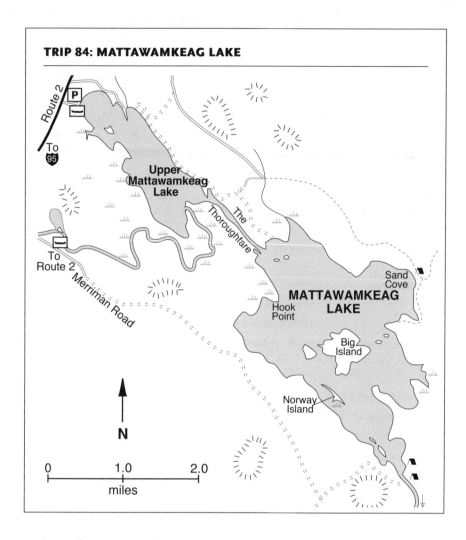

TRIP 84: MATTAWAMKEAG LAKE

From the Mattawamkeag River access, you wind around eastward, toward the lake. Occasional weedy fields interrupt the wooded shoreline, and boulders line the shore in places, some protruding out into the river. Although the banks sport high tree diversity, silver maple grows in profusion. Hemlock, balsam fir, spruce, white pine, northern white cedar, sugar maple, yellow birch, and many other species also grow along the fertile riverbank. Several potential campsites lurk under the dense canopy of large hemlock and other conifers.

Major game trails lead down to the water's edge; a white-tailed buck snorted at us from the dense undergrowth; and numerous beavers slapped the water with their tails as we paddled back to the access at sunset. In addition to flocks of cedar waxwings, several great blue herons, and a few ospreys, we came very close to a mature bald eagle before it flew from its aerie. Rounding a bend, just past an alder swamp, we surprised an American bittern standing in some grass, and it exploded into the air with a squawk. The river also harbors a population of yellow lampmussels (*Lampsilis cariosa*), a threatened mussel that thrives only in clear, undisturbed water.

As you paddle out onto Upper Mattawamkeag Lake, emerging from an extensive stand of rushes, note the tiered fields on the distant hillside. After clearing the river mouth, paddle around to the right, about 1 mile down through The Thoroughfare, to Mattawamkeag Lake. Watch carefully around the channel's edges, near what look like cattails, for an occasional patch of sweet flag, with its 3-inch-long dense flower spikes growing out of the stem's center. You can distinguish these leaves by their off-center midvein and spicy aroma. Horsetail, yellow pondlily, pickerelweed, and other aquatic plants crowd the edges of this shallow channel.

As you clear the channel, the forested Bug Islands appear, with emergent rocks all around, making this end of the lake quite scenic. Teddy Roosevelt stayed at the cottages on nearby Hook Point.

Paddling out into the middle and looking back, on a clear day you can see Katahdin off in the distance. Compared with Upper Lake, little development crowds the shores of Mattawamkeag. Due to the abundant wildlife, beautiful surroundings, and views of the mountains in Baxter State Park, the state has protected much of the lake's southern portion, including more than 7 miles of lakeshore and 126 acres on Big Island, home to a rare stand of old-growth timber. The purchase also includes 3 miles of riverfront on West Branch Mattawamkeag River.

Primarily deciduous trees cover the heavily forested shoreline, but spruce, balsam fir, and other conifers grow farther back. We saw lots of ospreys on Mattawamkeag, along with four bald eagles: two adults and two immature. They usually nest on Norway Island.

85 | Chesuncook Lake, West Branch Penobscot River, and Pine Stream Flowage

This trip covers a huge but outstanding paddling resource. You can trace Henry David Thoreau's 1850s journeys by paddling down West Branch Penobscot River then down the length of Chesuncook Lake. Although not for the faint of heart, this area epitomizes the northern Maine wilderness. You could also paddle Pine Stream Flowage, with its abundant waterfowl and moose, as a separate trip.

Location: Chesuncook Township, T2 R12 WELS, and six other areas
Maps: *Maine Atlas & Gazetteer,* Map 49: A4, A5, B4, B5, C3, C4, C5, D3, D4, D5 and Map 50: B1, C1, D1, D2, E1; USGS Caribou Lake North, Caribou Lake South, Chesuncook, Cuxabexis Lake, Harrington Lake, Longley Pond, Mud Pond, Penobscot Farm, Pine Stream Flowage, Ragmuff Stream, Rainbow Lake West
Area/Length: 26,200 total acres; West Branch Penobscot River, 20 miles one way; Pine Stream Flowage, 15 miles one way
Time: Multiday trip
Habitat Type: Huge, scenic lake; northern forest streams with marshlands
Fish: Brook trout, lake trout, landlocked salmon, white perch (see fish advisories, Appendix A)
Information: Chesuncook Lake House, chesuncooklakehouse.com
Take Note: Fill up with gas in Millinocket; frequent hazardous paddling conditions; North Maine Woods camping and entrance fees required, northmainewoods.org; camping only in designated sites; no fire permits required; little development on Chesuncook, more on Ripogenus and Caribou lakes along the Golden Road

GETTING THERE

West Branch Penobscot River. From Millinocket, at the T intersection of Routes 11 and 157 with Katahdin Avenue, turn right on Katahdin Avenue, go 0.2 mile, and turn left on Bates Street/Millinocket Lake Road/Baxter Park Road. Go 9.2 miles (cumulative: 9.4 miles) and turn left on Sawdust Pile Road, followed by an immediate right on Golden Road. Go 43.2 miles (52.6 miles), passing through the Caribou Checkpoint (pay fees), and turn left on a connector road. Go 0.8 mile (53.4 miles) and veer right on Poulin Road. Go 2.7 miles (56.1 miles) to the access on Lobster Stream. (45° 53.532′ N, 69° 33.888′ W)

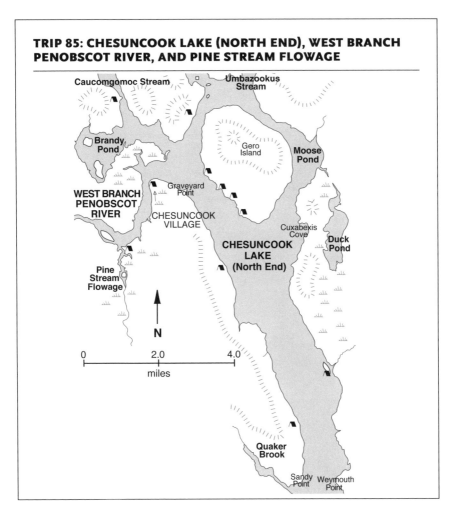

Ripogenus Lake. As above, except go 22.4 miles (cumulative: 31.8 miles) on Golden Road, turn right on Chesuncook Lake Road at Allagash Gateway Campground sign, and go 1.2 miles (33 miles) straight to the access. (45° 53.016′ N, 69° 14.160′ W)

Pine Stream Flowage. As above, except go 41.1 miles (cumulative: 50.5 miles) on Golden Road, passing through the Caribou Checkpoint (pay fees), and turn right on Village Road. Go 3.2 miles (53.7 miles) to the access by the bridge. (45° 56.238′ N, 69° 24.966′ W)

TRIP 85: CHESUNCOOK LAKE (SOUTH END)

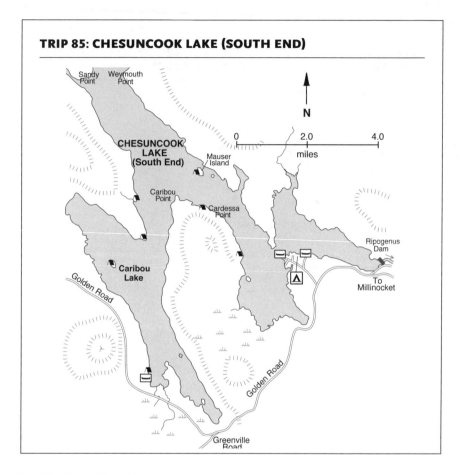

WHAT YOU'LL SEE

In many ways, Chesuncook Lake—Maine's third largest, after Sebago and Moosehead—and West Branch Penobscot River that feeds it represent quintessential northern Maine. Huge, wild, and beautiful, Chesuncook stretches 20 miles. Although only 1 to 3 miles wide, even modest winds can generate very rough conditions. Wind, of course, does not affect paddling on West Branch or on Pine Stream Flowage, which flows northward to the junction of Chesuncook and West Branch.

Chesuncook and West Branch Penobscot River. *Chesuncook*, an Abenaki word, means "place of the principal outlet" or "place where many streams empty in." The construction of dams between 1840 and 1920 turned broad, grassy meadows where a number of shallow streams converged, into a huge lake. When Henry David Thoreau paddled here in 1853 and 1857, a small lake existed, but with the completion of the Chesuncook dam in 1904, the rising

TRIP 85: WEST BRANCH PENOBSCOT RIVER AND PINE STREAM FLOWAGE

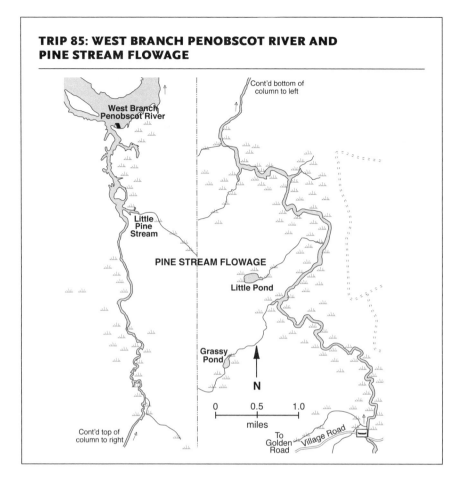

lake eliminated some West Branch and Pine Stream rapids and portions of many streams.

Subsequently, the larger Ripogenus Dam—built in 1920 to control the West Branch level for the transport of pulp mill logs, a practice banned in 1972—raised the water level enough that Ripogenus and Caribou lakes merged with Chesuncook. The largest privately owned dam in the United States, Ripogenus Dam stretches 795 feet wide and 83 feet high. In the early 1950s, the owners retrofit the dam with 37 megawatt-hydropower turbines.

A wonderful trip extends from Lobster Lake outlet stream along the Penobscot West Branch and into Chesuncook Lake. From the Lobster Stream access (see Lobster Lake, Trip 80), you paddle nearly 20 miles to Chesuncook Village on the lake. This West Branch section flows gently, with only a few stretches of quickwater, especially between Big Island and Little Ragmuff Stream.

Watch for moose along the river's winding course. We saw four during an

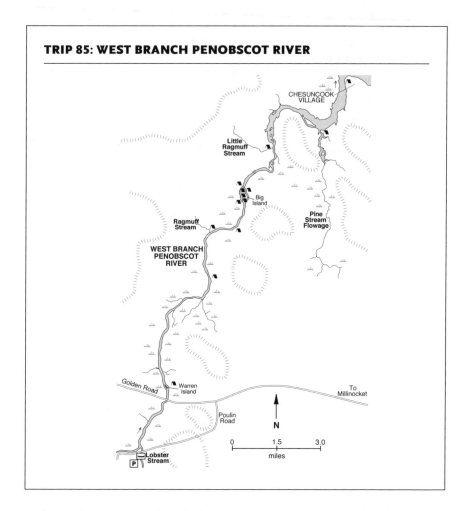

TRIP 85: WEST BRANCH PENOBSCOT RIVER

CHESUNCOOK-VILLAGE

Little Ragmuff Stream

Big Island

Pine Stream Flowage

Ragmuff Stream

WEST BRANCH PENOBSCOT RIVER

Golden Road   Warren Island

To Millinocket

Poulin Road

N

0   1.5   3.0
miles

Lobster Stream
P

early October trip, one a huge bull whose broad antlers reflected early morning light as we rounded a river bend. We also saw white-tailed deer, mergansers, ospreys, gray jays, migrating snow geese, loons, and kingfishers.

Balsam fir, spruce, northern white cedar, and white pine grow along the West Branch's heavily wooded shores, with alders and other shrubby vegetation closer to the water. You can explore several West Branch inlets on the way down to Chesuncook. More than a dozen campsites perch along the riverbanks between Lobster Stream and Chesuncook. Putting in late in the day, we camped at Warren Island just below the Golden Road—a place where Thoreau camped and is now sometimes called Thoreau Island. Another half-dozen campsites lie on and near Big Island, about 10 miles from the Lobster Stream access.

As you round the river's final bend, buildings of Chesuncook Village (accessible only by boat or floatplane) appear on the right. The village offers a

We see moose frequently in northern Maine. Note the line of flies on its nose.

number of lodging options, including the Chesuncook Lake House. The lake here does not appear huge because Gero Island—more than 3,000 acres of Maine Public Reserve land, with four beautiful campsites—obscures your view. The area north of Gero Island offers many hours of exploration, as well as connections to Caucomgomoc Lake (Trip 87) and Umbazooksus Lake. About a dozen other campsites lie on both sides of the lake, along inlet streams to the north, and on Mouser Island in the south.

The northwest-southeast orientation of Chesuncook Lake can generate very rough water, as winds tend to blow from the northwest or southeast. We fought strong winds for hours as we slowly made our way down the lake's eastern shore. Waves lapped over the bow even in modest winds; another boater told us he'd seen 4-foot waves here. We prefer to use sea kayaks—with spray skirts handy, if necessary—rather than open canoes.

Pine Stream Flowage. This small stream slowly meanders along, dropping a little more than 2 feet each mile, making it easy to paddle in both directions. You can paddle up and back or, with two vehicles, continue a short way on West Branch Penobscot River, followed by paddling down the length of Chesuncook Lake. If you choose to go up and back on a two-day trip, you could stay at the campsite at the junction of West Branch Penobscot River and Pine Stream Flowage.

This is the heart of moose country, and it's possible to see a dozen here on a trip. Joe Polis, Henry David Thoreau's guide back in the 1800s, shot a moose on their trip here. You would also see hundreds of ducks, as this is one of the most productive breeding grounds in Maine. Although the map shows only the streambed, during times of high water, Pine Stream flows out into the adjacent lowland marsh.

On one of our trips, we bumped into a retired state of Maine biologist who, for many years, paddled Pine Stream Flowage to conduct annual waterfowl surveys. Besides the abundant waterfowl, he commented on the abundance of moose.

The usual bog vegetation grows here in profusion, providing cover for waterfowl and forage for moose and other birds and animals. The northern boreal forest—comprising spruce, fir, pine, tamarack, and northern white cedar—sits well back from the water. This area has seen quite a bit of logging, which can best be appreciated by looking at an aerial view using Google Maps or Google Earth.

86 | Loon Lake, Big Hurd Pond, and Little Hurd Pond

Apart from the abundant wildlife, you'll likely have these remote ponds to yourself. Expect to see loons, ospreys, bald eagles, common terns, moose, and white-tailed deer.

Location: T6 R15 WELS
Maps: *Maine Atlas & Gazetteer*, Map 49: A2 and Map 55: E1; USGS Caucomgomoc Lake East, Caucomgomoc West, Ragmuff Stream
Area: Loon Lake, 1,140 acres; Big Hurd Pond, 250 acres; Little Hurd Pond, 180 acres
Time: All day or multiday trip
Habitat Type: Lake and shallow ponds with marshy coves
Fish: Brook trout, landlocked salmon, white perch (see fish advisories, Appendix A)
Information: The Pingree family and New England Forestry Foundation developed a 762,000-acre conservation easement, including the west shore of Loon Lake and Big Hurd Pond, newenglandforestry.org
Take Note: Fill up with gas in Millinocket; no personal watercraft; campfire permit required, 207-435-7963

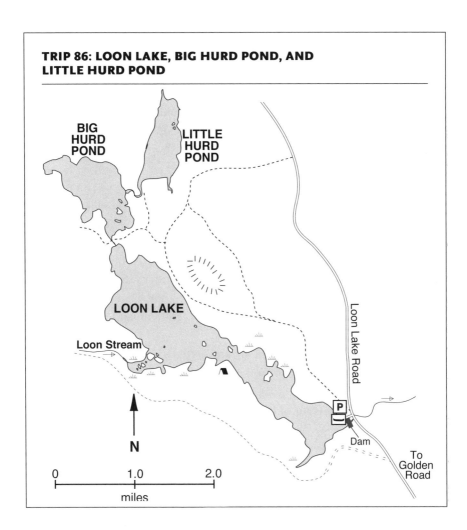

TRIP 86: LOON LAKE, BIG HURD POND, AND LITTLE HURD POND

BIG HURD POND

LITTLE HURD POND

LOON LAKE

Loon Stream

Loon Lake Road

P

Dam

To Golden Road

N

0   1.0   2.0
miles

GETTING THERE

From Millinocket, at the T intersection of Routes 11 and 157 with Katahdin Avenue, turn right on Katahdin Avenue, go 0.2 mile, and turn left on Bates Street/ Millinocket Lake Road/Baxter Park Road. Go 9.2 miles (cumulative: 9.4 miles) and turn left on Sawdust Pile Road, followed by an immediate right on Golden Road. Go 46.5 miles (55.9 miles), passing through the Caribou Checkpoint (pay fees), and turn right on Ragmuff Road. Go 14.4 miles (70.3 miles) and turn left on a connector road. Go 0.4 mile (70.7 miles) and turn left on Loon Lake Road. Go 1.2 miles (71.9 miles) and turn right. Go 2 miles (73.9 miles) to the access on the left. (46° 7.920′ N, 69° 36.186′ W)

WHAT YOU'LL SEE

Loon Lake. We set out on Loon Lake on a calm July evening, with scarcely a ripple on the water's surface, the only sound the steady dip of paddles and the plaintive cry of a loon on this aptly named lake. We left behind thoughts of the long drive on bumpy logging roads through clearcuts and third-or fourth-generation spruce and fir regrowth. Few people visit Loon Lake; most never make it this far or, if they do, pass by on their way to more famous paddling destinations.

Unlike nearby Allagash River and Allagash Lake, this wonderful place lies off the beaten path yet remains readily accessible by vehicle. Loon Lake offers about 10 miles of shoreline to explore, in addition to a paddleable section of Loon Stream inlet. Big Hurd Pond provides another 3.5 miles, plus islands.

Loon Lake and Big Hurd Pond have varied shorelines, with coves to explore, marshy areas providing great bird habitat, rock outcrops draped in moss and ferns, and majestic white pines overlooking the water. Though we could not find the nest, we saw an adult bald eagle and several immature. We lost count of ospreys and loons.

Loon Stream inlet—shallow, marshy, and dotted with islands—has abundant wildlife and remains our favorite section. Floating vegetation crowds the channel, and we saw nesting ring-necked ducks here. You can paddle some distance up the inlet stream, at least at high-water levels.

Big and Little Hurd Ponds. With high-water levels, the case when we visited in mid-July, you can paddle easily from Loon Lake into Big Hurd Pond. The Loon Lake level can drop considerably, though, making access into Big Hurd more difficult. Even at high water, watch out for rocks in the connecting channel.

Big Hurd Pond, small compared with Loon Lake, has a protected feel to it. When we paddled in from Loon Lake as the sun dipped down over western hills, the place seemed magical. Near the access from Loon Lake, several islands crop up, along with a few more near the pond's center. Mostly solid rock, the islands' huge granite boulders reach down into the water in places. Look for thick carpets of moss and lichen and copious blueberries in season.

To get from Big Hurd into Little Hurd Pond, paddle up a shallow stream then carry your boat about 100 feet over a rocky area and small ledge. In early morning, we saw four deer (three were bucks) and a moose. An unusual sight, two of the deer and the moose browsed close together along the Little Hurd Pond outlet. They would have fit into one camera frame. Common terns continually skimmed the pond's surface during our paddle here.

Although we saw lots of wildlife at Little Hurd, paddling here is not enjoyable. Extremely shallow, with few places deeper than 1 foot, the lake has a bottom of thick organic ooze. Currents created by paddling agitate the bottom, leaving a trail of thousands of tiny bubbles of marsh gas. Even a family of common goldeneye swimming along left a bubble trail. Little Hurd probably does not have too many centuries of life left before filling in and getting taken over by encroaching tamarack and bog vegetation.

87 | Caucomgomoc Lake, Rowe Pond, Round Pond, Daggett Pond and Poland Pond

These bodies of water are about two hours away from the nearest paved road; it could take even longer when the roads have ruts. If, however, you want a multiday wilderness experience, paddling here will provide it. You will see loons, ospreys, bald eagles, moose, otters, white-tailed deer, and lots more.

Location: T6 R14 WELS, T6 R15 WELS, T7 R14 WELS, T7 R15 WELS
Maps: *Maine Atlas & Gazetteer*, Map 55: D2, D3, E1, E2, E3; USGS Allagash Lake, Caucomgomoc Lake East, Caucomgomoc Lake West
Area: Caucomgomoc Lake, 5,081 acres; Rowe Pond, 250 acres; Round Pond, 375 acres; Daggett Pond, 461 acres; Poland Pond, 490 acres
Time: Multiday trip
Habitat Type: Shallow lake, ponds, and connecting streams with miles of shoreline
Fish: Brook trout, lake trout, landlocked salmon, white perch (see fish advisories, Appendix A)
Information: Loon Lodge, loonlodgemaine.com; the Pingree family and New England Forestry Foundation developed a 762,000-acre conservation easement, including the northeast shore of Caucomgomoc Lake, the east shore of Rowe Pond, and all of Round, Daggett, and Poland ponds, newenglandforestry.org
Take Note: Fill up with gas in Millinocket; paddle smaller ponds when winds blow on Caucomgomoc; no personal watercraft; campfire permit required, 207-435-7963

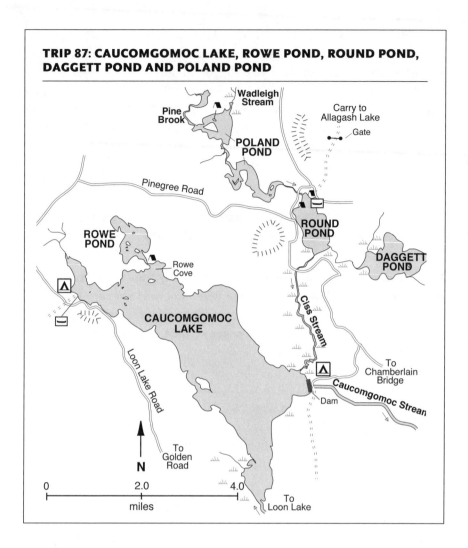

TRIP 87: CAUCOMGOMOC LAKE, ROWE POND, ROUND POND, DAGGETT POND AND POLAND POND

GETTING THERE

Caucomgomoc Lake. From the Loon Lake access road (see previous entry), go 7.4 miles (cumulative: 81.3 miles) north, turn right on Depot Road, and go to the end. (46° 13.332′N, 69° 39.768′ W)

Round Pond. From Depot Road, above, go 4.5 miles (cumulative: 85.8 miles) north on Loon Lake/Caucogomic/Cave roads, and turn right on Pingree Road. Go 6.3 miles (92.1 miles) and turn sharply left. Go 1.9 miles (94 miles) to the access on the right. (46° 15.222′ N, 69° 33.894′ W)

WHAT YOU'LL SEE

These bodies of water lie in the heart of northern Maine canoe country. While more famous for the Allagash Wilderness Waterway, this region also offers superb lake and pond paddling. Caucomgomoc Lake provides a good starting point, but with its northwest-southeast orientation, it often suffers from strong winds and rough water.

Caucomgomoc Lake and Rowe Pond. Caucomgomoc's west end, where the lake seems less large, and the east end, where one can travel up into Round, Daggett, and Poland ponds, appeal most to the quietwater paddler. The more adventuresome can reach Caucomgomoc by paddling or poling downstream (north) from Loon Lake (Trip 86) for 4 miles or can use Caucomgomoc as an Allagash Lake access (Trip 88). We put in on Caucomgomoc and spent several wonderful days exploring this area. We started out paddling the northwest inlet and the shoreline over to Rowe Pond, staying our first night at the Rowe Cove campsite.

Caucomgomoc Lake's 26-mile shoreline has a wild and highly varied feel. In the northwestern tip's narrow inlet channel, we spotted an otter, and we watched another for about half an hour between Rowe Cove and Caucomgomoc Dam. We saw lots of loons, several bald eagles, ospreys, moose, and deer along here. Gorgeous islands, including Henry's Island, which sports a small campsite, dot the surface of Rowe Pond. During an early morning paddle, we heard a group of coyotes howling off in the woods.

Ciss Stream and Round Pond. Ciss Stream enters the lake just northwest of Caucomgomoc Dam. With adequate water levels, Ciss Stream provides very enjoyable paddling up into Round, Daggett, and Poland ponds. The barely perceptible current will not impede your progress as the wide stream wends its way through a broad, flooded valley strewn with sun-whitened stumps and fallen trees. We watched ospreys fish along here with their characteristic hovering manner, we spooked a few ducks, and then we watched a huge bull moose at close range near the Round Pond entrance.

Loon Lodge perches on the northeast shore of Round Pond. This very nice and relatively new sporting camp offers various levels of accommodations, as well as boat-ferrying service partway into Allagash Lake (Trip 88). The only sporting camp in this part of Maine, it's ideal for paddlers seeking more luxurious accommodations.

Poland's drift logs add a playful diversion.

Daggett Pond. Round Pond provides access into two very nice ponds. At Round Pond's southeast end, you can paddle Little Ciss Stream east into Daggett Pond. Watch quietly for moose, deer, and otters as you round this gentle stream's many bends. Daggett Pond, 1.5 miles long and rich with wildlife, offers about 5 miles of beautiful, highly varied shoreline to explore. We watched three moose along the marshy shore at the pond's northwest end.

Firm ground comes right down to the water on the pond's more wooded eastern half. On the point of land extending into the pond along the northeastern shore sits Fort Daggett—not a fort at all, but an elegant summer camp built back in the early 1900s and rarely used today.

Poland Pond. Poland Pond, to the northwest of Round Pond, differs markedly from Daggett Pond but also provides a great day trip. You have to do a bit of upstream poling or pulling your boat through a few hundred yards of quickwater to get there. For wading and lining your boat upstream, be sure to wear water shoes or a pair of old sneakers to help negotiate the rocky, slippery bottom. At the remains of an old dam, carry your boat about 30 feet up over a small rise to get into the pond. Going back downstream, with high enough water you should be able to paddle the modest rapids below the carry.

Because the dam failed, dropping the water level, a band of younger vegetation grows along the shore, providing superb deer forage. We counted six deer, including two large bucks, as we paddled on the pond one mid-July day. Tamarack and other northern fen species grow along the pond's boggy sections.

A narrow channel at its midpoint divides long, narrow, highly convoluted Poland Pond. You may find downed logs blocking Pine Brook, which flows into the pond's northwest tip, but with a little work, you might be able to get through and explore farther north. At the pond's northeast tip, you can explore Wadleigh Stream inlet.

The smaller island at Poland Pond's north end also has a very nice campsite, from which you can walk over to a huge rock face and look out over the pond—often at deer or moose browsing on shoreline vegetation. The campsite has a small beach; campfires here require a permit from the Maine Forest Service.

---

88 | Allagash Lake and Johnson Pond

Exuding northern wilderness, Allagash Lake and Johnson Pond offer one of the best paddling experiences in Maine—that is, if you can get here, often over poor roads and having to portage in. You will be rewarded with sightings of moose, loons, bald eagles, ospreys, common terns, otters, beavers, and lots more.

Location: T7 R14 WELS, T8 R14 WELS
Maps: *Maine Atlas & Gazetteer*, Map 55: C3, C4, D3, D4; USGS Allagash Lake, Tramway
Area: Allagash Lake, 4,260 acres; Johnson Pond, 197 acres
Time: Multiday
Habitat Type: Clear, sand-bottomed lake
Fish: Brook trout, lake trout (see fish advisories, Appendix A)
Information: The Pingree family and New England Forestry Foundation developed a 762,000-acre conservation easement, including all of Johnson Lake and the remaining shore of Allagash Lake not owned by the state, newenglandforestry.org
Take Note: Fill up with gas in Millinocket; difficult driving conditions and lakes not easily accessible; entry streams low except in spring; no motors; camping only at authorized sites; no fire permits required

GETTING THERE

We prefer the access at the Allagash Lake Ranger Station in Northwest Piscataquis, but all accesses are difficult. Loon Lake Lodge will ferry you in for a fee.

Ranger Station. Approaching Round Pond coming from the Caucomgomoc Lake access (see previous trip), from the sharp left off Pingree Road (cumulative: 92.1 miles), go 1.9 miles (94 miles) north and turn left on the access road. Go about 2.5 miles (96.5 miles) to the end (there is a left turn about midway),

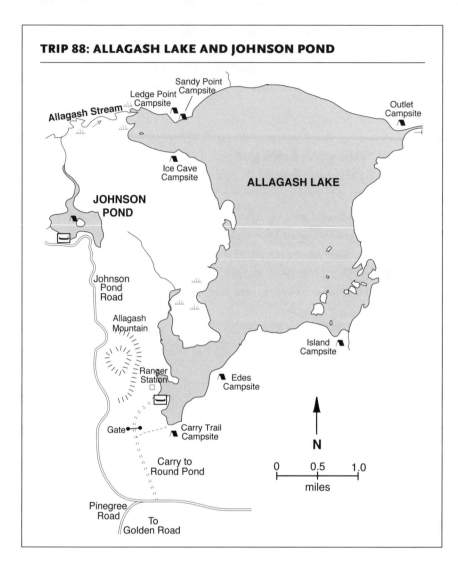

TRIP 88: ALLAGASH LAKE AND JOHNSON POND

Sandy Point
Campsite

Ledge Point
Campsite

Allagash Stream

Outlet
Campsite

Ice Cave
Campsite

ALLAGASH LAKE

JOHNSON
POND

Johnson
Pond
Road

Allagash
Mountain

Island
Campsite

Ranger
Station

Edes
Campsite

Gate

Carry Trail
Campsite

N

Carry to
Round Pond

0   0.5   1.0
miles

Pinegree
Road

To
Golden Road

and portage the last mile to the Ranger Station. (46° 17.400′ N, 69° 33.534′ W)

Johnson Pond. From the sharp left off Pingree Road above (cumulative: 92.1 miles), go 1.4 miles (93.5 miles) north and turn left on Johnson Pond Road. Go about 5.7 miles (99.2 miles) to the Johnson Pond access. Paddle down the outlet and Allagash Stream, portaging over beaver dams; you may have to walk through shallow water. (46° 18.996′ N, 69° 35.028′ W)

Allagash Stream. Continue beyond Johnson Pond, above, for about another 1.6 miles (100.8 miles) and turn right. Go about 1.8 miles (102.6 miles) to the access where Allagash Stream nears the road. Paddle downstream to the lake. The road may be bad. The water may be low; the upstream return trip will be difficult. (46° 20.394′ N, 69° 36.462′W)

WHAT YOU'LL SEE

Allagash Lake remains at the top of our list, one of our very favorite Maine lakes. While large and subject to heavy winds, the lake's geometry prevents waves from building up as much as on other large lakes in the region. Wind does not affect the large number of protected areas on the lake.

The lake nestles beneath Allagash and Poland mountains, with deep, wild forest all around. Moss-covered rocks line the shores of marshy inlets. You will not hear motors or automobiles or even see floatplanes landing here, as it is the only Maine lake that excludes all motors, even electric.

Most people travel to this region to paddle the Allagash Wilderness Waterway, created by the state in 1966, and they usually stick to the far better known waters: Allagash River and the string of connected lakes (Chamberlain, Eagle, Churchill) that some 10,000 paddlers travel each year. Far fewer take the side trip up Allagash Stream to Allagash Lake. Canoes may use up to 10 HP motors on most of the Allagash Wilderness Waterway but not on Allagash Lake.

When we visited, we spent most of our time in the southern end, protected from the wind, which seems almost ever-present in northern Maine. Two permitted campsites lie at the south end: Carry Trail and Edes. Large groups traveling through Allagash Lake from Round Pond and Caucomgomoc use the Carry Trail Campsite pretty heavily. For small groups, we prefer Edes, with its sandy beach, nice fire ring, and several flat tenting sites.

The cove extending from the south end up to the northwest is simply fantastic. On an early morning paddle, we watched deer browse along a grassy section of shoreline, and we surprised a young moose eating pond vegetation as we entered the small pond at the cove's north end. Along the way, take a close-up look at classic northern bog vegetation: tamarack, sphagnum, pitcher plants, sundew, cranberry, swamp rose, sheep laurel, leatherleaf, sweetgale, and—perhaps our favorite—the delicate rose pogonia orchid. We watched several families of common goldeneye along here; studied the graceful, ternlike flight of Bonaparte's gulls; saw ospreys and a broad-winged hawk; and watched loons from enough distance to avoid disturbing them.

Farther north, mosses and polypody cover the granite boulders separating sections of thickly wooded shoreline. The clean water and generally sandy bottom support numerous freshwater mussels that filter out microscopic food particles. The many little coves and inlets provide lots of opportunity to look for deer, moose, otters, mink, and other mammals that call this home.

Common terns nest on a few rocky islands, and we saw three gull species: ring-billed, herring, and Bonaparte's gulls—the last an uncommon summer resident in New England.

As the shoreline curves west, you will reach the Ice Cave Campsite. A short uphill hike takes you to several fascinating ice caves that can be quite refreshing on a hot, humid day. Bring a flashlight and prepare to get a little muddy as you squeeze down into the cold granite caves, where ice lasts well into the summer.

Also explore the numerous islands, with one campsite, in the southeast corner. Not on a route into or out of the lake, this campsite sees fewer visitors. Campsites at the north end, near the lake's inlet and outlet, receive heaviest use. Quite a few groups come through Allagash Lake as part of extended trips north on the Allagash River. During three days here, we saw an Outward Bound group and a large group from a wilderness-experience camp.

Johnson Pond. If you want to do more extended exploring, take a trip up Allagash Stream and a side stream to Johnson Pond. This fairly wide, deep section of Allagash Stream entering at the northeast tip flows slowly, although you will encounter a few riffles. Watch for a narrow stream coming in from the left about 1.5 miles from the lake. You can make your way up this tiny stream, although you have to pull your boat up over several beaver dams and pull yourself through thick alder swamps in places.

After the last barrier, the stream opens up gradually into Johnson Pond. A grassy marsh initially surrounds this narrow section, but it widens out into a simply gorgeous pond about two-thirds of a mile across with a large island in the center. A sizable campsite exists on the island, with several separate tent sites. Several outfitters store boats on the island for clients who arrive by float-plane then depart from here for Allagash River trips. When we visited back in 1994, merlins nested in a tree on the island. More common in northern Canada, these small, rare falcons look somewhat like small peregrine falcons.

89 | Lower South Branch Pond and Upper South Branch Pond

These two small lakes, among the smallest in this guide, sit in a valley surrounded by forested hillsides and spectacular Baxter State Park peaks. While you're here, take advantage of wonderful hiking opportunities. We saw a loon pair here.

Location: T5 R9 WELS
Maps: *Maine Atlas & Gazetteer*, Map 51: A1; USGS Wassataquoik Lake
Area: Lower South Branch Pond, 93 acres; Upper South Branch Pond, 84 acres
Time: 4 hours
Habitat Type: Small, deep, oligotrophic ponds in a spectacular setting
Fish: Brook trout (see fish advisories, Appendix A)
Information: Baxter State Park, baxterstateparkauthority.com, 207-723-5140; camping reservations required
Take Note: No motors; canoes for rent; this popular area includes a campground and sees a lot of traffic; illegal to remove fossils (or anything else) from the park

GETTING THERE

From I-95, Exit 264 northbound, go 0.4 mile left (west) on Route 158 and turn right on Route 11. Go 9.3 miles (cumulative: 9.7 miles) and turn left on Route 159, which becomes Grand Lake Road at Shin Pond then Perimeter Road at the Baxter Park gate (fee). Go 33 miles (42.7 miles), turn left at South Branch ponds sign, and go 2.2 miles (44.9 miles) to the access. (46° 6.546′ N, 68° 54.132′ W).

WHAT YOU'LL SEE

Spectacular. Awesome. Superlatives barely convey the beauty of these ponds and the surrounding mountains. The ponds perch in an alpine valley about 1,000 feet above sea level, and the surrounding mountain peaks rise another 2,500 feet, much of that via exposed rock faces.

The shorelines of South Branch ponds—each less than 1 mile in length, making them among the smallest bodies of water in this guide—lack variation, and the extremely oligotrophic, crystal clear waters are nearly devoid of life. In the right light, you can see down more than 20 feet. Apparently, though, the

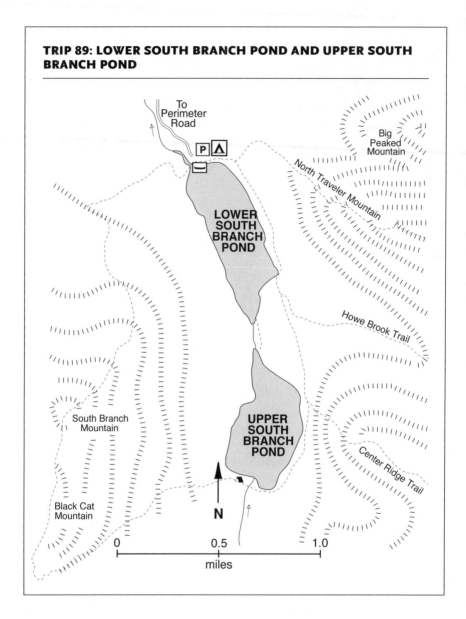

TRIP 89: LOWER SOUTH BRANCH POND AND UPPER SOUTH BRANCH POND

To Perimeter Road

Big Peaked Mountain

North Traveler Mountain

LOWER SOUTH BRANCH POND

Howe Brook Trail

UPPER SOUTH BRANCH POND

South Branch Mountain

Center Ridge Trail

Black Cat Mountain

N

0   0.5   1.0

miles

loon pair we saw on Upper South Branch Pond could find enough fish, and the freshwater mussels we spotted could find adequate microscopic life.

At Lower South Branch Pond's southeastern tip, you can portage into Upper South Branch Pond over a fairly flat, several-hundred-yard trail. The jagged, sheer granite cliffs of Baxter's Katahdin extend down into the water, making Upper Pond even more spectacular than Lower Pond. Steep, dramatic ridges of Traveler Mountain lie to the east. The charcoal-gray rhyolite on these ridges

Canoers take in glorious fall foliage on Lower South Branch Pond. Jerry and Marcy Monkman/Ecophotography

differs geologically from the pinkish Katahdin granite, which cooled very slowly deep underground, forming large crystals. Traveler Mountain rhyolite, lava from a volcanic eruption, solidified into finer-grained crystals about 400 million years ago.

The fossiliferous rock that you find here represents another interesting South Branch ponds geologic feature. Look along the shoreline for pieces of sandstone or shale embedded with fossils of small brachiopods, or marine animals superficially resembling clams. Glaciers carried these fossil-bearing rocks here, one of the few places in Maine where one can find fossils.

Hardwoods dominate the vegetation around South Branch ponds, including paper birch, red maple, sugar maple, and beech. A few white pine, red pine, spruce, and fir scatter amid the hardwoods. In the understory, you will see the large-leafed striped maple and beaked hazelnut, which produces an edible, filbertlike nut. Logging began here in the mid-1800s, first for white pine, then spruce, and finally pulpwood. The last logging ended in 1965, when the remaining logging rights ran out, according to the deeds negotiated by Percival Baxter when he acquired the land. Governor Baxter gave to the state of Maine 200,000 acres of land acquired over a 45-year period—one of the most impressive private land-protection efforts ever. We should all be thankful to Governor Baxter for his farsighted vision in preserving the beauty of this area.

From the campground, enjoy the spectacular hikes in this part of Baxter State Park. North Traveler Mountain Trail provides dramatic views down into South Branch ponds. Howe Brook Trail leads to a spectacular cascading waterfall on the side of Traveler Mountain. You can also backpack south along Notch Trail to Russell Pond and remote Wassataquoik Lake, which provides the most remote paddling in the park (rare blueback trout; canoes available for rent on an honor system).

90 | Grand Lake Matagamon

A large part of Grand Lake Matagamon lies within Baxter State Park, which allows motors on the lake but protects it from development. In this wildlife paradise, you should see loons, ospreys, moose, white-tailed deer, and many songbirds.

Location: Trout Brook Township, T6 R8 WELS
Maps: *Maine Atlas & Gazetteer*, Map 51: A2 and Map 57: E1, E2; USGS Frost Pond, Trout Brook Mountain
Area: 4,165 acres
Time: Multiday
Habitat Type: Large, deep lake with some marshy areas
Fish: Brook trout, lake trout, landlocked salmon (see fish advisories, Appendix A)
Information: Baxter State Park, baxterstateparkauthority.com, 207-723-5140; camping reservations required
Take Note: Wind can make paddling hazardous; no fire permits required at designated sites; camping fees

GETTING THERE
From I-95, Exit 264 northbound, go 0.4 mile left (west) on Route 158 and turn right on Route 11. Go 9.3 miles (cumulative: 9.7 miles) and turn left on Route 159, which becomes Grand Lake Road at Shin Pond. Go 25.9 miles (35.6 miles) to the access on the right, just before the Baxter State Park gate in North Penobscot. (46° 9.228′ N, 68° 48.390′ W)

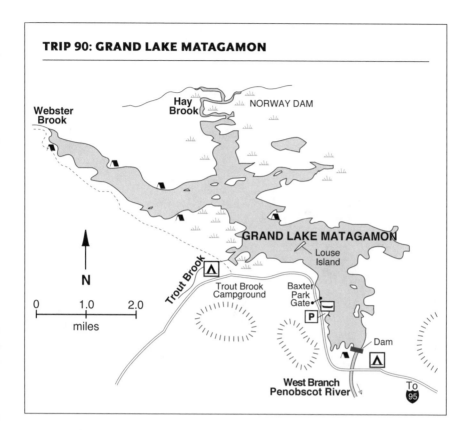

TRIP 90: GRAND LAKE MATAGAMON

Webster Brook

Hay Brook · NORWAY DAM

GRAND LAKE MATAGAMON

Louse Island

N

0   1.0   2.0
miles

Trout Brook

Trout Brook Campground

Baxter Park Gate

P

Dam

West Branch Penobscot River

To 95

WHAT YOU'LL SEE

About half of Grand Lake Matagamon lies within the boundaries of Baxter State Park. The park allows motors here and on Webster Lake but protects both from development. With 6.5 square miles of water coupled with its remoteness, Grand Lake Matagamon provides a large measure of solitude and would take two or more days to explore fully.

The park maintains five campsites on the lake; distances to the campsites from the access point are as follows: Togue Ledge, 2.5 miles; Boody Brook, 4.7 miles; Second Lake, 4.9 miles; Pine Point, 6.1 miles; Northwest Cove, 7.1 miles.

Grand Lake Matagamon has changed from the time Thoreau paddled it in the mid-1800s. Much of it remains wild, but the downed timber he had to negotiate drowned long ago, with higher lake levels produced by a new concrete dam. An obstacle course of exposed and barely submerged stumps remains in shallower areas, but you can now reach most of the lake by boat.

When Thoreau stopped on Louse Island, where he ate fried moose, he found all three species of native pine, and those three remain today. Besides the widely

Spruce grouse, an unwary bird, inhabits the northern boreal forest. Credit: Seokhee Kim, Creative Commons on Flickr

distributed red and white pines, you can find fair numbers of rare jack pines on Louse, as well as on other islands and along the shore. Maine represents the southern extension of the jack pine range, which grows almost to the Arctic Circle, the farthest north of any pine species. We distinguish it from other pines by its short, 1- to 1.5-inch-long needles. Note the persistent, thin, curved cones from 1 to 3 inches long, often with two cones growing on opposite sides of a branch. Seeds from these cones are important food for wildlife.

As you paddle out from the access, go left around the first island to view a thick stand of jack pine, along with paper birch and quaking aspen. In addition to breaking up the view, dozens of islands provide scenic spots for picnics, swimming, or just lounging around—bugs permitting.

Continuing around to the left, a series of coves appears, one of them connecting to Trout Brook, which leads up to Trout Brook Farm Campground in Baxter Park. When the wind is up on the main lake, one could put in at the campground and paddle down Trout Brook to the lake, through an extensive marshy area. When we paddled here, a pair of ospreys nested at the lake inlet.

More marshlands, seldom visited by boaters, appear just south and north of the inlet. Look for moose in early morning and evening in this largest expanse of marsh on the lake. Marsh and alder swamps in the sinewy north inlet, called Norway Dam, provide another good area for moose. We also saw many white-tailed deer along the shore in the middle of the day.

Balsam fir, topped with pointed spires, grow with great frequency in the Trout Brook area. Note the beautiful dark-purple cones, 2 to 4 inches long, pointing upward from the branches. An important browse plant for moose and white-tailed deer, dense balsam foliage provides refuge for spruce grouse and many smaller birds, as well. We watched flocks of cedar waxwings darting from the alders and firs to catch insects out over Trout Brook, with its absolutely crystal-clear water.

Several northern flickers had chipped out holes in the marshland's dead trees, inadvertently providing homes for numerous cavity-nesting birds, such as wood ducks, common and hooded mergansers, chickadees, nuthatches, wrens, tree swallows, bluebirds, and kestrels. Matagamon offers hours—even days—of birding and wildlife viewing.

Forested islands and boulders appropriate for picnicking, swimming, and sunning appear in profusion. Wildlife abounds, and solitude awaits those who explore the marshy coves and inlets. For an exciting and varied vacation, combine paddling here with hiking the extensive trails of Baxter State Park.

LOON: VOICE OF THE NORTHERN WILDERNESS

For us, no animal better symbolizes wilderness than the loon, whose haunting cry resonates through the night air on many northern lakes. The bird seems almost mystical, with its distinctive black-and-white plumage, daggerlike bill, and piercing red eyes. But like our remaining wilderness, the loon is threatened over much of its range. As recreational pressures increase, the loon gets pushed farther away. We who share its waters bear responsibility for protecting this wonderful bird.

The common loon, *Gavia immer*, a large diving bird that lives almost its entire life in water, visits land only to mate and to incubate eggs. Although adapted remarkably well to water, the loon has difficulty on land because its rearward leg position, which aids in swimming, prevents it from walking. Unlike most birds, the loon has solid bones, allowing it to dive to great depths. Its internal air sac controls how high it floats; by compressing this sac, a loon can submerge gradually, with barely a ripple, or swim with just its head above water.

Its heavy body and rearward legs make takeoff difficult. A loon may require a quarter-mile to build up enough speed to lift off, and it may need to circle a small lake several times to gain enough altitude to clear nearby hills. When migrating, a loon flies rapidly—up to 90 MPH—but cannot soar.

The loon generally mates for life and can live for 30 years. The female lays two eggs in early May, and both male and female incubate the moss-green eggs. It builds its nest close to shore, where a passing paddler can scare birds away and a motorboat wake can flood the nest with cold water. The loon most often nests on islands to hide the eggs from predators.

Loon chicks hatch covered in black down and usually enter the water a day after hatching. Chicks grow quickly on a diet of small fish and crustaceans. By two weeks of age, they reach half their adult size and can dive to relatively deep lake bottoms. Loon chicks remain dependent on their parents for about eight weeks and do not fly until ten to twelve weeks of age. Once they've left the nest, loons return to land after three or four years, when they reach breeding age. Young mature at sea, having followed their elders to saltwater wintering areas.

On the threatened or endangered list in most other Northeastern states, loons remain plentiful in Maine, although slow but steady growth has pla-teaued in the last ten years, with an estimated population statewide of about 4,000 adult birds. Breeding pairs are territorial, which limits the ultimate population size within the state. It remains unclear whether lingering lead shot and fishing weights on lake bottoms, as well as continued mercury ema-nations from coal-fired power plants, further dampen populations. According to the Tufts Wildlife Clinic, chicks die primarily from collisions with personal watercraft and motorboats, and adults die primarily from the ingestion of lead sinkers and jigs. Although we no longer use small lead weights for fishing or lead shot for waterfowl hunting, the large amounts of lead deposited on lake bottoms during the last 100 years lingers throughout Maine's loon habitat.

Besides lead poisoning, encroachment by humans, and nest predation by raccoons and skunks, loons suffer mortality in many other ways. Anglers must avoid leaving spent monofilament line behind, as it, too, causes loon deaths. Because paddlers can easily disturb loons, watch for warning displays during nesting season, early May through mid-July. If a nest fails, loons may try up to two more times, although the later a chick hatches, the lower its chance of survival.

The loon has lived in the Northeast longer than any other bird—an estimated 60 million years. Let's make sure this wonderful species remains protected so future generations may listen to its enchanting music on a still, moonlit night. For more information on how to protect the loon, visit Maine Audubon's website, maineaudubon.org. The society has conducted annual loon counts since 1983.

91 | Sawtelle Deadwater and Mud Pond

The impounded Sawtelle Deadwater, backed up behind a small dam, lies within the Francis D. Dunn Wildlife Management Area. Although set aside for waterfowl production, it's a great place to spot moose and other marshland species. You will see wood ducks, ring-necked ducks, kingfishers, great blue herons, ospreys, moose, muskrat, and possibly beavers and otters.

Location: T6 R7 WELS
Maps: *Maine Atlas & Gazetteer*, Map 51: A3, A4 and Map 57: E3; USGS Hay Lake
Area/Length: 218 acres; 6 miles one way, including Sawtelle Brook and Mud Pond
Time: 6 hours
Habitat Type: Long, narrow, marshy stream through extensive wetland
Fish: Brook trout (see fish advisories, Appendix A)

Take Note: Camping at the Seboeis River campsite 0.7 mile before Scraggly Lake turnoff; campfire permit required, 207-435-7963

GETTING THERE

From I-95, Exit 264 northbound, go 0.4 mile left (west) on Route 158 and turn right on Route 11. Go 9.3 miles (cumulative: 9.7 miles) and turn left on Route 159, which becomes Grand Lake Road at Shin Pond. Go 16.4 miles (26.1 miles) and turn right on Scraggly Lake Road. Go 1.8 miles (27.9 miles) to the access on the left. (46° 9.552′ N, 68° 39.930′ W)

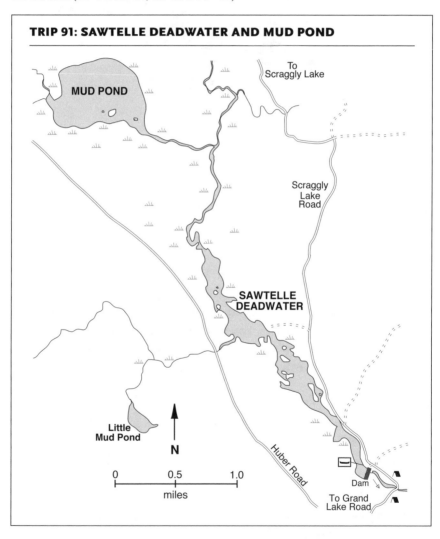

TRIP 91: SAWTELLE DEADWATER AND MUD POND

MUD POND

To Scraggly Lake

Scraggly Lake Road

SAWTELLE DEADWATER

Little Mud Pond

N

0   0.5   1.0
miles

Huber Road

Dam

To Grand Lake Road

WHAT YOU'LL SEE

A dam built years ago to power a sawmill created Sawtelle Deadwater. With the mill's removal in 1955, the wildlife biologist Francis Dunn of the Department of Inland Fisheries & Wildlife urged the state to manage the area as waterfowl habitat. The land purchase, completed in 1985, created the Francis D. Dunn Wildlife Management Unit. You will see nesting boxes for wood ducks and hooded mergansers, and you may find some wild rice that the department planted. We saw many ducks each time we visited.

The winding marshy channel of Sawtelle Deadwater provides one of the best spots to see moose throughout the summer, until late August. Paddling here in early August we counted six, some on shore, others wading in the water and muck. We also have seen otters, muskrat, and beavers.

You also may see an unusual invertebrate of the phylum Bryozoa. These colonial bryozoans, *Pectinatella*, more commonly grow farther south; we have seen them in only a few Maine ponds. Look for globular masses attached to submerged sticks or rocks. The individual units (called zooids) appear as small bumps on the mass, and the colony looks like a jellied pineapple. Each zooid's ciliated tentacles filter out microscopic food particles; these tentacles retract at lightning speed into the protective ectocyst. Colonies can grow to the size of a watermelon by summer's end. *Pectinatella* grows only in relatively pure water. Look amid the rocks in the outlet below the dam for colonies; we also saw a smaller number upstream on submerged logs.

Lush growths of alder, cattail, pickerelweed, bulrushes, arrowhead, sweet-gale, American eelgrass, American white waterlily, yellow pondlily, water-shield, pondweed, and bladderwort populate the area. Farther away from the water, common tree species include northern white cedar, tamarack, white pine, paper birch, bigtooth aspen, red maple, balsam fir, and red spruce. On the right side as you paddle upstream, look for a sizable grove of red pine. One time while paddling here, we had to portage over a small beaver dam on the stream.

Look for kingfishers diving into the water after 2- to 3-inch fish, of which the birds consume many each day. Mature females sport a rust-colored chest band; males and immature females do not. We also saw numerous great blue herons and several ospreys.

Grassy islands populate the wide southern section of Sawtelle Deadwater. Some you can paddle around; others lead to dead ends—at least by midsummer. As you paddle north, the deadwater narrows gradually to a channel 20- to

A muskrat, unconcerned by our presence, munches on vegetation.

30-feet wide. You eventually will reach the remains of an old bridge, and several hundred yards past that the channel divides. We did not paddle very far up the right fork, but if you take the left fork, you can paddle about two-thirds of a mile up to Mud Pond. We might have chosen to call it Muck Pond. Your paddle can easily penetrate a foot or two into the organic ooze at the bottom of this wide, shallow pond. We saw a moose cow and calf browsing along the western shore, and if you spend any time at all here, you should see deer enjoying the copious vegetation.

92 | Scraggly Lake (Northern)

Scraggly Lake's out-of-the-way location, irregular shoreline, and dozen or so islands, along with inlet and outlet streams, make for an outstanding multiday trip. In this wildlife management area protecting remnant old-growth forest, expect to see loons, moose, possibly mink, and lots more.

Location: T7 R8 WELS
Maps: *Maine Atlas & Gazetteer*, Map 57: E2, E3; USGS Hay Lake, Trout Brook Mountain
Area: 842 acres
Time: All day or multiday trip
Habitat Type: Deep, clear lake with forested hillsides
Fish: Brook trout, lake trout, landlocked salmon, smallmouth bass, white perch, chain pickerel (see fish advisories, Appendix A)
Take Note: No personal watercraft; official campsites do not require fire permits

GETTING THERE

From I-95, Exit 264 northbound, go 0.4 mile left (west) on Route 158 and turn right on Route 11. Go 9.3 miles (cumulative: 9.7 miles) and turn left on Route 159, which becomes Grand Lake Road at Shin Pond. Go 16.4 miles (26.1 miles) and turn right on Scraggly Lake Road. Go 1.8 miles (27.9 miles) to the access on the right. (46° 13.938′N, 68° 44.922′ W)

WHAT YOU'LL SEE

Scraggly Lake lies just northeast of Baxter State Park, entirely within 10,000 acres owned by the Maine Bureau of Public Lands, which manages not only for timber but also for wildlife, important plant communities (including several tracts of old-growth forest), and recreational opportunities.

By almost any standards, Scraggly Lake, with its crystal-clear water and highly varied shoreline, is a treasure. Deep coves and a long, sinewy inlet to the southwest provide more than twelve miles of shoreline to explore, along with dozens of islands. In late spring and early summer, take care—especially near the islands—so as not to disturb nesting loons.

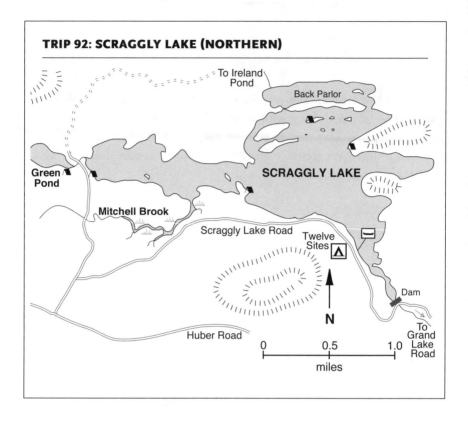

TRIP 92: SCRAGGLY LAKE (NORTHERN)

To Ireland Pond

Back Parlor

Green Pond

SCRAGGLY LAKE

Mitchell Brook

Scraggly Lake Road

Twelve Sites

Dam

N

Huber Road

To Grand Lake Road

0   0.5   1.0

miles

On the lake's west arm, you can paddle up Mitchell Brook for about 1 mile, including both forks. The quiet, meandering channel with barely perceptible current flows through a northern bog ecosystem replete with pitcher plants, sundew, sphagnum, leatherleaf, cranberry, bog rosemary, and the feathery light-green tamarack—the first tree to take hold as a mat of sphagnum and bog vegetation extends into a body of water. When we explored here just after sunrise in August, the first rays of mist-filtered sunlight illuminated thousands of dew-covered spider webs on the low bog vegetation, giving the place a magical, jewel-like appearance.

On the northern shore of Scraggly's western arm, we watched a mink for several minutes as it peered out at us from the protective cover of a fallen tree. Keep an eye out for mink along the shoreline of ponds, where they hunt for food: fish, chipmunks, frogs, and such.

Numerous rocky islands contribute to the beauty of the lake's northern section. At one point, you can walk several yards over a narrow spit of land into the long east-west arm at the north end. Or, at the northeast end, you can

We often see white-tailed deer come down for a drink on Maine's lakeshores.

paddle into the deep cove. Note the lone, ancient, old-growth white pine on a point of land that extends into the lake. If you get out of your boat, you will see this last remnant of the stately white-pine forest that once dominated the land was almost cut down many decades—perhaps more than a century—ago, and that the wedge cut has gradually grown over. With a trunk of more than 3 feet in diameter, the tree could be 500 years old.

We saw plenty of signs of moose but no moose, although we did see several white-tailed deer browsing along the shore and chest-deep in the water, munching on pipewort—an aquatic plant that sends long, narrow stems and buttonlike flowers above the water's surface. We also saw great blue herons, black ducks, wood ducks, common mergansers, pileated woodpeckers, and quite a few loons.

Except in boggy areas, the pebbly shoreline and sandy bottom support lots of freshwater mussels. White pine, hemlock, cedar, red spruce, balsam fir, white and yellow birch, white ash, and sugar maple populate the shoreline. An 80-acre section of old-growth hemlock forest—the largest such remnant forest in the state, with trees up to 400 years old—occurs about 1 mile west of the lake, in the Scraggly Lake Management Unit.

Two significant stands of mixed-age woodland, making up 137 total acres, grow north of the lake, around Ireland Pond. Though not truly old growth because some cutting occurred, many large, individual, old-growth trees of various species grow here, including red spruce, hemlock, balsam fir, white pine, sugar maple, and yellow birch. Although Huber Road provides gated access to Ireland Pond, the adventurous could take a day trip, hiking from Scraggly Lake into this scenic 35-acre pond.

93 | Deboullie Pond, Pushineer Pond, Gardner Pond, and Togue Pond

These four spectacular ponds within the Deboullie Public Reserved Lands form the northernmost entry in this book. As you might expect, they see fewer visitors than many other trips. Expect to spot loons, ospreys, bald eagles, ravens, moose, beavers, and much more.

Location: T15 R9 WELS
Maps: *Maine Atlas & Gazetteer*, Map 63: A1; USGS Deboullie Pond, Gardner Pond
Area: Deboullie Pond, 266 acres; Pushineer Pond, 55 acres; Gardner Pond, 288 acres; Togue Pond, 388 acres
Time: Multiday trip
Habitat Type: Small, deep ponds
Fish: Brook trout, blueback trout, lake trout, landlocked salmon in Togue Pond (see fish advisories, Appendix A)
Take Note: Camping and use fees; no personal watercraft on Deboullie Pond; campfire permit required, 207-435-7963

GETTING THERE
From Portage, at the junction of Route 11 and West Road, go 1 mile west on West Road and turn left on Fish Lake/Rocky Brook roads. Go 6 miles (cumulative: 7 miles) and turn right on Hewes Brook Road; follow signs for Red River Camps. Go 12.6 miles (19.6 miles) and take the left fork. Go 8 miles (27.6 miles), turn right, and go 0.1 mile (27.7 miles) to the Pushineer Pond access. (46° 57.528′N, 68° 50.268′ W).

TRIP 93: DEBOULLIE POND, PUSHINEER POND, GARDNER POND, AND TOGUE POND

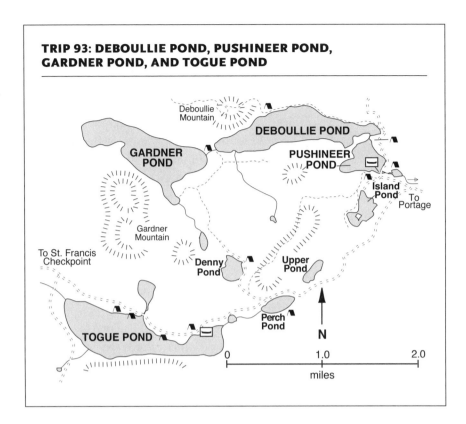

WHAT YOU'LL SEE

Tucked away in the northern reaches of the Pine Tree State, and a long drive from southern Maine, this cluster of small but beautiful, deep ponds provides opportunity for a wonderful North Maine Woods experience.

Deboullie, Gardner, and Togue ponds, along with about a dozen smaller ponds, nestle among steep mountainsides in a 20,000-acre section of Maine Public Reserved Lands. Due to the steepness, some significant patches of old-growth forest remain. Although timber harvesting in the reserve occurs on a limited basis, clearcuts are reserved for habitat improvement.

Like most public reserved land in Maine, the state acquired Deboullie Management Unit primarily through land swaps with private landowners. When Maine divided its land into hundreds of 6-mile-square townships and auctioned them off during the eighteenth and nineteenth centuries, each township retained a small portion of widely scattered land in public ownership. Beginning in the 1970s, the state consolidated many small parcels through swaps with private landowners. The state now has more than 600,000 acres of public reserved lands in 154 units, ranging in size from 60 to 47,000 acres.

Deboullie and Pushineer Ponds. Put in on Pushineer Pond at its eastern end. A short section of stream connects Pushineer and Deboullie ponds, with a slight elevation rise into Deboullie. We paddled right through the two slight riffles from Pushineer, but beavers sometimes dam this stream.

In French, *deboullie* means "rock slide," and one can easily see the appropriateness of the name as you scan the pond. A large talus slope creeps down along the north shore, and several exposed cliffs look out over the pond. The cliffs and talus slopes here provide habitat for a number of rare plant species.

Deep woods surround Deboullie and Pushineer ponds; shorelines grow thick with spruce, fir, birch, and red maple. Farther from shore, yellow birch and sugar maple mix with conifers. Along the shore, look for mountain ash (in the rose family), whose flower clusters provide nice spots of white during June and whose bright, orange-red berries add variety to early autumn colors. A dense band of alder crowds the shore, making disembarking difficult. The shore itself contains sharp chunks of granite. Use care paddling here, as these rocks can put deep scratches in your boat.

A wonderful, though steep hike traverses from Deboullie Pond to the top of Deboullie Mountain and a fire lookout tower, which affords spectacular views of the north woods. The trail starts about two-thirds of the way up the pond's north shore. Keep an eye out for a campsite and a small stream that enters the pond here. The trail climbs about 800 feet in 0.6 mile, taking about 0.5 hour. You also can reach this trail from the campsite area at Deboullie Pond's east end.

Deboullie, Pushineer, and Gardner ponds have native populations of threatened blueback trout: a char, in the same genus as brook and lake trout. Blueback char (*Salvelinus alpinus oquassa*), found in only nine bodies of water in Maine, descends from anadromous, or sea-run, arctic char that became isolated from the sea during the most recent glaciation.

Gardner Pond. From the campsite on Deboullie's far western tip, an easy portage trail leads into Gardner Pond. If Deboullie is beautiful, Gardner is spectacular, wild, and dramatic, with tall, jagged, basalt cliffs and large patches of scree. When we paddled here, ravens called from hidden cliff aeries below Gardner Mountain. A 42-acre patch of old-growth, spruce-fir forest lies between Gardner Mountain's peak and the pond. Deboullie Management Unit has five patches of old-growth, spruce-fir forest totaling 153 acres.

We watched an osprey dive for a fish and a bald eagle soar over Gardner Mountain. You can explore a few yards up the small inlet creek at the western

Deboullie Mountain affords a superb view of Deboullie and Pushineer ponds on the right, and Black Pond on the left.

end of Gardner Pond. Look here for the tiny sundew plant, whose sticky hairs trap small insects. See "Carnivorous Plants: The Table is Turned," on page 102 for more on carnivorous plants.

Togue Pond. Less visually striking and somewhat less remote than Deboullie and Gardner ponds, Togue Pond lies south of Gardner. Unlike Deboullie and Gardner, the state stocks Togue Pond with salmon to improve recreational fishing, and you will see motorboats here.

Togue Pond's shoreline differs significantly from that of Deboullie and Gardner ponds. Northern white cedar, more prevalent here, extends right down to the water's edge, in contrast with the alder that dominates the shoreline of the more northern ponds.

Appendix A: Fish Advisories

Information presented here is adapted from the Maine Center for Disease Control and Prevention website and applies to fish that you catch in Maine waters. See:
• maine.gov/dhhs/mecdc/environmental-health/eohp/fish/2kfca.htm
• maine.gov/dhhs/mecdc/environmental-health/eohp/fish/documents/meffguide.pdf

Fish and other seafood, especially those fish whose oils are rich in omega-3 fatty acids, should be part of everyone's diet. Not all seafood is safe, however, mainly because mercury, a very toxic metal, accumulates in some game fish. Generally, the larger the fish and the closer to the top of the food chain, the more mercury. Also, for some waters, PCBs and dioxins are also a concern. Those waters are listed separately below. If you have specific questions, call Maine Department of Environmental Protection at 1-866-292-3474. A serving size is approximately 6 ounces of cooked fish for the average-sized adult.

Healthy Sport Fish and Seafood for the Whole Family
• Atlantic mackerel
• Sea-run smelt
• Farm-raised and wild-caught salmon
• Canned salmon
• Hatchery-reared trout
• Sardines
• Mussels, clams, and scallops
• Light canned tuna
• Haddock, hake, cod, and pollock
• Flounder and sole
• Lobster (but not the tomalley) and shrimp
• Imitation crab and lobster
• Fish sticks

U.S. Food & Drug Administration (FDA) advises adults may eat 2 servings per week from the list above without ill effect.

Sport Fish with Eating Limits

- Freshwater/lake smelt
- Landlocked salmon
- Brook trout

Limit for pregnant and nursing women, and children under age 8: 1 serving per month.
Limit for everyone else: 1 serving per week.

Sport Fish with Very Strict Eating Limits

All other fish, including:

- Northern pike and chain pickerel
- Largemouth and smallmouth bass
- White perch
- Lake and brown trout
- Striped bass and bluefish
- Swordfish, shark, king mackerel, and tilefish

Pregnant and nursing women, and children under age 8: Do not eat these fish.
Limit for everyone else: 2 servings per month.

Advisories for Specific Bodies of Water

Pregnant and nursing women, and children under age 8, should not eat fish from these waters. Others should follow the listed guidelines.

Androscoggin River, Gilead to Merrymeeting Bay: 6 to 12 fish servings per year

Dennys River, Meddybemps Lake to Dead Stream: 1 to 2 fish servings per month

Kennebec River, Augusta to The Chops: Do not eat any fish

Kennebec River, Shawmut Dam to Augusta: 5 trout servings per year; 1 to 2 bass servings per month

Kennebec River, Madison to Fairfield: 1 to 2 fish servings per month

Little Madawaska River and tributaries, Madawaska Dam to Grimes Mill Road: Do not eat any fish

Meduxnekeag River: 2 fish servings per month

North Branch Presque Isle River: 2 fish servings per month

Penobscot River below Lincoln: 1 to 2 fish servings per month

Prestile Stream: 1 fish serving per month

Red Brook in Scarborough: 6 fish servings per year

Salmon Falls River below Berwick: 6 to 12 fish servings per year

Sebasticook River, East and West Branches and main stem, and Corinna/Hartland to Winslow: 2 fish servings per month

Appendix B:
Further Reading

Appalachian Trail Guide to Maine, 15th ed. Augusta, Maine: Maine Appalachian Trail Club, 2009.

Arlen, Alice. *Maine Sporting Camps: The Year-Round Guide to Vacationing at Traditional Hunting and Fishing Lodges*, 3rd ed. Woodstock, Vermont: Countryman Press, 2003.

Brame, Rich, and David Cole. *Soft Paths: How to Enjoy the Wilderness Without Harming It*, 4th ed. Mechanicsburg, Penn.: Stackpole Books, 2011.

Daugherty, Michael. *AMC's Best Sea Kayaking in New England: 50 Coastal Paddling Adventures from Maine to Connecticut*. Boston: Appalachian Mountain Club Books, 2016.

Fiske, John. *AMC River Guide: Maine*, 4th ed. Boston: Appalachian Mountain Club Books, 2008.

Gibson, John. *In High Places with Henry David Thoreau: A Hiker's Guide with Routes & Maps*. Woodstock, Vermont: Countryman Press, 2013.

Huber, J. Parker. *The Wildest Country: Exploring Thoreau's Maine*, 2nd ed. Boston: Appalachian Mountain Club Books, 2008.

Hutchinson, Derek C. *Basic Book of Sea Kayaking*, 2nd ed. Guilford, Conn.: Falcon, 2007.

Jacobson, Cliff. *Canoeing and Camping: Beyond the Basics*, 3rd ed. Guilford, Conn.: Falcon, 2007.

Johnson, Shelley. *The Complete Sea Kayakers Handbook*, 2nd ed. McGraw Hill, 2011.

Kish, Carey Michael. *AMC's Best Day Hikes Along the Maine Coast*. Boston: Appalachian Mountain Club Books, 2015.

Kish, Carey Michael. *Maine Mountain Guide: AMC's Comprehensive Guide to Hiking Trails of Maine, Featuring Baxter State Park and Acadia National Park*, 10th ed. Boston: Appalachian Mountain Club Books, 2012.

Leave No Trace information and materials, Leave No Trace Center for Outdoor Ethics, www.lnt.org.

Maine Atlas & Gazetteer, 34th ed. Yarmouth, Maine: DeLorme, 2015.

Marchand, Peter J. *AMC Nature Guide to the Northern Forest.* Boston: Appalachian Mountain Club Books, 2010.

Monkman, Jerry, and Marcy Monkman. *Outdoor Adventures: Acadia National Park.* Boston: Appalachian Mountain Club Books, 2017.

Roberts, Harry, and Steve Salins. *Basic Essentials Canoe Paddling.* Guilford, Conn.: Falcon, 2007.

Seidman, David. *The Essential Sea Kayaker: A Complete Guide for the Open Water Paddler*, 2nd ed. Camden, Maine: Ragged Mountain Press, 2001.

Wivell, Ty. *Discover Maine: AMC's Outdoor Traveler's Guide to the Pine Tree State.* Boston: Appalachian Mountain Club Books, 2006.

List of Waterways

AMC in the Maine Woods

The Maine Woods Initiative is the Appalachian Mountain Club's strategy for land conservation in the 100-Mile Wilderness region. This innovative approach to conservation combines outdoor recreation, resource protection, sustainable forestry, and community partnerships. To date, AMC has purchased and permanently conserved more than 75,000 acres of forest land, created more than 130 miles of recreational trails, opened three sporting camps to the public, established a Forest Stewardship Council (FSC)-certified sustainable forestry operation, and developed partnerships with local Piscataquis County schools.

This AMC land, which includes 22,000 acres of ecological reserve, is permanently protected and open to the public. Together with adjacent properties, such as Baxter State Park and the new Katahdin Woods and Waters National Monument, this creates a 63-mile conservation corridor from Moosehead Lake to Katahdin, comprising nearly 650,000 contiguous acres of conservation land open to public recreational use. AMC's land is held under multiple conservation easements with the Maine Bureau of Parks and Lands, The Nature Conservancy, and the Forest Society of Maine, and is managed for recreation, ecological protection, sustainable forestry, and scientific research. (See page 257 for a map of the 100-Mile Wilderness, including AMC's Maine Woods Initiative.)

AMC's conservation and recreation land buffers 17 miles of the Appalachian Trail corridor and permanently conserves more than 100 square miles of the Maine Woods, including more than two dozen ponds, 20 miles of streams, the 3,521-foot Baker Mountain, the 300-acre Caribou Bog, and multiple stands of late-successional forests, wetlands, and other critical wildlife habitat. It is an incredible landscape that is forever conserved for future generations.

AMC's three Maine Wilderness Lodges, Gorman Chairback, Little Lyford, and Medawisla, provide ideal bases for exploring AMC's property and the broader Moosehead Lake/100-Mile Wilderness region. There are limitless opportunities for hiking, paddling, fly fishing, and wildlife watching, and the connecting multiuse trail network provides unique lodge-to-lodge skiing, hiking, and cycling.

To learn more about the Maine Woods Initiative, visit outdoors.org/mwi.

AMC Books Updates

AMC Books strives to keep our guidebooks as up-to-date as possible to help you plan safe and enjoyable adventures. If after publishing a book we learn that trails are relocated or routed or contact information has changed, we will post the updated information online. Before you hit the trail, check for updates at outdoors.org/publications/books/updates.

While hiking or paddling, if you notice discrepancies with the description or map, or if you find any other errors in the book, please let us know by submitting them to amcbookupdates@outdoors.org or in writing to Books Editor, c/o AMC, 5 Joy Street, Boston, MA 02108. We will verify all submissions and post key updates each month.

AMC Books is dedicated to being a recognized leader in outdoor publishing. Thank you for your participation.

About the Authors

ALEX WILSON

Alex Wilson is an avid canoeist and naturalist and a widely published writer on energy, building technology, and environmental issues. He lives in Dummerston, Vermont.

JOHN HAYES

John Hayes, now retired, is the former director of sustainability at Pacific University in Oregon and former professor of environmental science at Marlboro College in Vermont. Besides paddling all over New England, New York, Pennsylvania, and New Jersey, he has paddled in the Pacific Northwest, in Minnesota's Boundary Waters, in the Okefenokee Swamp in Georgia, across the Everglades, and in Belize. In all, he has canoed and kayaked more than 5,000 miles.

APPALACHIAN MOUNTAIN CLUB

At AMC, connecting you to the freedom and exhilaration of the outdoors is our calling. We help people of all ages and abilities to explore and develop a deep appreciation of the natural world.

AMC helps you get outdoors on your own, with family and friends, and through activities close to home and beyond. With chapters from Maine to Washington, D.C., including groups in Boston, New York City, and Philadelphia, you can enjoy activities like hiking, paddling, cycling, and skiing, and learn new outdoor skills. We offer advice, guidebooks, maps, and unique lodges and huts to inspire your next outing. You will also have the opportunity to support conservation advocacy and research, youth programming, and caring for 1,800 miles of trails.

We invite you to join us in the outdoors.

YOUR CONNECTION TO THE OUTDOORS

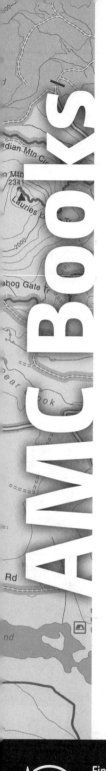

AMC's Best Sea Kayaking in New England

Michael Daugherty

This concise guide, written by a Registered Maine Guide and inveterate paddler, features 50 of the best sea kayaking adventures in New England, from Maine's Bold Coast to the mouth of the Connecticut River. Many trips can be done in a day or turned into an overnight for all ability levels.

$18.95 • 978-1-62842-006-7

Maine Mountain Guide, 10th Edition

Carey Michael Kish

For more than 50 years, *Maine Mountain Guide* has been the trusted resource for hikers visiting the state's spectacular peaks. This new edition has been thoroughly revised and updated, with 200 new trails, expanded coverage of Baxter State Park, and new in-text maps.

$23.95 • 978-1-934028-30-8

Outdoor Adventures: Acadia National Park

Jerry and Marcy Monkman

Now with an enhanced focus on recreation, *Outdoor Adventures Acadia National Park* (formerly *Discover Acadia National Park*) spotlights 50 hiking, biking, and paddling trips for all ability levels. Covering the popular Mt. Desert Island, as well as the hidden gems of Isle au Haut and Schoodic Peninsula, this is the definitive guide to enjoying the best of New England's only national park.

$22.95 • 978-1-62842-057-9

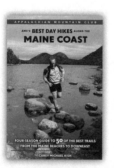

AMC's Best Day Hikes along the Maine Coast

Carey Michael Kish

From the editor of AMC's popular *Maine Mountain Guide*, this new book leads readers on 50 hikes that can be completed in less than a day, exploring the full length of Maine's rugged coast, from the Portland area to Quoddy Head State Park, the easternmost point in the United States.

$18.95 • 978-1-934028-92-6